Everyman, I will go with thee,
and be thy guide

John Locke

TWO TREATISES
OF GOVERNMENT

Edited by
MARK GOLDIE
Churchill College, Cambridge

EVERYMAN
J. M. DENT · LONDON
CHARLES E. TUTTLE
VERMONT

Consultant Editor for this volume
David Berman (Trinity College, Dublin)
© Text, introduction and other critical apparatus
J. M. Dent 1993

This title first published in Everyman 1924
New edition first published 1993

17 19 20 18

J. M. Dent
Orion Publishing Group
Orion House, 5 Upper St Martin's Lane,
London WC2H 9EA
and
Tuttle Publishing
Airport Industrial Park, 364 Innovation Drive,
North Clarendon, VT 05759-9436, USA

Printed in Great Britain by
Clays Ltd, Elcograf S.p.A.

British Library Cataloguing-in-Publication Data
is available upon request.

ISBN-13 978-0-4608-7356-7

The Orion Publishing Group's policy is to use papers that
are natural, renewable and recyclable products and
made from wood grown in sustainable forests. The logging
and manufacturing processes are expected to conform to
the environmental regulations of the country of origin.

www.orionbooks.co.uk

CONTENTS

NOTE ON THE AUTHOR AND EDITOR

JOHN LOCKE was born on 29 August 1632 and educated at Westminster School, then at Christ Church, Oxford, where he graduated in 1656. He was elected a Student (Fellow) there in 1658 and was Lecturer in Greek, Rhetoric and Moral Philosophy between 1660 and 1664. From 1667 until 1682 he was physician and secretary to Anthony Ashley Cooper (later Earl of Shaftesbury). He was elected a Fellow of the Royal Society in 1668, was Secretary to the Lords Proprietors of Carolina in 1668–75 and Secretary to the Council of Trade and Plantations in 1673–5. During 1675–9 he travelled in France. He was active as 'assistant pen' and political agent for Shaftesbury and the Whigs from 1679 to 1683. Exiled in Holland in 1683–9, he was expelled from his Christ Church Studentship in 1684. He was a Commissioner on the Board of Trade from 1696 to 1700. He died on 28 October 1704.

MARK GOLDIE is Director of Studies in History and Fellow of Churchill College, Cambridge. He is co-editor of *The Cambridge History of Political Thought 1450–1700* and *The Cambridge History of Eighteenth-Century Political Thought*.

CHRONOLOGY OF LOCKE'S LIFE

Year	Age	Life
1632		Born at Wrington, Somerset, 29 August
1647–52	15	Attends Westminster School, London
1652–6	20	Undergraduate at Christ Church, Oxford. Graduated BA 1656, MA 1658. Continued in Oxford until 1667
1658	26	Elected Student (Fellow) of Christ Church
1661–4	28	Lecturer in Greek, Rhetoric and Moral Philosophy. Writes first political essay, *Two Tracts on Government*
1663	31	Writes *Essays on the Law of Nature*
1665–6	33	Secretary to an embassy to Brandenburg
1667	35	Joins Lord Ashley's household in London. Usually resident in London until 1675
1668	36	Fellow of the Royal Society
1669–75		Secretary to the Lords Proprietors of Carolina
1671	39	Begins writing *An Essay Concerning Human Understanding*

CHRONOLOGY OF HIS TIMES

Year	Literary Context	Historical Events
1637		Rebellion in Scotland against King Charles I
1640		Meeting of the Long Parliament
1641		The Irish Rebellion
1642–51		The British Civil Wars
1649		Execution of Charles I; England a republic
1651	Hobbes, *Leviathan*	
1653–8		Oliver Cromwell rules as Lord Protector
1660		Restoration of King Charles II
1662		Act of Uniformity, enforcing Anglican worship
1666		Great Fire of London
1667	Milton, *Paradise Lost*	
1672		Lord Ashley appointed Lord Chancellor and created Earl of Shaftesbury

Year	Age	Life
1672–3	40	Secretary for Presentations (to Church livings)
1673–4	41	Secretary to the Council of Trade and Plantations
1675–9	43	Travels in France
c.1680–83	47	Writes *Two Treatises of Government*
1683–9	51	In exile in Holland, mainly in Amsterdam until early 1687, then in Rotterdam
1684	52	Expelled from Studentship of Christ Church

Year	Literary Context	Historical Events
1672-3		Declaration of Indulgence (royal edict of religious toleration)
1673		Conversion to Catholicism of the King's brother, James, Duke of York, made public. Shaftesbury ousted
1674-9		Rule of the Anglican Cavaliers under the Earl of Danby
1678	John Bunyan, *Pilgrim's Progress*	Popish Plot revealed: alleged Catholic conspiracy against Charles II
1679	Death of Thomas Hobbes	
1679-81		Exclusion Crisis: attempt to exclude James, Duke of York, from inheriting the throne. Party names 'Tory' and 'Whig' coined
1680	Publication of Sir Robert Filmer's *Patriarcha*	
1681		Oxford Parliament meets and is quickly dismissed
1682		Tory coup against Whig leadership in the City of London. Flight of Shaftesbury to Holland
1683		Rye House Plot; execution of Algernon Sidney and Lord William Russell; death of Shaftesbury

Year	Age	Life
1685	53	Writes *A Letter Concerning Toleration*
1689	57	Appointed Commissioner of Excise Appeals. Publishes *Two Treatises, Essay Concerning Human Understanding* and *Letter Concerning Toleration*
1690	58	Settles at Oates in Essex in Masham household
1693	61	Publishes *Some Thoughts Concerning Education*
1695	63	Advises on the ending of press censorship and the great recoinage. Publishes *The Reasonableness of Christianity*
1696–1700	64	Member of the Board of Trade and Plantations
1704	72	Death at Oates, 28 October. Buried in High Laver churchyard, Essex

Year	Literary Context	Historical Events
1685		Death of Charles II; accession of James II. Rebellion of the Duke of Monmouth: defeated at Sedgemoor and executed
1687	Publication of Isaac Newton's *Principia*	
1688		Glorious Revolution: overthrow of James II
1689		Accession of William III and Mary II. Act of Toleration. Bill of Rights. War against Louis XIV of France
1690		Battle of the Boyne: William defeats James in Ireland
1694		Triennial Act (regular parliaments). Foundation of Bank of England
1701		Act of Settlement, ensures (Protestant) Hanoverian succession
1702		Death of William III; accession of Queen Anne
1704		Duke of Marlborough's victory over France at Blenheim

INTRODUCTION

The many books and articles published every year about Locke are testimony to his stature in contemporary political controversy. His reputation is such that interpreters are keen to conscript him on behalf of modern doctrines. His *Two Treatises of Government* remains influential today chiefly because it is regarded as the foundational text of liberalism. Yet there is fierce disagreement about what liberalism means and about what Locke's intentions were. Let us begin with the historical Locke.

A PATH FROM CONSERVATISM

Locke was fifty-seven when he published the *Two Treatises* in the autumn of 1689. He had just returned to England from exile in Holland, where he had fled in 1683, marked out as a seditious agent of a Whig conspiracy against King Charles II. The Stuart regime, continued by Charles's Catholic brother James II, had collapsed in 1688 in the face of William of Orange's invading army and desertion to William's cause by the English political elite. This 'Glorious Revolution' culminated in the decision of a parliamentary Convention to install William as king. A few months later the *Two Treatises* appeared, demolishing the theory of monarchical absolutism and defending the right of resistance against tyrants.

Yet Locke had not always held such views. As a young man he had been deeply conservative. Political circumstances and intellectual reconsideration propelled him in a more radical direction. It was a trajectory which ran against the grain of his temperament, for he was always cautious, anxious and prim.

He came from a West Country background, near Bristol. Stones in graveyards usually mark a death: in Wrington churchyard a stone marks the site of Locke's birth. His grandfather was a successful clothier, his father an attorney of minor gentry status, a Puritan and Parliamentarian who took arms against King Charles I in the Civil War. Commentators tend to deduce that this milieu predisposed Locke towards liberalism. Yet this is misleading, for the Presbyterian gentry who started the Civil War were appalled by its republican outcome and by the Pandora's box of religious sectarianism and social levelling they unwittingly let loose. They yearned to restore the 'mixed and balanced constitution' of king, lords and commons, and a godly discipline in the Church. In 1659, during the chaos that followed the death of Lord Protector Cromwell, Locke wrote despairingly of 'this great bedlam England'.

When Charles II was restored to the throne in 1660, controversy arose concerning the civil magistrate's right to impose religious conformity. Locke, then a tutor at Christ Church in Oxford, drafted his first political essay, an attack on a senior colleague who pleaded for liberty of conscience. The *Two Tracts on Government*, unpublished until 1967, insisted that the magistrate had a right to impose anything not clearly precluded by God in Scripture. 'The supreme magistrate in every nation . . . must necessarily have an absolute and arbitrary power over all the indifferent actions of his people.' Any alternative would 'turn us loose to the tyranny of a religious rage'. More generally Locke displayed a pessimistic, Augustinian sense that government was ordained by God to restrain sinful humanity. 'The stubbornness and peevishness of the people' will need 'severe applications of authority'. He dwelt on the perils of anarchy and civil war, and the necessity of firm rule. 'The indelible memory of our late miseries, and the happy return of our ancient freedom and felicity, are proofs sufficient to convince us where the supreme power of these nations is most advantageously placed.' As Hobbes put this point in *Leviathan*, 'sovereign power is not so hurtful as the want of it'. Locke cited *Romans* 13, the familiar biblical text on obedience to superiors, which instructs us to obey 'the powers that be' for they are 'ordained by God'. It is true that, in pondering the origins of political power, Locke suggested it might derive from the community, but, like several theorists inclined to absolutism before him, such as Suarez, Grotius and Hobbes, he argued that the social contract totally transferred the authority of the community to the ruler.

Locke later repudiated these opinions, but many of his contemporaries, throughout the Restoration, adhered to them. In due course such people would be called Tories, staunch defenders of monarchical right and religious intolerance.

There were probably several influences which turned Locke in new directions. In 1660 he met the natural philosopher ('scientist', as we would now say) Robert Boyle, whose religious views were more tolerant, though the early Royal Society, to which Locke was elected in 1668, did not necessarily reflect liberal positions. It is perhaps significant that Locke did not enter the Church, the usual pattern for Oxford dons, though he remained a practising member of the established Church of England throughout his life. In due course his clerical friends were mainly of the 'latitudinarian' type, who sought a relaxation of the harsh religious settlement imposed in 1662 by the Act of Uniformity. In 1665 he acted as secretary to an embassy to Germany, and at Cleves observed that it was possible for Lutherans, Calvinists and Catholics to live and worship in harmony.

Decisive in the history of Locke's opinions was his sixteen-year association with Lord Ashley, later first Earl of Shaftesbury and Lord Chancellor, later still, out of office and implacably hostile to Charles II's Court, and, finally, a traitor in exile. They met in 1666, when Locke, who trained in medicine, saved Ashley's life by a delicate liver operation. Ashley was also of West Country Presbyterian background, and was a great landowner. Locke joined his household, acting as political adviser, tutor and librarian; he walked beside his lordship's coach, and prompted him during speeches in the House of Lords. Through Shaftesbury Locke learnt a great deal about commercial and colonial matters, in particular the Americas, and invested in slave-trading companies. Locke served as secretary to the Council of Trade and Plantations, and assisted the Lords Proprietors of Carolina, for whom he helped draft *The Fundamental Constitutions of Carolina* (1669). In 1667 he wrote an *Essay on Toleration*, which marked a decisive change of mind, and in 1672 helped his master defend the King's Declaration of Indulgence, which temporarily granted freedom of worship by royal edict.

THE EXCLUSION CRISIS

In 1672 Charles II came closest to escaping the strait-jacket of the Anglican Royalist vision of the post-Civil War polity. Soon, however, fiscal and political necessity forced him to capitulate to the Earl of Danby, architect of what became Toryism. By 1678 Charles and Danby stood accused of religious persecution, crypto-Catholicism, raising a standing army and corrupting parliament by bribing 'placemen'. Shaftesbury's *Letter from a Person of Quality* (1675), which Locke may have drafted, was a manifesto of the emergent Whig party. It denounced the project of making government 'absolute and arbitrary', a regime in which 'priest and prince' must be 'worshipped as divine in the same temple'.

The English elite feared both Puritan revolution and Catholic domination. Between 1678 and 1681, the period of the Popish Plot and Exclusion Crisis, the latter fear predominated. James, the heir presumptive, had converted to Catholicism, and revelations of a Catholic plot revived the mythology of England's national destiny as the flagship of Protestantism in the struggle against Counter-Reformation Catholicism. The Whigs were carried on a tide of anti-Popish fever, and attempted in three successive parliaments to prevent James from inheriting the crown. Notwithstanding their electoral successes, Charles defeated the Whigs by deploying his prerogative power to postpone and dismiss parliaments, and by marshalling a majority in the House of Lords. After 1681 Charles called no further parliaments, and England was given over to a ferociously savage purge against Whig dissidents and religious Dissenters. It was the high tide of Anglican Toryism.

The Exclusion Crisis raised fundamental theoretical issues: whether parliaments were subordinate to the crown and whether they could alter the royal succession. In 1679–80 the Tory leadership, rallying to the crown, published the works of Sir Robert Filmer, a Civil War Royalist who had died in 1653. Filmer's *Patriarcha, or the Natural Power of Kings* was far more characteristic of seventeenth-century absolutist thought than was Hobbes's *Leviathan*, and it became the textbook of divine right Toryism. Filmer argued that we are born unfree and unequal, and that political society is not grounded in the consent of the people, but in the ordination of God, as revealed in the natural order of patriarchy. The original power of monarchs lay in Adam's rights as father and husband. Likewise, the sacred rights of royal heirs were inviolable. Filmer also claimed that an investigation of the origins of English parliaments showed that they had begun in the Middle Ages as extensions of the king's great council, and so existed only by the will and pleasure of the crown.

Whig polemicists responded to both parts of Filmer's doctrine, some focusing on the natural law argument, others on the constitutional. Three books challenged the patriarchalist case: *Patriarcha non Monarcha* (1681), by Locke's close friend James Tyrrell; the *Discourses Concerning Government* (published in 1698), by the republican Algernon Sidney, who was executed in 1683, partly on the evidence of his manuscript; and Locke's *Two Treatises*. The constitutionalist Whigs, notably William Petyt and William Atwood, turned to history. They posited an Ancient Constitution, a pristine Anglo-Saxon polity in which popular representation, in the 'witenagemot', was an entrenched right. Parliament was heir of the witenagemot, not a belated feudal council, and the Norman Conquest had not breached the continuity of English liberties. Subsequent history was punctuated by struggles to preserve the constitution from the encroachments of despotic monarchs. This doctrine entailed a celebration of the simplicity and communal virtue of the Germanic tribes whom Tacitus had praised in contrast to the corrupt Roman Empire. Here lay the origins of 'Whig historiography' – history written as the contest of patriots against despots (Pocock, 1987). Although Locke said little about this theme, he endorsed its outlook, for he denied any significance to the Norman Conquest (177) and asserted that monarchy was originally elective (106, 223; I, 93–5).*

DATING THE *TWO TREATISES*

The preface of the *Two Treatises* announced its purpose as being to justify King William 'in the consent of the people'. Later generations assumed that Locke wrote his book in 1689 to defend

* Numbers in brackets refer to paragraphs in the Second Treatise, except when preceded by 'I' to indicate the First Treatise. References by author and date to books by modern commentators can be followed up in the Suggestions for Further Reading.

the Glorious Revolution. But this was not so. Far from being written in the aftermath of a successful revolution as a plea for new allegiances, it was in fact produced some years earlier. It was originally a clandestine and audacious tract justifying an insurrection planned in the darkest days of Charles II's drift towards absolutism. During the 1950s Peter Laslett demonstrated conclusively that the *Two Treatises* was not written shortly before its publication. Part of his evidence lies in textual clues. For instance, in one passage (later corrected) Locke refers to 'King James', meaning 'the First', but without a number, so he most likely wrote it before James II's accession in 1685; and in another he refers to 'the late [i.e. recent] relation of Ceylon', which can be identified as a book published in 1681. Laslett's central claim, however, was that the *Two Treatises* was pre-eminently an attack upon Filmer, who, around 1680, the Whigs urgently needed to counter.

Nobody now doubts Laslett's general case, but less secure is his claim that the whole work was composed in 1679–81, and that Locke wrote the Second Treatise first, and then wrote the First Treatise, impelled by the need for a more detailed criticism of Filmer. What is doubtful is that the refutation of Filmer and the exclusion of James provided the sole intellectual motives behind Locke's *whole* composition. There are indications that the two treatises are separable, and that they were written in the order of their publication. Locke's title page announces that the First Treatise overthrows Filmer's false principles, while the Second is a general essay on the 'true original, extent, and end of civil government'.

In the First Treatise, which he probably wrote in 1679–81, Locke makes no claim for a right of resistance. He had no reason to call for insurrection at that stage; indeed, there were powerful reasons for not doing so. The Whigs were winning elections; they hoped to drive the King, through parliamentary pressure, to capitulate. They needed to pass an Exclusion Act, which would be followed by further legislation naming a successor, perhaps the King's illegitimate but Protestant son, the Duke of Monmouth. Even in opposition, Shaftesbury's campaign initially was impeccably loyalist: the crown must be rescued from Catholic conspiracies, and no changes were needed to the constitution. Also Shaftesbury's clique was not the most radical political force at this time. Algernon Sidney was intent on a republic, and Henry Nevile's

Plato Redivivus (1681) argued that if the crown's powers were drastically curtailed, it would not matter if the next king were a Catholic. Shaftesbury opted for a more conservative position: change the future king, not the powers of kingship. It is hard to find anybody arguing for a recourse to arms against Charles II before the close of 1681.

Only by 1681 was it becoming apparent that constitutional means were blocked. Charles dismissed the Oxford parliament in March just one week after it had assembled. His government began a campaign of rigged treason trials against Whig activists, who were despatched to the executioner. Some temporarily escaped because the juries were appointed by Whig sheriffs. But in 1682 Whig sheriffs, chosen by popular vote in London, were replaced by Tories in a *coup d'état* against the City. Shaftesbury fled to Holland. The Court also forced the rewriting of borough charters, which made it easier to control local officers and MPs, and to purge the towns of dissidents. Finally the government, abetted by zealous Tories, embarked on a wholesale persecution of religious Dissenters, who were fined, jailed and expelled from public offices. During 1682–3 a small group of Whigs was driven to conspire to overthrow King Charles and his brother. Their plot was exposed, and judicial fury was let loose. Sidney and Lord Russell were executed, both refusing on the scaffold to disown the doctrine of resistance to tyrants. Author by now of a book which would have cost him his life, Locke fled.

It was not Filmer, but the treason trials, the City *coup* and the persecution which drove Locke to adopt the revolutionary position of the Second Treatise. Although Locke worked on his manuscript at various times, he almost certainly composed it between 1681 and 1683. He put aside his First Treatise, a pedantic commentary on a rival ideologue's book.* Events had moved on, and he now needed a fundamental essay about the limits of government and the right of citizens to challenge tyranny – bloodily if necessary. The same vehement commitment led also to another tract of fundamental importance, his *Letter Concerning Toleration*, which he wrote in Holland in 1685.

* The Second Treatise is of immeasurably greater importance than the First. Readers seeking a brief inroad into the First Treatise should read chapters 1, 5, and 9, and also paragraphs 8, 40–2, and 55–9.

SIR ROBERT FILMER AND PATRIARCHALISM

In turning now to the substance of Locke's arguments in the *Two Treatises*, we need to begin with his critique of patriarchalism. Filmer held that Adam's power was the archetype of all human rulership. To his notion about God-given parental and marital rights Filmer added a doctrine of sovereignty, derived from Bodin and shared with Hobbes, by which absolute dominion over the lives and estates of subjects was a logically necessary attribute of rulers. The theory of sovereignty is a lasting legacy of early modern royalism, but it is difficult now to take the patriarchalist aspect of Filmer seriously. Yet his theory was well attuned to the social facts of seventeenth-century England, which was a household society. The household was an economic as well as a family unit, a 'petty commonwealth' which included servants and apprentices, under their 'petty monarch', the father, husband and master. Catechisms explained the Fifth Commandment ('Honour thy father and thy mother') as encompassing 'several sorts of parent': natural; spiritual (priests and bishops); political (kings and magistrates); and 'domestical' (masters of servants and labourers). Locke himself was said to belong to Shaftesbury's 'family', and he speaks of a 'family' as including servants (77, 86). The *Two Treatises* is markedly concessive to patriarchalism. The earliest political societies, as Aristotle and Hooker argued, probably evolved from family households, and patriarchs became kings (74–6, 105, 107, 110, 162).

Nonetheless, Locke cuts down to size Filmer's celebration of masculine potency. (Freudians have interpreted Locke's liberalism as an act of intellectual castration of the patriarchs of traditional society.) Parents, Locke insists, have duties of nurture and education towards their children rather than rights of despotic control over them (58, 63, 67). The human child is God's 'workmanship', and sexual intercourse is merely the vehicle of God's creativity. Locke indeed is fastidiously disturbed at the suggestion that rights might be generated in a moment of animal sexuality (56; I, 54).

What Locke chiefly insists on is that patriarchy can tell us nothing about political obligation: paternal and political power have different purposes and spheres (2, 71, 77, 86, 169–70). The authority of the prince and the magistrate is simply not the same as that of a father, husband or master. For instance, the sovereignty of Queen Elizabeth I would not have been compromised had she married (I, 47). We owe lifelong honour and gratitude to parents, but that is not political subjection, and fathers cannot dictate the political allegiances of their children (66–70, 170). Locke, in short, accuses Filmer of using a false analogy between the family and the state.

Some feminists have applauded Locke. He berates Filmer for glossing the Fifth Commandment as if it had been about paternal and not parental power, for Filmer foreshortens the Commandment to read 'honour thy father', leaving out the mother (52–3, 64; I, 44–9, 66). He attacks Filmer's biological assumption that men are the sole agents in procreation, and women mere empty vessels waiting to be filled (I, 55); he allows that women might retain some property rights in marriage (83); and he countenances divorce (81). Others, however, have seen Locke as entrenching the characteristic patriarchalism of the modern era (Pateman, 1988). He dethrones Filmer's domineering father, but creates instead a political fraternity of men. By claiming that political power is radically separable from paternal power, he leaves intact the 'natural' ordering of the hierarchical family. He assumes that female subordination is pre- and non-political. The husband is 'naturally' in charge, as 'the abler and the stronger' (82).

THE STATE OF NATURE

Locke declares that we are all by nature free and equal (95). To be in a condition of freedom and equality, prior to government, is to be in the state of nature. It is not an unsocial condition, for people are naturally drawn together into families and communities; it is a circumstance in which people acquire property and engage in commerce (14). It is not, as it was for Hobbes, a brutish condition, though it is an unstable one. In order to preserve our lives, liberties and estates, we choose to come out of the state of nature and enter into civil society by an act of consent known as the social contract – usually referred to by Locke as a 'compact' (97). The idea of a state of nature and of a social contract is central to the political philosophy of a train of writers, signally Grotius, Pufendorf, Hobbes, Locke, Rousseau and Kant.

The notion of a natural state was open to objections. Chief of these was that it is a figment of the political imagination, for, as Filmer emphasized, we are born under government, and there is little evidence for a primordial, ungoverned arcadia (14–15). In the seventeenth century, moreover, the Filmerians could assert that the history of the earliest societies was fully known because it was reported in Scripture. To deny the continuity of government from the creation of Adam down through the kings of Israel would be to question the authority of the Bible.

Although Locke accepts the contemporary belief that the world began in 4004 BC, and his First Treatise uses traditional Old Testament chronologies, he rejects Filmer's insistence on historicity. The state of nature may be construed as a description of the fundamental character of the human condition, and not as an historical circumstance. It is the state we naturally *are* in, not *were* in (4). As with Hobbes, though in a less menacing way, Locke's state of nature is immanent in our contemporary political condition, always lurking just beneath its surface. The carapace of legal order is fragile. The state of nature recurs within political communities when the government becomes tyrannical; a ruler (or any citizen) who makes war on the people does not differ from a marauding thug in the state of nature (11, 172, 181). Furthermore, Locke points out that governments remain in a state of nature in relation to one another, having no common sovereign to whom they might appeal to settle their differences (14, 145). Locke, however, somewhat confuses the issue by also suggesting that the state of nature was indeed an historical state. He read widely in travel literature, and his account of the state of nature was partly an essay in anthropology. The native Indians of America and Peru lived in settled, loose-knit communities, capable of mutual trust and binding contracts, although they did not, he claims, live under civil government, choosing chieftains only in times of war (14, 102).

Locke is anxious to add two caveats to the idea of equality and liberty in the state of nature. He asserts only an equality of right, for he accepts that there should be many inequalities, conferred by age, virtue, birth, beneficence, gratitude (4, 54) – and property. (Marxists, accordingly, hold that Locke entrenched the liberal piety of 'equality under the law', while masking vicious economic inequalities.) The second caveat is that although the state of nature is a condition of 'perfect freedom', this does not mean an anarchic wilfulness, a liberty to do anything we desire. Liberty does not mean licence (6, 22, 57). The state of nature is unbounded by human laws, yet it remains bounded by a law of nature, which is God's law (4, 6, 8). Locke's philosophy was profoundly imbued with Christian convictions: he was no secular thinker (Dunn, 1969). He was firmly in a tradition of moral philosophy that ultimately gives a theological gloss to Plato and Cicero. True freedom consists in a life governed by the rational intellect, and not in slavery to the passions. We are put on earth to fulfil our best nature; we are here to do God's business. Accordingly, political freedom consists in a lack of impediments to conducting a godly life. In this sense it is inappropriate, some say, to connect Locke with 'liberalism' at all, for he does not believe in freedom of action in a moral vacuum.

THE LAW OF NATURE

The American Declaration of Independence asserts that certain truths about humankind's fundamental status are 'self-evident'. That document stands in the natural law tradition which posits a body of knowable laws and rights which transcend particular human regimes. Since these stand outside, and prior to, the written, positive laws of states, they cannot be known from ordinary law books. They are usually held to be discernible by any rational and reflective person. In the Christian tradition they are said to be deducible from God's arrangement of the world, or capable of immediate intuition because implanted by God in our consciences. In the Second Treatise Locke is remarkably optimistic about our ability to discern the law of nature: reason teaches us what that law is (6, 12, 124). He endorses an intuitionist position, speaking of these laws as 'writ in the hearts of all mankind' (11, 56; I, 86).

Locke holds that we can confirm the validity of our intuitions by reading the word of God in Scripture, for God speaks through both His words and His works. Locke often links 'God and nature', 'reason and revelation' (25, 52, 168). Here he seems to stand squarely in the tradition of the medieval Catholic scholastic philosophers, such as Thomas Aquinas, though equally he may be said to prefigure the Enlightenment deists' tendency to reduce divine revelation to aphoristic confirmations of the truths of natural reason.

Locke minimizes the content of the law of nature, in a way that the theologians would not: for instance, marriage is merely a contract, a matter of variable human practice, not of fixed natural law (78, 81–3). In general he follows Grotius and Pufendorf who, while avoiding the complete scepticism about human values expressed by the sixteenth-century Pyrrhonians, Montaigne and Charron, constructed only a minimal foundation of natural law, based on the core interests which human beings experience as the conditions of their existence (Tuck, 1979). For Locke, as for Grotius and Pufendorf, the law of nature arises from the perceived needs of God's creatures, who seek to preserve themselves, both materially in their subsistence and morally in their personhood. This is why government's central purpose is to protect 'life, liberty and estate'.

The most important corollary of Locke's natural law theory is the general right of punishment in the state of nature. Because we are all competent judges of the law of nature, so we are all authorized executioners of it. When we suffer injury we may deter future crime and exact reparation. This is not only a matter of self-defence, for anybody, not just the victim, may punish a malefactor, if necessary with death, since a breach of natural law is a crime against all humanity (7–8, 16–19, 128). This doctrine is known as the 'universal executive power of the law of nature' and Locke concedes it may be thought a 'very strange doctrine' (9). He had in mind the standard absolutist argument that, since the Sixth Commandment says 'Thou shalt not kill', the sovereign can acquire the right of capital punishment only by direct gift from God, and not from the people, who have no such right. Locke insists that people do have that right; Scripture says that after Cain murdered Abel, anybody might execute Cain (11). People transfer their right to the civil sovereign, who, in normal times, undertakes acts of retribution on their behalf. But, crucially, they recover that natural right when the sovereign invades the properties he was established to protect and contradicts the purpose of his institution.

There is a deep puzzle about Locke's commitment to natural law in the *Two Treatises*, for in his book *An Essay Concerning Human Understanding* (which philosophers today regard as Locke's most important work), he rejected precisely the naive belief that God has furnished our minds with moral certainties. Book I of the *Essay* is an assault on innate ideas: it declares the mind at birth to be a *tabula rasa*, a blank slate; knowledge comes only from experience. Locke scholars labour to reconcile his 'realism' or 'essentialism' (the idea that there are universal intuitive, or deductive, axioms of morality) and his 'nominalism' (that, as Hobbes put it, 'good and evil are but names', and that names, or laws, are no more than the commands of a known law-giver – most notably, they are God's commands, to which are attached rewards and punishments). The irreconcilability of the *Essay* and the *Two Treatises* is, as Locke himself was painfully aware, the central failure of his intellectual life.

His problem remains ours. In the face of the world's tyrants and of 'crimes against humanity' we desperately seek a stable (and enforceable) code of irreducible human rights, but we are hampered not least by the conceptual problem that lofty talk of universal natural rights might turn out to be, as Bentham called it, 'nonsense upon stilts'.

CONSENT

Despite our clear grasp of natural law, our corrupt nature leads us to breach it; and despite our right to execute the law of nature, we act prejudicially in our own cause (124–8). As we saw earlier, the state of nature is an unstable condition, in which reason is apt to give way to force and fraud; we are thereby reduced to a state of war (19, 123, 137). The avoidance of this condition is our reason for forming civil society. To form a political society is to quit the executive power of the law of nature and place the right of judgment, appeal and execution in the hands of government (21, 88–9, 123, 127–31). Like other contractarians, Locke holds that political society is formed by an act of consent which constitutes the social contract (95, 97). The only legitimate foundation for any political rule is its voluntary acceptance by the citizens.

Locke believes that any government not founded in consent is incompatible with civil society: an absolute monarchy is an undeclared state of war, an unstable truce until such time as the people shall bring it down (90). Thus Locke draws a distinction between civil society and government; the former is not reducible to the latter (though despotisms attempt it), and the latter indeed ought to be merely the agent of the former.

Political institutions are not to be justified on the grounds that they are God-given, or natural, or traditional, or even useful; the only source of legitimacy is the rational will of those who choose to live under them. However, the idea of consent is open to a series of empirical and conceptual objections. As with the state of nature, there is the question of the historicity of the contract (100, 114). Locke's critics said that the making of a social contract never actually occurred. In part, Locke responds in the spirit of modern theorists of consent, who offer a pure 'thought experiment': the contract is an act of political imagination in which we place ourselves in an 'original position' and ask what kind of society it would be rational to choose. But, on the other hand, Locke also argues that the founding of polities anew, by the people's choice, has historically often occurred (103, 115).

He recognizes that many existing governments have their origin in force, fraud, conquest, usurpation and patriarchy. He concedes that we are born under government, but not that this fact alone creates obligation: *de facto* power is not the same as morally legitimate power (100, 103, 113–14, 116). However, all governments may be redeemed by consent. A conqueror or usurper can acquire legitimacy by the consent of the conquered, as can a patriarchal monarch by that of his sons (24, 74–5, 175). The compact is a jural event, not necessarily undertaken *ab initio*; it is an act of political will.

The next difficulty is what constitutes a sufficiently manifest expression of a person's consent, for we do not ordinarily make a formal declaration of our membership of a polity. At first sight Locke's distinction between express and tacit consent solves this dilemma, by suggesting that continued residence under a government and enjoyment of its protection, may be deemed tacit consent (119–20). This had plausibility in an age when there were vacant lands across the seas and thousands of Puritans could renounce England by emigrating to America; even today, the right to emigrate is taken as a criterion of a free society. Another suggestion is that inheritance of property constitutes consent (73, 120). Macpherson (1962) takes this to indicate that for Locke only the propertied were true citizens, and that his commonwealth was only for the bourgeoisie. It is true that Locke gives inheritance as an example. Yet he is emphatic that only express consent can make a person a citizen, as a precondition for inheritance, and that inheritance alone does not bind sons to their fathers' allegiances; he also implies that tacit consent refers only to the limited obligation of domiciled foreigners (73, 116–17, 121–2). To the question of what, for Locke, constitutes the act of consent, a plausible answer lies in oaths of allegiance (62, 151). These were a prevalent feature of his society. An oath was imposed in 1606 to distinguish true Englishmen from Catholics who owed allegiance to the Pope. The Engagement Oath to the new republic in 1649, nominally required of every adult male, provoked a crisis of conscience and a debate to which Hobbes's *Leviathan* was partly addressed. The new oath of 1689 extended to all office-holders, schoolteachers and clergymen. In a paper of 1690 Locke lent his weight to the imposition of a stricter oath, requiring express recognition of the Revolution's legitimacy.

The next puzzle is how Locke's apparent requirement for universal consent – nobody is a citizen unless they have given their consent – can be reconciled with restricted political participation. Even though in one passage he speaks expansively of law-making through majority rule (95–7), it is evident that Locke was no democrat. He showed no interest in conferring the vote on all adult males (let alone females), and he accepts that in England legislation lies in a parliament composed of a king and lords as well as commons. There is, however, no contradiction here: the foundational act which forms political society is different from everyday acts of legislation (96–9). The former is universal; the latter is by majorities within the established assembly. There is no difficulty for Locke about universal consent to be bound by a majority of those who represent us, or even by oligarchies. There is, however, a proviso: majorities are not themselves unbounded, for the laws they make must not breach natural law or the fundamental purposes of political society. (Locke may conceivably have envisaged something like the American system in which what he calls the 'fundamental law' or 'original grant' is embodied in a written constitution that checks the activities of legislators (134, 153).) Locke has sometimes been seen as inclining to a dictatorial 'majoritarian democracy', rather as Rousseau has been seen as a 'totalitarian democrat'. But Locke gives no general licence to the corporate community, majoritarian or otherwise, to enact what it pleases. The canons of right and wrong transcend the will of parliaments and peoples. There are things that even the most unambiguous popular mandate cannot legitimately do.

The final problem with consent is of a more abstract kind. It is not difficult to imagine people choosing to accept all manner of governments: slavery and absolutism, as well as, in private life, domestic and sexual subjection. While Hobbes tended to regard any actual assent as an admissible act of consent, Locke did not. There are occasions when we apparently give our consent, but in a deeper and more real sense do not. In the first place, we must distinguish consent from submission: the latter is an enforced 'consent', a necessity, and does not bind (176). It is sensible to obey a highwayman with a gun, but our submission confers no legitimacy (186). A woman may submit to rape to avoid injury, but she has not consented. Equally, we may submit to a conqueror, and bide our time until resistance has a chance of success.

There is a second way in which we can distinguish rational from actual consent. If I buy goods which turn out to be faulty, I may cancel my contract of purchase, because no rational person would consent to buy unfit goods. I have, so to speak, been coerced by my ignorance. But we are now in difficult territory. It is easy to agree that parents should decide for their children because minors are not capable of rational consent. But it is problematical to say that an adult's actual consent may not equate with his or her real or rational consent. In modern political theory the idea of 'false consciousness' is sometimes used to explain why groups of people fail to choose what rational, far-sighted people should choose. Locke often wrote about the way superstitions, inherited prejudices, intellectual fashions, and officially sanctioned public doctrines threaten us with mental slavery and prevent us making rational judgments (I, 58). This train of thought can be traced from Locke through Rousseau to Marx. Hobbes (and Bentham), by contrast, are more ready to defer to what people actually choose, since they have little patience with the notion of univocal rational human purposes. In this sense Hobbes and Bentham may be argued to be more 'liberal' than Locke.

For Locke there are regimes to which we cannot consent (23, 131, 164). He means 'cannot, if we are not to renounce our humanity', for the free exercise of our rational will is fundamental to our dignity as humans. Our civil liberty constitutes part of our moral liberty. Locke reiterates an Aristotelian idea that counterpoises the life of an autonomous personality to the less-than-human life of one who is merely the instrument of another: the political relation of ruler–citizen is contrasted with the sub-political relation of master–slave (17, 22–4, 163, 172, 174). Rousseau, Kant and Hegel would later develop this same notion. Locke repeatedly uses the word 'arbitrary' to characterize the irrational, coercive will of masters and tyrants. Liberty consists in being free of the arbitrary will of another; in legitimate civil society we obey only ourselves, because we have consented to the laws (22). Good laws are not restrictions, but enlargements of freedom (57).

THE CONSTITUTION

Within the bounds of natural law, the people may establish whatever form of government they like (106, 132, 135, 141, 220, 243). Whatever the form, government is fiduciary, a trust (149, 156). Its powers are delegated to it by the people, and may be recalled, dismantled, or altered by them (149). Unlike other Whigs, Locke held that the contract takes place only between citizens and not between king and people: rulers are merely servants and officials (152). Locke divides forms of government in the traditional way: the rule of one, few or many – monarchy, aristocracy or democracy – or, preferably, a mixed form. This typology was inherited from Aristotle and the Roman republicans, and transmitted by the scholastics and humanists. According to Locke, any of the three 'pure' forms may be legitimate, and may become despotic (201). Legislative power *could* rightfully be placed solely in the hands of a monarch (135). This suggests the theoretical possibility of Locke's allowing absolute monarchy. In 1672 he practically did so when supporting the royal edict of toleration against an intolerant parliament. What makes a tyranny is not a particular form of government but the abuse of the public good (135–7). In practice, however, it would be folly to erect a pure monarchy, for earthly kings are not sufficiently godlike to act justly, and Locke frequently equates 'absolute' with 'arbitrary'. He likewise thinks democracy is scarcely advisable. Prudence dictates that the best form is a mixed government. In a parochial way Locke takes for granted the existing arrangements of the English mixed constitution, in which the legislature consists of king, lords and commons, and hence only *in part* of popular representatives (157). Locke sees parliament, despite its unelected elements and the narrow franchise, as representing the whole nation (135), just as a modern parliament may be said to represent children and those who did not bother to vote. His only hint at franchise reform is the suggestion that representation should be more demographically balanced, so that 'rotten boroughs' (decayed towns with small populations) should be disfranchised (157–8).

Locke has sometimes been credited with the doctrine of the separation of powers. In its modern form, chiefly derived from Montesquieu's *Spirit of the Laws* (1748), this is the idea that there are three distinct functions of government – legislative, executive and judiciary – which enhance liberty by balancing each other. Their separation is articulated in the American constitution, but only partially in the British, so that in modern times there is a danger in Britain that the legislature is too weak in the face of the executive power of the prime minister, who, arguably, has inherited most of the powers of the Stuart crown. Locke speaks of legislative, executive and federative powers (88, 143–8). By the last he means the conduct of foreign relations (146), which we would regard as part of the executive power. While he is insistent on the distinction between legislative and executive, he accepts the English model with its partial separation – for the monarch and the ministers, who constitute the executive, also belong to the legislature in parliament (144, 151, 159). However, he warns that where the executive power controls the legislature, or where the judiciary is perverted by the executive power, tyranny inevitably follows (20, 91, 214). The danger in late Stuart England was that the crown would engross the legislative power by undermining or evading parliament, and the judicial power by sacking and bullying judges.

Although Locke's chief fear is of absolute monarchy, he insists that legislatures may also be despotic (149, 168, 218, 227). He probably had in mind the Cavalier Parliament which sat, without a general election, from 1661 to 1679, and passed a body of oppressive legislation, particularly to impose religious conformity. A parliament that sits perpetually becomes corrupt, and law-makers should regularly return to the discipline of being ordinary citizens (138, 143). Moreover, Locke is surprisingly generous to prerogative power, the personal powers of the monarch. It is neither possible nor desirable for the legislature always to be sitting, and there may be emergencies requiring rapid decision-making (159–68). Not every circumstance can be anticipated by laws, and Locke values wisdom and prudence in rulers. In politics the art of governing is as important as abstract principles (42, 147, 154, 160). The crucial prerogative power is that of summoning and dismissing parliaments. For, fundamental though the legislative power is, paradoxically it requires executive action to convoke it. If the monarch abuses this power, it is a sure mark of tyranny (153–6, 167).

THE RIGHT OF RESISTANCE

Locke is at his most polemical when he describes the evils of despotism (92–3; I, 58). Nothing is more salutary than Locke's insistence that rulers are subject to popular moral judgment, and that it is just as patriotic to resist internal as external aggression (231). The word 'terrorism' today is usually applied only to violence against the state by disaffected citizens. Locke reminds us that states sometimes sponsor terrorism against their own citizens.

Tyranny brings about the dissolution of government, and frees people to establish a new and better one. When Locke describes the marks of tyranny he comes closest to narrating the events of his own time. Government is dissolved when a prince hinders the legislature from meeting (155, 215). Here he had in mind either

Charles II's refusal to allow a newly elected parliament to sit during 1679–80, or the abrupt dismissal of the Oxford Parliament in 1681 and the failure to call elections thereafter. Government is dissolved when the legislators, or 'ways of election', are corrupted (216, 218, 222): this alludes to Charles's use of 'placemen' in parliament, or to the dismissal of London's elected Whig sheriffs in 1682, or to James II's pressure on MPs to do his bidding. Government is dissolved when property is invaded (221): this is probably a reference to the punitive sequestrations of money and goods from Dissenters caught worshipping illegally. It is dissolved when a prince submits his state to a foreign power (217) – an allusion to Charles's and James's subservience to Louis XIV of France. It is dissolved when a religion which is not that of the people is surreptitiously favoured (210), a reference to the Catholic threat. And, finally, it is dissolved if the prince abandons his kingdom (219), as James did in 1688.

Locke provides a roll-call of those who conspire with absolutist princes. Tyrants are invariably surrounded by sycophants, ambitious ministers, and self-interested factions, and also by priests whose divine right doctrines prostitute religion in the service of an authoritarian state (94, 210, 239; I, 1–5). More generally, tyranny is the rule of arbitrary caprice, of force without right, of private rather than public good (19, 199, 202). Since the social contract is a bargain – we would not choose to be worse off by it – any government which does not preserve our lives, liberties and property cannot be that to which we gave our consent (131, 222). In these circumstances government is dissolved and a state of war ensues (17, 90, 131, 205, 211). It is not the people who dissolve government, but the tyrant who does so: it is he who rebels against righteousness, and thereby 'unkings' himself. Revolution is a restoration of natural right against rebellion by the tyrant (226–7, 239). A tyrant is no longer a political agent; he is a private person, a pirate and robber, a murderous animal (11, 16, 172, 202, 228). At this point Locke's 'universal executive power of the law of nature' comes back into play. The people transfer the right of judging, and of executing judgment, to the sovereign, but always retain a reversionary right, when the rule of law is denied them (13, 20). When that happens, any person may, once more, exact retribution. Locke's 'strange doctrine' is fundamental to his shocking insistence that any person may kill a tyrant. He licenses political assassination.

The assassin as a righteous agent of God was as dangerous a figure in the seventeenth century as today. Under the doctrine of 'antinomianism', godliness allows the elect to overthrow, or ignore, ordinary laws and governments. Locke does not condone an antinomian approach; he offers no sectarian religious justification, no licence grounded arbitrarily in Scriptural verses. Scripture must harmonize with reason and nature. Yet he echoes the radical Reformation tradition which found biblical support for tyrannicide, culminating in John Milton's citation of Ehud's slaying of King Eglon as a precedent for the execution of Charles I after the Civil War. Locke speaks of an 'appeal to heaven', and makes play of Jephtha, who was chosen leader by the people, and revolted against the Ammonites (21, 109, 168, 176, 241-2).

Understandably, therefore, some commentators stress Locke's radicalism. Ashcraft (1986) shows him engaged in a career of conspiracy and under surveillance by government spies. He argues that Locke's radicalism extended to a social critique, that he appealed to the trading and artisanal class, and to the minor gentry, against the idle rich, and that he had affinities with the Levellers of the 1640s. Much of this case is persuasive, for in two ways Locke's argument was strikingly radical. First, the right of revolution lies with every private citizen acting alone or collectively. There is no theory of the 'lesser magistrates', of nobles or parliament, as the agents of revolution. Most earlier radicals had cautiously avoided placing revolutionary violence in the hands of the lower orders. Second, Locke's theory of dissolution was too radical for most contemporaries. At the beginning of 1689 the Convention parliament hurried to install William of Orange as king with a minimum of disruption to the existing constitution. A minority, however, argued that the entire constitution was now in the melting pot, and Locke seems to share this view. His is not a theory about parliament's redressing a constitutional balance unhinged by a wayward king. He argues that in a revolution, power reverts to the community as a whole, which may establish whatever form of government it pleases (Franklin, 1978). His fellow Whig, Atwood, the only person who mentioned Locke's book in the debate on allegiance during 1689-93, criticized him for unnecessarily dissolving government into the hands of the 'confused multitude'.

Nonetheless, we should be cautious about seeing Locke as a revolutionary in too expansive or heroic a way. First, he is anxious to deny that his theory encourages anarchy and rebelliousness. Not every injury by a prince should be redressed, for 'a long train of actings' must be visible; not a mere caucus of malcontents, but the whole body of the people, must judge of the oppression; and a people must first exhaust all possibility of legal redress (168, 203–10, 223–5, 230). Second, the social bearing of Locke's philosophy is consonant with the hierarchies of his day. He served a great aristocrat and wrote for landed gentlemen. He distances himself from such populist rebels as Spartacus, Cade, Massaniello, even Cromwell (196; I, 79, 121). The *Two Treatises* is a work of political, not of social, revolution. (For this reason Locke has acquired a new cachet in Eastern Europe. The rebels of 1989 disliked identifying with 'revolution', because that word has strong Marxian overtones of proletarian revolution – and these rebels were overthrowing Marxist states. The events of 1989 constituted a Lockean revolution. A people, constituted as a political community, not as a class, withdrew their assent, and undertook resistance; civil society was not dissolved, but government was.) Locke remarks that an oppressed people is not bound to risk all until it has good hopes of success; a people may submit and bide its time for many years (176). The Greek Christians, although for two centuries under Turkish rule, had not lost their right of resistance (192).

Third, despite being at the intellectual extreme of the Revolution debate in 1689, Locke became complacent about post-Revolutionary governments. It is true that he sponsored the ending of press censorship (1695), yet he sat on the Board of Trade when other Whigs were renewing a polemic against the Court, and his new patron was Lord Somers, a leader of the establishment 'Junto' Whigs, whom radicals saw as betraying Whig principles for the sake of power. When William Molyneux used Locke's book in 1698 to deny that Ireland had consented to English conquest, Locke distanced himself from the argument. One explanation for Locke's compliance was his acute sense of the paramountcy of King William's war to defend Protestantism against French Catholic absolutism. Fourth, Locke kept faith with the traditional Ancient Constitution, with its executive monarchy and hereditary nobility (213, 223). Despite the theoretical right to erect a new form of government, in practice he did not want this to happen. In 1689 he told a friend that the Convention should be 'restoring our ancient government, the best possibly that ever was'. In short, Locke was about as conservative as a revolutionary could be (Marshall, 1994).

PROPERTY

In 1703 Locke wrote that property was nowhere better explained than in the *Two Treatises*. The intensity of interpretative dispute about the fifth chapter of the Second Treatise stems not only from Locke's ambiguities but also from the urgency with which issues of property rights, entrepreneurship, equality, welfare and taxation are discussed today. An important stimulus to debate was provided by Macpherson (1962), who argued, in Marxist terms, that Locke defended unlimited property appropriation and in so doing legitimated the capitalist ethic at its inception. (Locke's text apart, it is true that he lived amidst a financial and commercial revolution which saw the foundations of modern fiscal institutions and joint-stock enterprises.) Ironically, 'New Right' defenders of the free market adopt an interpretation similar to Macpherson's, though the moral significance they give it is starkly divergent. By contrast, Tully (1980) has argued for the presence of communitarian and welfarist features in Locke's argument.

These differing approaches are reflected in two key philosophical texts of contemporary liberalism, which claim an allegiance to the Lockean tradition. In *Anarchy, State and Utopia* (1974), Robert Nozick offers a libertarian and anti-statist vision, in which welfare taxation is seen as a tyranny over private property rights. By contrast, John Rawls's *Theory of Justice* (1972) suggests that consenting citizens would rationally choose an outcome that includes a degree of egalitarianism and 'safety nets' for the disadvantaged.

In Western thought there have been, broadly, four doctrines concerning property (which, before modern times, were usually couched in theological language). The first is the communistic position: God gave the earth and its fruits to mankind in common and nobody has the right to private appropriation. This was taught by the medieval Franciscans, who denounced the wealth and pomp of the Church. It reappeared in Thomas More's *Utopia*, and, during Locke's youth, in the writings of the Digger leader Gerrard Winstanley. The second doctrine is at the opposite pole: God gave the world as private property directly to Adam and, by inheritance, to Adam's heirs (I, 21-43). This view was upheld by Filmer and, partially, in the feudal notion of the king as sole proprietor in his kingdom, under whom all subjects are tenants. Filmer's purpose (like Hobbes's) was to defend the right of early Stuart monarchs to tax their subjects without the consent of parliament. The remaining two doctrines also uphold private property, but they concede that God originally gave the world to mankind in common (*Genesis* 1:28), before authorizing its division into private property. The third entails that the rights thus generated are absolute and exclusive: the property of individuals is 'theirs' in an unequivocal and unencumbered way. Grotius argued that people consented to divide the world into private properties, with all the inequalities that followed. The fourth doctrine holds that alongside private rights there persist obligations to the community, especially to ensure subsistence for all, so that private property is subject to constraints. Aquinas ruled that it is not theft if the starving person takes what is necessary to live.

Locke plainly subscribed to neither the first nor the second doctrine. The difficult question is, did he hold the third or the fourth? We may first survey the textual evidence for the third, and then consider ways in which he mitigates a stringent private right doctrine.

1. Locke claims that a person acquires property in whatever he has 'mixed his labour with' (27). He awards high moral standing to those who work hard; accumulating property is the just fruit of their labour, since God gave the world to 'the industrious and rational' (34, 48). In his *Essay on the Poor Law* (1697) he takes a fiercely coercive view towards the feckless. Commentators have connected Locke's linkage of austerity and prosperity to the Calvinist idea of the 'calling' and to Max Weber's thesis about the 'Protestant work ethic'.

2. Locke apparently casts aside traditional moral constraints

laid upon property accumulation. These constraints were the spoil and sufficiency limitations: the propertied had a duty not to take so much that some goods would spoil, and were to leave enough behind to provide sufficiently for others (27, 31, 33, 46). Locke appears to argue that the invention of money obviated these constraints, for hoarded money would not spoil, whereas hoarded sheep carcasses would. Although Locke substitutes a labour theory for Grotius's consent theory to explain the origin of property, he does introduce a quasi-contract for the invention of money (36–7, 47). Industrious people, still in the state of nature, may thereby accumulate legitimate fortunes, and such enlarged possessions entail no injury to anyone (48, 50).

3. Locke repeatedly insists that the purpose of political society is to protect private property (94, 95, 124, 139, 171, 222). He offers no utopian idealization of political community, only a minimalist politics grounded in the 'umpirage' which the sovereign supplies in adjudicating disputes and in preserving from disturbance the settled enjoyment of our lives, liberties and estates (87). One crucial corollary is that governments cannot tax without consent (139–42).

4. Locke uses the 'nobody worse off' principle. We do not intend to be worse off by making the social contract. And in fact we are all better off, because private property, through incentive and entrepreneurship, makes people more productive, and, in a richer economy, even the poor are benefited, so that nobody is worse off under a system of inequality. Locke defends enclosure of common lands on the ground of greater productivity. He also remarks that a labourer in England's advanced economy is richer than the king of an American tribe (41). Adam Smith was to make a similar point a century later.

5. Locke upholds the grossly unequal property relations of his own time (46, 48, 50). In the aftermath of the Civil War he had strong motives for detaching his political radicalism from suspicion that he was a harbinger of social levelling. His message was that a gentleman could support an uprising against the king without fearing for his property. The *Fundamental Constitutions of Carolina*, which he helped Shaftesbury to draft, constructed a hierarchic society of carefully graded land holdings, including an hereditary aristocracy.

6. Locke justifies colonial exploitation. His preoccupation with America partly stems from his belief that the rights of the 'laborious' colonists entitle them to the unproductive 'wastelands' of the Indians. Those who can make America fruitful have a better right to own the land (41). In later American history the *Two Treatises* was used in courtrooms against native land rights.

However, there are significant elements in Locke's text which tend another way, and suggest the fourth doctrine concerning property.

1. By 'property' Locke does not mean simply material goods. He speaks of having property in one's person, life, liberty and religion, as well as estates (27, 123, 173, 209). To have a right of property is to exact from others the duty of recognizing our personhood. Labour is a creative act by which we impress our conscious will on the brute things of the earth, and it is labour that puts the value on things (40). Labour is necessary to our being, not just because we must eat, but because we must make of ourselves a distinctive moral character. Property rights must be framed around the rights of personality, to which every rational being is entitled. Later radical readers of Locke took him to be insisting upon a universal right to work.

2. Locke emphasizes that we are God's property. God laboured to create us and therein lies His property right. We are an expression of God's divine being, of God's 'workmanship', and God is the sole true proprietor of the world (6; I, 39). Consequently we are not free to act as we please, with our lives or goods. For example, it is sinful to commit suicide, for we do not fully own ourselves (6). Among the obligations we bear, as property owners, is to respect the needs of others, who are God's workmanship.

3. Locke is clear that the right of subsistence remains: the impoverished must be fed (25, 70, 183). There are important passages in the First Treatise about our duty to a 'needy brother' (I, 41–3). The holding of property, like the exercise of government, is a trust, a stewardship: we are permitted private property only so that the earth may fructify for the common good.

4. Locke exhibits a doctrine of communal rights which have been called 'use rights' or 'claim rights'. The original common

ownership in *Genesis* 1:28 was such that everybody had a right of access to use God's gifts. In Locke's society, and ours, this notion persisted in 'commons': public, unenclosed land, which anybody could use (28). An instance of 'use rights' today is public rights of way: the farmer owns the land, but not absolutely, for he cannot exclude members of the community from walking across it. Locke holds that in modern times such commons were secured by 'compact' and law, so that no enclosure could occur without the community's consent (35). Historians have documented the long struggle of the early-modern English to maintain their communal rights against enclosers.

5. Locke perhaps takes one further step, arguing that once we enter political society, the legislature legitimately intervenes. The sovereign is bound to arrange property rights in such a way that they do not hinder productive labour and so that subsistence will be available for all. Locke argues that, in his society, unlike in ancient times, there is a land shortage (except in America) and so the sufficiency principle is breached; governments may therefore redress the balance. Positive law thus enforces natural law entitlements, and he speaks of governments 'regulating' property (3, 30, 45, 50, 120).

If these propositions about community rights can be sustained from Locke's text, there is an ironic outcome. It is Filmer, the Royalist absolutist, with his emphasis on Adam's absolute proprietorship, who is closer than Locke, the supposed modern liberal, to the modern capitalist doctrine of indefeasible property rights. Locke, by contrast, would turn out to be what we would now call a social democrat.

THE HISTORY OF SOCIETY

We can place Locke's argument about property in the context of his account of the history of civilization. He traces the passage of humankind from primitive simplicity to economic modernity. Sometimes he lauds primitive virtue and a golden age (94, 110, 111), but the march of economic history and the development of human institutions are inexorable. The earliest peoples lived in hunter-gatherer societies; then came settled agriculture. Money, trade and greater abundance followed, and in turn unequal property distributions, land scarcity and greater quarrelsomeness. These circumstances required sophisticated legal institutions. As states enlarged, so opportunities for political corruption increased, and the unencumbered prerogatives of patriarchal chieftains gave way to the constitutional apparatus of modern states (31–2, 36–8, 45, 94, 105, 107, 110, 162). In a more complex form these ideas would become the theory of economic stages proposed by Adam Smith and the Scottish Enlightenment philosophers and, in turn, by Marx. It is a theory which shows how the economic structure of a society shapes its laws, institutions and culture.

One aspect of this theme is Locke's concern for demographic growth. His contemporaries were fearful about under-population; a century later people began to fear over-population – an anxiety forcefully expressed in the writings of Thomas Malthus. Locke holds that the trajectory of world history is towards a fully peopled earth; this is part of God's purpose. The earliest ages of the world exhibited low population densities and low productivity. The empty wildernesses of biblical times have given way to a peopling of the four corners of the earth, except in America, where peopling is urgent. It is the duty of modern states to encourage population growth, and it is a characteristic of despotisms that they are less populous and less productive. Free societies are demographically expansionist societies, and they are richer; they fulfil the providential unfolding of world history (74; I, 33, 41, 59).

Allied to this theme is Locke's preoccupation with agricultural 'improvement'. He writes in the tradition of the Puritan economic reformers in the circle of Samuel Hartlib in the 1640s, which was developed in his own time by the economist William Petty. They envisaged progress toward highly productive agriculture. Locke's vision in the *Two Treatises* remains agrarian rather than industrial (Wood, 1984). His concern is with productive labour through better tillage and husbandry. States should not seek territorial expansion for its own sake, but more intensive use of existing land (32, 34, 37, 42).

Locke sees private property and money as necessary instruments for economic growth, in order that the whole community would be enriched. He is not concerned to celebrate private

wealth, but to enhance the 'common stock'. Private appropriation is simply the means to make God's fruits grow (26, 34,
37). Thus, enclosed land (taken out of the commons) would,
through intensive cultivation, yield ten times greater the quantity
of goods. Locke cannot abide the waste of uncultivated land
(37–8, 42, 45–6). He mentions that in Spain people may
cultivate land they do not own if the owner has left that land to
waste (36). Ownership is secondary to the fundamental purpose
of 'improvement' for the benefit and 'conveniency' of all
mankind.

Whatever the importance for Locke of private property and
personal effort, there is nothing especially 'individualist' about his
vision. Indeed, in order to achieve 'improvement', governments
may have to be regulatory and interventionist. Locke hopes for a
'godlike' prince who will galvanize the 'honest industry' of the
nation (42). His contemporaries and friends, such as Boyle and
Newton, intended their 'natural philosophy' to help fulfil human
destiny by the recovery of the *prisca theologia*, the original enlightenment and perfection which God gave to Adam before the Fall.
Locke believes that the same intellectual effort could be applied
to the art of government. He is somewhat apocalyptic in identifying
history's destination as the full peopling and full cultivation of the
earth. He remarks that 'in the beginning all the world was America',
but he also implies that in the end it will be Devonshire (37, 49).
Condemned to labour by the Fall, humanity can recover the
cornucopia of the Garden of Eden by its 'honest industry' (32; I,
45). Just as God offers a charter for the eternal salvation of fallen
humanity, so He offers a charter for our temporal, economic
salvation. In politics it is our duty, singly and as a commonwealth,
to fulfil God's temporal charter, for God gave humankind 'all
things richly to enjoy'.

MARK GOLDIE

NOTE ON THE TEXT

Locke scholarship was transformed by the publication in 1960 of a new and authoritative text edited by Peter Laslett. This was based on Locke's own copy of the third edition, published in 1698, which he and his secretary carefully corrected by hand, and which is today owned by Christ's College, Cambridge. It includes significant additions and alterations. This therefore is the most authentic text, the one that Locke authorized for posterity. Some eighteenth- and early nineteenth-century editions, especially that by the republican scholar Thomas Hollis in 1764, on the whole made a good job of being faithful to Locke's final intentions. But after the 1880s several printings (including the previous Everyman edition) went back to the first edition of 1690, in the understandable belief that this must be closest to Locke's original (but lost) manuscript. In fact Locke was angry with his printer for a botched job. In his will he wrote, 'Mr Churchill has published several editions but all very incorrect'.

The present edition is the first modernized version of the whole *Two Treatises* based on Locke's corrected text. It is derived from Laslett's edition and has been checked against the copy-text at Christ's College; the comparison reveals a handful of trivial imperfections in Laslett's text. I am grateful to the Master and Fellows of Christ's for permission to work with Locke's copy. There have been three previous editions which have provided a modernized version of the Christ's College text of the Second Treatise only: those by J. W. Gough (Oxford: Blackwell, 1946); R. I. Cox (Arlington Heights, Illinois: Croft's Classics, 1982); and David Wootton (London: Penguin, 1993, which includes extracts from the First Treatise). Most recent American editions, including T. I. Cook's (New York: Hafner, 1947) and C. B. Macpherson's (Indianapolis: Hackett, 1980) derive from Hollis's sixth edition.

The present edition revises Laslett's text to make it more user-friendly for modern readers. Spelling and capitalization have been modernized, and words in italics (which occur profusely in seventeenth-century texts) have been converted to roman. However, Locke's punctuation has been retained, except that the usage of apostrophes has been modernized and inverted commas have been supplied for quotations. He did not always punctuate as we would, and seventeenth-century sentences can be very long, but his liberal use of punctuation usually renders his text readily explicable, and to have revised it would have risked introducing misreadings of his meaning. I have retained Locke's vocabulary, which is occasionally archaic: he uses such words as 'methinks', 'saith', 'begat', 'hath' and 'seemeth'; I have also kept his characteristic ' 'tis'. Note also that, like his contemporaries, Locke generally referred to the civil ruler as the 'prince' or 'magistrate', and that he usually speaks of the 'commonwealth' rather than the 'state'. I hope to have rendered the text accessible to modern readers while preserving the character of a book recognizably belonging to a time other than our own. Students who wish for the full scholarly apparatus provided by Laslett may refer to his edition, published by Cambridge University Press (1960; second edition, 1967; student edition, 1988).

Locke explained at the end of his preface that his citations from his adversary, Sir Robert Filmer, were taken from the editions newly published in 1679–80. The present edition omits these and replaces them with page references, in square brackets, to Johann P. Sommerville's edition of Filmer's *Patriarcha and Other Writings* (Cambridge University Press, 1991). For Locke's quotations from Richard Hooker's *Of the Laws of Ecclesiastical Polity* I have supplied page references to A. S. McGrade's edition (Cambridge University Press, 1989). Citations from the Bible and other sources have been rendered in modern form and, where appropriate, placed in brackets; in square brackets where Locke did not himself provide a reference. Locke's quotations are not always accurate but I have left them as they are. Some surmises have been necessary as to where Locke intended quotation marks to occur. Where Locke writes 'F.', 'Sir R. F.', 'our A.', 'ch.', 'chap.' and so on, I have expanded these to 'Filmer', 'Sir Robert Filmer', 'our author', 'chapter' and so on. Compounds such as 'any one' and 'every one' have been elided to conform to modern usage. I can detect no pattern in Locke's variant usage of 'freemen', 'free men' and 'free-men', and have rendered all such cases as 'free men'. Hebrew words have been transliterated (for which I am grateful to Dr Naomi Tadmor); unfamiliar Latin phrases are provided with translations in square brackets. All material in square brackets has been editorially interpolated; there are no editorial footnotes to the text and all the footnotes are Locke's and comprise quotations from Hooker. Locke's text is 103,000 words long: 48,000 in the First Treatise and 55,000 in the Second. The First Treatise is an incomplete work and ends abruptly: Locke tells us in his preface that the lost manuscript would have amounted to 'more than all the rest'.

For their advice I am indebted to John Dunn, Iain Hampsher-Monk, Howell Lloyd, Christine MacLeod, John Marshall, Jonathan Scott, Sylvana Tomaselli, James Tully, Robert Wokler and John Yolton.

M. G.

TWO
TREATISES
OF
Government:
In the Former,
The False Principles and Foundation
OF
Sir *Robert Filmer*,
And His FOLLOWERS,
ARE
Detected and Overthrown.
The Latter is an
ESSAY
CONCERNING
The True Original, Extent, and End
OF
Civil-Government.

LONDON: Printed for *Awnsham* and *John Churchill*, at the *Black Swan* in *Pater-Noster-Row.* 1 6 9 8.

This title page of the third edition of the *Two Treatises* (1698), the last published in Locke's lifetime, is reproduced with the permission of the Syndics of Cambridge University Library. This particular copy came from the collection of Lord Acton, the Victorian historian who planned to write the definitive history of freedom.

In his own copy of the 1698 edition Locke wrote out a passage in Latin from Livy's *History of Rome*, Book 9, Chapter 1. It is a strikingly savage condemnation of despotism. In English the passage reads roughly as follows.

But if the poor are left no human rights when they encounter the mighty, then I shall turn to the Gods as avengers of overweaning pride. I shall pray that they turn their anger upon those who are content neither with their own property, nor with what they take from others. Their savagery is not satisfied by the death of the guilty. They will be satisfied only if we offer them our blood to drink and our entrails to tear out.

THE PREFACE

Reader,

Thou hast here the beginning and end of a discourse concerning government; what fate has otherwise disposed of the papers that should have filled up the middle, and were more than all the rest, 'tis not worthwhile to tell thee. These, which remain, I hope are sufficient to establish the throne of our great restorer, our present King William; to make good his title, in the consent of the people, which being the only one of all lawful governments, he has more fully and clearly than any prince in Christendom: and to justify to the world, the people of England, whose love of their just and natural rights, with their resolution to preserve them, saved the nation when it was on the very brink of slavery and ruin. If these papers have that evidence, I flatter myself is to be found in them, there will be no great miss of those which are lost, and my reader may be satisfied without them. For I imagine I shall have neither the time, nor inclination to repeat my pains, and fill up the wanting part of my answer, by tracing Sir Robert again, through all the windings and obscurities which are to be met with in the several branches of his wonderful system. The king, and body of the nation, have since so thoroughly confuted his hypothesis, that, I suppose, nobody hereafter will have either the confidence to appear against our common safety, and be again an advocate for slavery; or the weakness to be deceived with contradictions dressed up in a popular style, and well turned periods. For if anyone will be at the pains himself, in those parts which are here untouched, to strip Sir Robert's discourses of the flourish of doubtful expressions, and endeavour to reduce his words to direct, positive, intelligible propositions, and then compare them one with another, he will quickly be satisfied there was never so much glib nonsense put together in well sounding English. If he think it not worthwhile to examine his works all through, let him make an experiment in that part where he treats of usurpation; and let him try whether he can, with all his skill, make Sir Robert intelligible, and consistent with himself, or common sense. I should not speak so plainly of a gentleman, long since past answering, had not the pulpit, of late years, publicly owned his doctrine, and made it the current divinity of the times. 'Tis necessary those men, who taking on them to be teachers, have so dangerously misled others, should be openly showed of what authority this their patriarch is, whom they have so blindly followed, that so they may either retract what upon so ill grounds they have vented, and cannot be maintained, or else justify those principles which they preached up for gospel; though they had no better an author than an English courtier. For I should not have writ against Sir Robert, or taken the pains to show his mistakes, inconsistencies, and want of (what he so much boasts of, and pretends wholly to build on) Scripture proofs, were there not men amongst us, who, by crying up his books, and espousing his doctrine, save me from the reproach of writing against a dead adversary. They have been so zealous in this point, that if I have done him any wrong; I cannot hope they should spare me. I wish, where they have done the truth and the public wrong, they would be as ready to redress it and allow its just weight to this reflection, *viz.* that, there cannot be done a greater mischief to prince and people, than the propagating wrong notions concerning government, that so at last all times might not have reason to complain of the drum ecclesiastic. If anyone, concerned really for truth, undertake the confutation of my hypothesis, I promise him either to recant my mistake, upon fair conviction; or to answer his difficulties. But he must remember two things;

First, that cavilling here and there, at some expression, or little incident of my discourse, is not an answer to my book.

Secondly, that I shall not take railing for arguments, nor think either of these worth my notice: though I shall always look on myself as bound to give satisfaction to anyone who shall appear to be conscientiously scrupulous in the point, and shall show any just grounds for his scruples.

I have nothing more, but to advertise [to] the reader, that 'A' stands for our author. 'O' for his *Observations on Hobbes, Milton, etc.* And that a bare quotation of pages always means pages of his *Patriarcha*, edit[ion of] 1680.*

*[Locke's system of referencing is not followed here. See 'Note on the Text'.]

THE FIRST TREATISE OF GOVERNMENT

Chapter 1
THE INTRODUCTION

1. Slavery is so vile and miserable an estate of man, and so directly opposite to the generous temper and courage of our nation; that 'tis hardly to be conceived, that an Englishman, much less a gentleman, should plead for it. And truly, I should have taken Sir Robert Filmer's *Patriarcha* as any other treatise, which would persuade all men, that they are slaves, and ought to be so, for such another exercise of wit, as was his who writ the encomium of Nero, rather than for a serious discourse meant in earnest, had not the gravity of the title and epistle, the picture in the front of the book, and the applause that followed it, required me to believe, that the author and publisher were both in earnest. I therefore took it into my hands with all the expectation, and read it through with all the attention due to a treatise, that made such a noise at its coming abroad, and cannot but confess myself mightily surprised, that in a book, which was to provide chains for all mankind, I should find nothing but a rope of sand, useful perhaps to such, whose skill and business it is to raise a dust, and would blind the people, the better to mislead them, but in truth is not of any force to draw those into bondage, who have their eyes open, and so much sense about them as to consider, that chains are but an ill wearing, how much care soever hath been taken to file and polish them.

2. If anyone think I take too much liberty in speaking so freely of a man, who is the great champion of absolute power, and the idol of those who worship it; I beseech him to make this small allowance for once, to one, who, even after the reading of Sir Robert's book, cannot but think himself, as the laws allow him, a free man: and I know no fault it is to do so, unless anyone better skilled in the fate of it, than I, should have it revealed to him, that this treatise, which has lain dormant so long, was, when it appeared

in the world, to carry by strength of its arguments, all liberty out of it; and that from thenceforth our author's short model was to be the pattern in the mount [*Hebrews* 8:5], and the perfect standard of politics for the future. His system lies in a little compass, 'tis no more but this, 'that all government is absolute monarchy'. And the ground he builds on, is this, 'that no man is born free'.

3. In this last age a generation of men has sprung up among us, who would flatter princes with an opinion, that they have a divine right to absolute power, let the laws by which they are constituted, and are to govern, and the conditions under which they enter upon their authority, be what they will, and their engagements to observe them never so well ratified by solemn oaths and promises. To make way for this doctrine they have denied mankind a right to natural freedom, whereby they have not only, as much as in them lies, exposed all subjects to the utmost misery of tyranny and oppression, but have also unsettled the titles, and shaken the thrones of princes: (for they too, by these men's system, except only one, are all born slaves, and by divine right, are subjects to Adam's right heir); as if they had designed to make war upon all government, and subvert the very foundations of human society, to serve their present turn.

4. However we must believe them upon their own bare words, when they tell us, we are all born slaves, and we must continue so; there is no remedy for it: life and thraldom we entered into together, and can never be quit of the one, till we part with the other. Scripture or reason I am sure do not anywhere say so notwithstanding the noise of divine right, as if divine authority hath subjected us to the unlimited will of another. An admirable state of mankind, and that which they have not had wit enough to find out till this latter age. For however Sir Robert Filmer seems to condemn the novelty of the contrary opinion [3], yet I believe it will be hard for him to find any other age or country of the world, but this which has asserted monarchy to be *jure divino* [by divine right]. And he confesses that 'Hayward, Blackwood, Barclay, and others, that have bravely vindicated the right of kings in most points', never thought of this, 'but with one consent admitted the natural liberty and equality of mankind' [3].

5. By whom this doctrine came at first to be broached, and brought in fashion amongst us, and what sad effects it gave rise

to, I leave to historians to relate, or to the memory of those who were contemporaries with Sibthorp and Manwaring to recollect. My business at present is only to consider what Sir Robert Filmer who is allowed to have carried this argument furthest, and is supposed to have brought it to perfection, has said in it; for from him everyone, who would be as fashionable as French was at Court, has learned, and runs away with this short system of politics, *viz.* 'men are not born free, and therefore could never have the liberty to choose either governors, or forms of government. Princes have their power absolute, and by divine right, for slaves could never have a right to compact or consent. Adam was an absolute monarch, and so are all princes ever since'.

Chapter 2
OF PATERNAL AND REGAL POWER

6. Sir Robert Filmer's great position is, that 'men are not naturally free'. This is the foundation on which his absolute monarchy stands, and from which it erects itself to a height, that its power is above every power, *caput inter nubila* [its head is in the clouds], so high above all earthly and human things, that thought can scarce reach it; that promises and oaths, which tie the infinite deity, cannot confine it. But if this foundation fails, all his fabric falls with it, and governments must be left again to the old way of being made by contrivance, and the consent of men ('Ανθρωπίνη κτίσις) making use of their reason to unite together into society. To prove this grand position of his, he tells us, 'men are born in subjection to their parents', and therefore cannot be free [7]. And this authority of parents, he calls 'royal authority' [6], 'fatherly authority', 'right of fatherhood' [6, 10]. One would have thought he would in the beginning of such a work as this, on which was to depend the authority of princes, and the obedience of subjects, have told us expressly what that fatherly authority is, have defined it, though not limited it, because in some other treatises of his he tells us, 'tis unlimited, and unlimitable;*

---

*'In grants and gifts that have their original from God or nature, as the power of the father hath, no inferior power of man can limit, nor make any law of prescription against them' [283]. 'The Scripture teaches, that supreme power was originally in the father without any limitation' [139].

he should at least have given us such an account of it, that we might have had an entire notion of this 'fatherhood', or 'fatherly authority', whenever it came in our way in his writings. This I expected to have found in the first chapter of his *Patriarcha*. But instead thereof, having, first, *en passant*, made his obeisance to the *arcana imperii* [secrets of state] [3]; secondly, made his compliment to the 'rights and liberties of this, or any other nation' [4], which he is going presently to null and destroy; and, thirdly, made his leg to those learned men, who did not see so far into the matter as himself [4]. He comes to fall on Bellarmine, and, by a victory over him, establishes his 'fatherly authority' beyond any question [5]. Bellarmine being routed by his own confession [6], the day is clear got, and there is no more need of any forces: for having done that, I observe not that he states the question, or rallies up any arguments to make good his opinion, but rather tells us the story, as he thinks fit, of this strange kind of domineering phantom, called the fatherhood, which whoever could catch, presently got empire, and unlimited absolute power. He assures us how this fatherhood began in Adam, continued its course, and kept the world in order all the time of the patriarchs till the Flood, got out of the ark with Noah and his sons, made and supported all the kings of the earth till the captivity of the Israelites in Egypt, and then the poor fatherhood was under hatches, till 'God by giving the Israelites kings, re-established the ancient and prime right of the lineal succession in paternal government' [9]. This is his business from page [7] to [9]. And then obviating an objection, and clearing a difficulty or two with one half reason, 'to confirm the natural right of regal power' [11], he ends the first chapter. I hope 'tis no injury to call a half quotation a half reason, for God says, 'honour thy father and mother' [*Exodus* 20:12]; but our author contents himself with half, leaves out 'thy mother' quite, as little serviceable to his purpose. But of that more in another place.

7. I do not think our author so little skilled in the way of writing discourses of this nature, nor so careless of the point in hand, that he by oversight commits the fault that he himself, in his *Anarchy of a Mixed Monarchy*, objects to Mr Hunton in these words: 'where first I charge the author that he hath not given any definition, or description of monarchy in general; for by the rules

of method, he should have first defined' [135]. And by the like rule of method Sir Robert should have told us, what his father-hood or fatherly authority is, before he had told us, in whom it was to be found, and talked so much of it. But perhaps Sir Robert found, that this fatherly authority, this power of fathers, and of kings, for he makes them both the same [12], would make a very odd and frightful figure, and very disagreeing, with what either children imagine of their parents, or subjects of their kings, if he should have given us the whole draught together in that gigantic form, he had painted it in his own fancy: and therefore like a wary physician, when he would have his patient swallow some harsh or corrosive liquor, he mingles it with a large quantity of that, which may dilute it; that the scattered parts may go down with less feeling, and cause less aversion.

8. Let us then endeavour to find what account he gives us of this 'fatherly authority', as it lies scattered in the several parts of his writings. And first, as it was vested in Adam, he says, 'not only Adam, but the succeeding patriarchs, had by right of fatherhood royal authority over their children' [6]. 'This lordship which Adam by command had over the whole world, and by right descending from him the patriarchs did enjoy, was as large and ample as the absolute dominion of any monarch which hath been since the Creation' [7]. 'Dominion of life and death, making war, and concluding peace' [7]. 'Adam and the patriarchs had absolute power of life and death' [16]. 'Kings, in the right of parents, succeed to the exercise of supreme jurisdiction' [10]. 'As kingly power is by the law of God, so it hath no inferior law to limit it, Adam was lord of all' [19]. 'The father of a family governs by no other law, than by his own will' [35]. 'The superiority of princes is above laws' [35]. 'The unlimited jurisdiction of kings is so amply described by Samuel' [35] [1 *Samuel* 8:11-18]. 'Kings are above the laws' [41] [quoting King James I, *The Trew Law of Free Monarchies*]. And to this purpose, see a great deal more which our author delivers in Bodin's words: 'it is certain, that all laws, privileges, and grants of princes, have no force, but during their life; if they be not ratified by the express consent, or by sufferance of the prince following, especially privileges' [162] [quoting Bodin, *Six Books of the Commonwealth*, Book 1, Chapter 8]. 'The reason why laws have been also made by kings, was this;

when kings were either busied with wars, or distracted with public cares, so that every private man could not have access to their persons, to learn their wills and pleasure, then were laws of necessity invented, that so every particular subject might find his prince's pleasure deciphered unto him in the tables of his laws' [41]. 'In a monarchy, the king must by necessity be above the laws' [44]. 'A perfect kingdom is that, wherein the king rules all things according to his own will' [44] [Aristotle, *Politics*, Book 3, Chapter 16]. 'Neither common nor statute laws are, or can be, any diminution of that general power, which kings have over their people by right of fatherhood' [52]. 'Adam was the father, king, and lord over his family; a son, a subject, and a servant or slave, were one and the same thing at first. The father had power to dispose or sell his children or servants; whence we find, that at the first reckoning up of goods in Scripture, the manservant, and the maidservant, are numbered among the possessions and substance of the owner, as other goods were' [237]. 'God also hath given to the father a right or liberty, to alien his power over his children to any other; whence we find the sale and gift of children to have been much in use in the beginning of the world, when men had their servants for a possession and an inheritance, as well as other goods, whereupon we find the power of castrating and making eunuchs much in use in old times' [282]. 'Law is nothing else but the will of him that hath the power of the supreme father' [226]. 'It was God's ordinance that the supremacy should be unlimited in Adam, and as large as all the acts of his will; and as in him, so in all others that have supreme power' [284].

9. I have been fain to trouble my reader with these several quotations in our author's own words, that in them might be seen his own description of his 'fatherly authority', as it lies scattered up and down in his writings, which he supposes was first vested in Adam, and by right belongs to all princes ever since. This 'fatherly authority' then, or 'right of fatherhood', in our author's sense is a divine unalterable right of sovereignty, whereby a father or a prince hath an absolute, arbitrary, unlimited, and unlimitable power, over the lives, liberties, and estates of his children and subjects; so that he may take or alienate their estates, sell, castrate, or use their persons as he pleases, they being all his slaves, and he lord or proprietor of everything, and his unbounded will their law.

10. Our author having placed such a mighty power in Adam, and upon that supposition, founded all government, and all power of princes, it is reasonable to expect, that he should have proved this with arguments clear and evident, suitable to the weightiness of the cause. That since men had nothing else left them, they might in slavery have such undeniable proofs of its necessity, that their consciences might be convinced, and oblige them to submit peaceably to that absolute dominion, which their governors had a right to exercise over them. Without this, what good could our author do, or pretend to do, by erecting such an unlimited power, but flatter the natural vanity and ambition of men, too apt of itself to grow and increase with the possession of any power? And by persuading those, who, by the consent of their fellow men, are advanced to great, but limited degrees of it, that by that part which is given them, they have a right to all, that was not so; and therefore may do what they please, because they have authority to do more than others, and so tempt them to do what is neither for their own, nor the good of those under their care, whereby great mischiefs cannot but follow.

11. The sovereignty of Adam, being that on which, as a sure basis, our author builds his mighty absolute monarchy, I expected, that, in his *Patriarcha*, this his main supposition would have been proved and established with all that evidence of arguments, that such a fundamental tenet required; and that this, on which the great stress of the business depends, would have been made out with reasons sufficient to justify the confidence with which it was assumed. But in all that treatise, I could find very little tending that way; the thing is there so taken for granted without proof, that I could scarce believe myself, when upon attentive reading that treatise, I found there so mighty a structure raised upon the bare supposition of this foundation. For it is scarce credible, that in a discourse where he pretends to confute the 'erroneous principle' of man's 'natural freedom', he should do it by a bare supposition of Adam's authority, without offering any proof for that authority. Indeed he confidently says, that 'Adam had royal authority' [6], and [7]; 'absolute lordship and dominion of life and death' [7]; 'a universal monarchy' [16]; 'absolute power of life and death' [16]. He is very frequent in such assertions, but what is strange in all his whole *Patriarcha*, I find not one pretence

of a reason to establish this his great foundation of government; not anything that looks like an argument, but these words: 'to confirm this natural right of regal power, we find in the Decalogue, that the law which enjoins obedience to kings, is delivered in the terms, "honour thy father", as if all power were originally in the father' [11-12] [*Exodus* 20:12]. And why may I not add as well, that in the Decalogue, the law that enjoins obedience to queens, is delivered in the terms of 'honour thy mother', as if all power were originally in the mother? The argument, as Sir Robert puts it, will hold as well for one as t'other. But of this, more in its due place.

12. All that I take notice of here, is, that this is all our author says in this first, or any of the following chapters, to prove the absolute power of Adam, which is his great principle; and yet, as if he had there settled it upon sure demonstration, he begins his second chapter with these words, 'by conferring these proofs and reasons, drawn from the authority of the Scripture' [12]. Where those 'proofs and reasons' for Adam's sovereignty are, bating [excepting] that of 'honour thy father' above mentioned, I confess, I cannot find, unless what he says, 'in these words we have an evident confession', *viz.* of Bellarmine [*De Romano Pontifice*, Book 1, Chapter 2], 'that creation made man prince of his posterity' [6], must be taken for proofs and reasons drawn from Scripture, or for any sort of proof at all: though from thence by a new way of inference in the words, immediately following, he concludes the 'royal authority' of Adam, sufficiently settled in him.

13. If he has in that chapter, or anywhere in the whole treatise, given any other proofs of Adam's royal authority, other than by often repeating it, which, among some men, goes for argument, I desire anybody for him to show me the place and page, that I may be convinced of my mistake, and acknowledge my oversight. If no such arguments are to be found, I beseech those men, who have so much cried up this book, to consider whether they do not give the world cause to suspect, that it's not the force of reason and argument, that makes them for absolute monarchy, but some other by interest, and therefore are resolved to applaud any author, that writes in favour of this doctrine, whether he support it with reason or no. But I hope they do not expect that rational

and indifferent men should be brought over to their opinion, because this their great doctor of it, in a discourse made on purpose, to set up the absolute monarchical power of Adam, in opposition to the natural freedom of mankind, has said so little to prove it, from whence it is rather naturally to be concluded, that there is little to be said.

14. But, that I might omit no care to inform myself in our author's full sense, I consulted his *Observations on Aristotle, Hobbes, etc.* to see whether in disputing with others he made use of any arguments, for this his darling tenet of Adam's sovereignty, since in his treatise of the *Natural Power of Kings*, he hath been so sparing of them. In his *Observations on Mr Hobbes's 'Leviathan'*, I think he has put, in short, all those arguments for it together, which in his writings I find him anywhere to make use of; his words are these. 'If God created only Adam, and of a piece of him made the woman, and if by generation from them two, as parts of them all mankind be propagated: if also God gave to Adam not only the dominion over the woman and the children that should issue from them, but also over the whole earth to subdue it, and over all the creatures on it, so that as long as Adam lived, no man could claim or enjoy anything but by donation, assignation, or permission from him, I wonder', etc. [187]. Here we have the sum of all his arguments, for Adam's sovereignty, and against natural freedom, which I find up and down in his other treatises; and they are these following; God's creation of Adam, the dominion he gave him over Eve: and the dominion he had as father over his children, all which I shall particularly consider.

Chapter 3
OF ADAM'S TITLE TO SOVEREIGNTY
BY CREATION

15. Sir Robert in his preface to his *Observations on Aristotle's 'Politics'*, tells us, 'a natural freedom of mankind cannot be supposed without the denial of the creation of Adam' [237]: but how Adam's being created, which was nothing but his receiving a being immediately from omnipotency, and the hand of God, gave Adam a sovereignty over anything, I cannot see, nor

consequently understand, how a supposition of natural freedom is a denial of Adam's creation, and would be glad [if] anybody else (since our author did not vouchsafe us the favour) would make it out for him. For I find no difficulty to suppose the freedom of mankind, though I have always believed the creation of Adam; he was created, or began to exist, by God's immediate power, without the intervention of parents or the pre-existence of any of the same species to beget him, when it pleased God he should; and so did the lion, the king of beasts before him, by the same creating power of God: and if bare existence by that power, and in that way, will give dominion, without any more ado, our author, by this argument, will make the lion have as good a title to it as he, and certainly the ancienter. No! for Adam had his title 'by the appointment of God', says our author in another place [144]. Then bare creation gave him not dominion, and one might have supposed mankind free without denying the creation of Adam since 'twas God's appointment made him monarch.

16. But let us see, how he puts his creation and this appointment together. 'By the appointment of God', says Sir Robert, 'as soon as Adam was created he was monarch of the world, though he had no subjects, for though there could not be actual government till there were subjects, yet by the right of nature it was due to Adam to be governor of his posterity: though not in act, yet at least in habit, Adam was a king from his creation' [144-5]. I wish he had told us here what he meant by 'God's appointment'. For whatsoever providence orders, or the law of nature directs, or positive revelation declares, may be said to be by God's appointment, but I suppose it cannot be meant here in the first sense, i.e. by providence; because that would be to say no more, but that 'as soon as Adam was created' he was *de facto* monarch, because 'by right of nature it was due to Adam, to be governor of his posterity'. But he could not *de facto* be by providence constituted the governor of the world at a time, when there was actually no government, no subjects to be governed, which our author here confesses. 'Monarch of the world' is also differently used by our author, for sometimes he means by it a proprietor of all the world exclusive of the rest of mankind, and thus he does in the same page of his preface before cited, 'Adam', says he, 'being commanded to multiply and people the earth and to subdue it, and

having dominion given him over all creatures, was thereby the monarch of the whole world, none of his posterity had any right to possess anything but by his grant or permission, or by succession from him' [236].

(2) Let us understand then by 'monarch' proprietor of the world, and by 'appointment' God's actual donation, and revealed positive grant made to Adam (*Genesis* 1:28), as we see Sir Robert himself does in this parallel place, and then his argument will stand thus, 'by the positive grant of God; as soon as Adam was created, he was proprietor of the world, because by the right of nature it was due to Adam to be governor of his posterity'. In which way of arguing there are two manifest falsehoods. First, it is false that God made that grant to Adam, as soon as he was created, since though it stands in the text immediately after his creation, yet it is plain it could not be spoken to Adam till after Eve was made and brought to him, and how then could he be 'monarch by appointment as soon as created', especially since he calls, if I mistake not, that which God says to Eve (*Genesis* 3:16): 'the original grant of government', which not being till after the Fall, when Adam was somewhat, at least in time, and very much, distant in condition from his creation, I cannot see, how our author can say in this sense, that by 'God's appointment, as soon as Adam was created he was monarch of the world'. Secondly, were it true that God's actual donation 'appointed Adam monarch of the world as soon as he was created', yet the reason here given for it would not prove it, but it would always be a false inference, that God, by a positive donation 'appointed Adam monarch of the world, because by right of nature it was due to Adam to be governor of his posterity': for having given him the right of government by nature, there was no need of a positive donation, at least it will never be a proof of such a donation.

17. On the other side the matter will not be much mended, if we understand by 'God's appointment' the law of nature, (though it be a pretty harsh expression for it in this place) and by 'monarch of the world', sovereign ruler of mankind; for then the sentence under consideration must run thus: 'by the law of nature, as soon as Adam was created he was governor of mankind, for by right of nature it was due to Adam to be governor of his posterity', which amounts to this, he was governor by right of nature,

because he was governor by right of nature. But supposing we should grant, that a man is by nature governor of his children, Adam could not hereby be monarch as soon as created; for this right of nature being founded in his being their father, how Adam could have a natural right to be governor before he was a father, when by being a father only he had that right, is, methinks, hard to conceive, unless he will have him to be a father before he was a father, and to have a title before he had it.

18. To this foreseen objection, our author answers very logically, 'he was governor in habit, and not in act' [144–5]; a very pretty way of being a governor without government, a father without children, and a king without subjects. And thus Sir Robert was an author before he writ his book, not 'in act' 'tis true, but 'in habit', for when he had once published it, it was due to him by the right of nature, to be an author, as much as it was to Adam to be governor of his children when he had begot them; and if to be such a monarch of the world, an absolute monarch 'in habit, but not in act', will serve the turn, I should not much envy it to any of Sir Robert's friends that he thought fit graciously to bestow it upon, though even this of act and habit, if it signified anything but our author's skill in distinctions, be not to his purpose in this place. For the question is not here about Adam's actual exercise of government, but actually having a title to be governor: government, says our author, was due to Adam by the right of nature. What is this right of nature? A right fathers have over their children by begetting them; *generatione jus acquiritur parentibus in liberos* [by generation parents acquire a right over their children], says our author out of Grotius [226] [*Of the Laws of War and Peace*, Book 2, Chapter 5, section 1]. The right then follows the begetting as arising from it, so that according to this way of reasoning or distinguishing of our author, Adam, as soon as he was created, had a title only 'in habit, and not in act', which in plain English is, he had actually no title at all.

19. To speak less learnedly, and more intelligibly, one may say of Adam, he was in a possibility of being governor, since it was possible he might beget children, and thereby acquire that right of nature, be it what it will, to govern them, that accrues from thence, but what connection has this with Adam's creation, to make him say, that 'as soon as he was created, he was monarch

of the world'? For it may be as well said of Noah, that as soon as he was born, he was monarch of the world, since he was in possibility (which in our author's sense is enough to make a monarch, a monarch in habit,) to outlive all mankind but his own posterity. What such necessary connection there is betwixt Adam's creation and his right to government, so that a natural freedom of mankind cannot be supposed without the denial of the creation of Adam, I confess for my part I do not see; nor how those words, 'by the appointment', etc. [289], however explained, can be put together to make any tolerable sense, at least to establish this position, with which they end, *viz.* 'Adam was a king from his creation'; a king, says our author, 'not in act, but in habit', i.e. actually no king at all.

20. I fear I have tired my reader's patience, by dwelling longer on this passage than the weightiness of any argument in it, seems to require: but I have unavoidably been engaged in it by our author's way of writing, who huddling several suppositions together, and that in doubtful and general terms makes such a medley and confusion, that it is impossible to show his mistakes, without examining the several senses, wherein his words may be taken, and without seeing how, in any of these various meanings, they will consist together, and have any truth in them; for in this present passage before us, how can anyone argue against this position of his, that 'Adam was a king from his creation', unless one examine, whether the words, 'from his creation', be to be taken, as they may, for the time of the commencement of his government, as the foregoing words import, 'as soon as he was created he was monarch', or, for the cause of it, as he says, 'creation made man prince of his posterity'? [6]. How further can one judge of the truth of his being thus king, till one has examined whether king be to be taken, as the words in the beginning of this passage would persuade, on supposition of his private dominion, which was by God's positive grant, 'monarch of the world by appointment'; or king on supposition of his fatherly power over his offspring which was by nature, due by the right of nature, whether, I say, king be to be taken in both, or one only of these two senses, or in neither of them, but only this, that creation made him prince, in a way different from both the other? For though this assertion, that Adam was king from his creation, be true in

no sense, yet it stands here as an evident conclusion drawn from the preceding words, though in truth it be but a bare assertion joined to other assertions of the same kind, which confidently put together in words of undetermined and dubious meaning, look like a sort of arguing, when there is indeed neither proof nor connection: a way very familiar with our author, of which having given the reader a taste here, I shall, as much as the argument will permit me, avoid touching on hereafter, and should not have done it here, were it not to let the world see, how incoherences in matter, and suppositions without proofs put handsomely together in good words and a plausible style, are apt to pass for strong reason and good sense, till they come to be looked into with attention.

Chapter 4
OF ADAM'S TITLE TO SOVEREIGNTY BY
DONATION, *GENESIS* 1:28

21. Having at last got through the foregoing passage, where we have been so long detained, not by the force of arguments and opposition, but the intricacy of the words, and the doubtfulness of the meaning; let us go on to his next argument, for Adam's sovereignty. Our author tells us in the words of Mr Selden, that 'Adam by donation from God (*Genesis* 1:28), was made the general lord of all things, not without such a private dominion to himself, as without his grant did exclude his children. This determination of Mr Selden', says our author, 'is consonant to the history of the Bible, and natural reason' [217] [*Mare Clausum*, Book 1, Chapter 4]. And in his preface to his *Observations on Aristotle* he says thus; 'the first government in the world was monarchical in the father of all flesh, Adam being commanded to multiply and people the earth, and to subdue it, and having dominion given him over all creatures, was thereby the monarch of the whole world, none of his posterity had any right to possess anything, but by his grant or permission, or by succession from him; the earth, saith the Psalmist, "hath he given to the children of men", which shows the title comes from fatherhood' [236] [Psalm 115:16].

22. Before I examine this argument, and the text on which it is founded, it is necessary to desire the reader to observe, that our author, according to his usual method, begins in one sense, and concludes in another; he begins here with Adam's propriety, or 'private dominion, by donation'; and his conclusion is, 'which shows the title comes from fatherhood'.

23. But let us see the argument. The words of the text are these; 'And God blessed them, and God said unto them, be fruitful and multiply and replenish the earth and subdue it, and have dominion over the fish of the sea, and over the fowl of the air, and over every living thing that moveth upon the earth' (*Genesis* 1:28). From whence our author concludes, that 'Adam, having here dominion given him over all creatures, was thereby the monarch of the whole world' [236]. Whereby must be meant, that either this grant of God gave Adam property, or as our author calls it, 'private dominion' over the earth, and all inferior or irrational creatures, and so consequently that he was thereby monarch; or, secondly, that it gave him rule and dominion over all earthly creatures whatsoever, and thereby over his children, and so he was monarch: for, as Mr Selden has properly worded it, 'Adam was made general lord of all things', one may very clearly understand him, that he means nothing to be granted to Adam here but property, and therefore he says not one word of Adam's monarchy. But our author says, 'Adam was hereby monarch of the world', which properly speaking, signifies sovereign ruler of all the men in the world, and so Adam, by this grant, must be constituted such a ruler. If our author means otherwise, he might, with much more clearness have said, that 'Adam was hereby proprietor of the whole world'. But he begs your pardon on that point, clear distinct speaking not serving everywhere to his purpose, you must not expect it in him, as in Mr Selden, or other such writers.

24. In opposition therefore to our author's doctrine, that Adam was monarch of the whole world, founded on this place, I shall show.

(1) That by this grant (*Genesis* 1:28), God gave no immediate power to Adam over men, over his children, over those of his own species, and so he was not made ruler, or monarch by this charter.

(2) That by this grant God gave him not private dominion over the inferior creatures, but right in common with all mankind; so

neither was he monarch, upon the account of the property here given him.

25. (1) That this donation (*Genesis* 1:28), gave Adam no power over men, will appear if we consider the words of it. For since all positive grants convey no more than the express words they are made in will carry, let us see which of them here will comprehend mankind, or Adam's posterity; and those, I imagine, if any, must be these, 'every living thing that moveth', the words in Hebrew are, *hayah ha-romeset* i.e. *bestiam reptantem* [a creeping beast], of which words the Scripture itself is the best interpreter. God having created the fishes and fowls the fifth day, the beginning of the sixth, he creates the irrational inhabitants of the dry land, which, verse 24, are described in these words, 'let the earth bring forth the living creature after his kind; cattle and creeping things, and beasts of the earth, after his kind', and verse 25, 'and God made the beasts of the earth after his kind, and cattle after their kind, and everything that creepeth on the earth after his kind'; here in the creation of the brute inhabitants of the earth, he first speaks of them all under one general name, of living creatures, and then afterwards divides them into three ranks, (1) cattle, or such creatures as were or might be tame, and so be the private possession of particular men; (2) *hayah* which verses 24 and 25 in our Bible, is translated 'beasts', and by the Septuagint θηρία, 'wild beasts', and is the same word, that here in our text, verse 28, where we have this great charter to Adam, is translated 'living thing', and is also the same word used (*Genesis* 9:2), where this grant is renewed to Noah, and there likewise translated 'beast', (3) the third rank were the creeping animals, which [*Genesis* 1] verses 24 and 25 are comprised under the word *ha-romeset*, the same that is used here verse 28 and is translated 'moving', but in the former verses 'creeping', and by the Septuagint in all these places, ἑρπετά or 'reptiles'; from whence it appears that the words which we translate here in God's donation, verse 28, 'living creatures moving', are the same which in the history of the creation, verses 24, 25, signify two ranks of terrestrial creatures, *viz.* 'wild beasts' and 'reptiles', and are so understood by the Septuagint.

26. When God had made the irrational animals of the world, divided into three kinds, from the places of their habitation, *viz.*

fishes of the sea, fowls of the air, and living creatures of the earth, and these again into cattle, wild beasts, and reptiles, he considers of making man, and the dominion he should have over the terrestrial world, verse 26, and then he reckons up the inhabitants of these three kingdoms, but in the terrestrial, leaves out the second rank *ḥayah*, or wild beasts: but here, verse 28, where he actually executes this design, and gives him this dominion, the text mentions 'the fishes of the sea, and fowls of the air', and the terrestrial creatures in the words, that signify the wild beasts and reptiles, though translated 'living thing that moveth', leaving out cattle. In both which places, though the word that signifies 'wild beasts' be omitted in one, and that which signifies 'cattle' in the other, yet, since God certainly executed in one place, what he declares he designed in the other, we cannot but understand the same in both places, and have here only an account, how the terrestrial irrational animals, which were already created and reckoned up at their creation, in three distinct ranks of cattle, wild beasts, and reptiles were here, verse 28, actually put under the dominion of man, as they were designed (verse 26) nor do these words contain in them the least appearance of anything, that can be wrested, to signify God's giving to one man dominion over another, Adam over his posterity.

27. And this further appears from *Genesis* 9:2, where God renewing this charter to Noah and his sons, he gives them dominion over the fowls of the air, and the fishes of the sea, and the terrestrial creatures, expressed by *ḥayah* and *ha-remes* wild beasts and reptiles, the same words that in the text before us (*Genesis* 1:28) are translated 'every moving thing, that moveth upon the earth', which by no means can comprehend man, the grant being made to Noah and his sons, all the men then living, and not to one part of men over another: which is yet more evident from the very next words ([*Genesis* 9] verse 3) where God gives every *remes*, 'every moving thing', the very words used chapter 1:28, to them for food. By all which it is plain, that God's donation to Adam, chapter 1:28, and his designation, verse 26, and his grant again to Noah and his sons, refer to, and contain in them, neither more nor less, than the works of the creation the fifth day, and the beginning of the sixth, as they are set down from the 20th, to the 26th verse inclusively of the first chapter and so comprehend

all the species of irrational animals of the terraqueous globe, though all the words whereby they are expressed in the history of their creation, are nowhere used in any of the following grants, but some of them omitted in one, and some in another. From whence I think it is past all doubt, that man cannot be comprehended in this grant, nor any dominion over those of his own species be conveyed to Adam. All the terrestrial irrational creatures are enumerated at their creation, verse 25, under the names, 'beasts of the earth, cattle and creeping things', but man being not then created, was not contained under any of those names, and therefore, whether we understand the Hebrew words right or no, they cannot be supposed to comprehend man in the very same history, and the very next verses following, especially since the Hebrew word *remes* which if any in this donation to Adam, chapter 1:28, must comprehend man, is so plainly used in contradistinction to him, as *Genesis* 6:20; [*Genesis*] 7:14, 21, 23; *Genesis* 8:17, 19. And if God made all mankind slaves to Adam and his heirs, by giving Adam dominion over 'every living thing that moveth on the earth', chapter 1:28, as our author would have it, methinks Sir Robert should have carried his monarchical power one step higher, and satisfied the world, that princes might eat their subjects too, since God gave as full power to Noah and his heirs, chapter 9:2, to eat 'every living thing that moveth', as he did to Adam to have dominion over them, the Hebrew words in both places being the same.

28. David, who might be supposed to understand the donation of God in this text, and the right of kings too, as well as our author, in his comment on this place, as the learned and judicious Ainsworth calls it, in the 8th Psalm, finds here no such charter of monarchical power, his words are, 'thou hast made him', i.e. man the son of man, 'a little lower than the angels, thou madest him to have dominion over the works of thy hands, thou hast put all things under his feet, all sheep and oxen and the beasts of the field, and the fowl of the air, and fish of the sea, and whatsoever passeth through the paths of the sea'. In which words, if anyone can find out that there is meant any monarchical power of one man over another, but only the dominion of the whole species of mankind, over the inferior species of creatures, he may, for ought I know, deserve to be one of Sir Robert's 'monarchs in habit', for the rareness of the

discovery. And by this time, I hope it is evident, that he that gave 'dominion over every living thing that moveth on the earth', gave Adam no monarchical power over those of his own species, which will yet appear more fully in the next thing I am to show.

29. (2) Whatever God gave by the words of this grant, *Genesis* 1:28, it was not to Adam in particular, exclusive of all other men: whatever dominion he had thereby, it was not a private dominion, but a dominion in common with the rest of mankind. That this donation was not made in particular to Adam, appears evidently from the words of the text, it being made no more than one, for it was spoken in the plural number, God blessed them, and said unto them, have dominion. God says unto Adam and Eve, have dominion; thereby, says our author, 'Adam was monarch of the world': but the grant being to them, i.e. spoke to Eve also, as many interpreters think with reason, that these words were not spoken till Adam had his wife, must not she thereby be lady, as well as he lord of the world? If it be said that Eve was subjected to Adam, it seems she was not so subjected to him, as to hinder her dominion over the creatures, or property in them: for shall we say that God ever made a joint grant to two, and one only was to have the benefit of it?

30. But perhaps 'twill be said, Eve was not made till afterward: grant it so, what advantage will our author get by it? The text will be only the more directly against him, and show that God in this donation, gave the world to mankind in common, and not to Adam in particular. The word 'them' in the text must include the species of man, for 'tis certain 'them' can by no means signify Adam alone. In the 26th verse, where God declares his intention to give this dominion, it is plain he meant, that he would make a species of creatures, that should have dominion over the other species of this terrestrial globe: the words are, 'and God said, let us make man in our image, after our likeness, and let them have dominion over the fish', etc. 'They' then were to have dominion. Who? Even those who were to have the image of God, the individuals of that species of man that he was going to make, for that 'them' should signify Adam singly, exclusive of the rest, that should be in the world with him, is against both Scripture and all reason: and it cannot possibly be made sense, if 'man' in the former part of the verse do not signify the same with 'them' in the latter, only 'man'

there, as is usual, is taken for the species, and 'them' the individuals of that species: and we have a reason in the very text. God makes him 'in his own image after his own likeness', makes him an intellectual creature, and so capable of dominion. For wherein soever else the image of God consisted, the intellectual nature was certainly a part of it, and belonged to the whole species, and enabled them to have dominion over the inferior creatures; and therefore David says in the 8th Psalm [5–6] above cited, 'thou hast made him little lower than the angels, thou hast made him to have dominion'. 'Tis not of Adam King David speaks here, for verse 4, 'tis plain, 'tis of man, and the son of man, of the species of mankind.

31. And that this grant spoken to Adam was made to him, and the whole species of man, is clear from our author's own proof out of the Psalmist. ' "The earth", saith the Psalmist [115:16], "hath he given to the children of men"; which shows the title comes from fatherhood': these are Sir Robert's words in the preface before cited, and a strange inference it is he makes, 'God hath given the earth to the children of men', *ergo* 'the title comes from fatherhood' [236]. 'Tis pity the propriety of the Hebrew tongue had not used 'fathers of men' instead of 'children of men', to express mankind: then indeed our author might have had the countenance of the sound of the words, to have placed the title in the fatherhood. But to conclude, that the fatherhood had the right to the earth, because God gave it 'to the children of men', is a way of arguing peculiar to our author. And a man must have a great mind to go contrary to the sound as well as sense of the words, before he could light on it. But the sense is yet harder, and more remote from our author's purpose: for as it stands in his preface, it is to prove Adam's being monarch, and his reasoning is thus, 'God gave the earth to the children of men', *ergo* 'Adam was monarch of the world' [236]. I defy any man to make a more pleasant conclusion than this, which cannot be excused from the most obvious absurdity, till it can be shown, that by 'children of men', he who had no father, Adam, alone is signified; but whatever our author does, the Scripture speaks not nonsense.

32. To maintain this property and private dominion of Adam, our author labours in the following page [217] to destroy the community granted to Noah and his sons, in that parallel place, *Genesis* 9:1–3, and he endeavours to do it two ways.

(1) Sir Robert would persuade us against the express words of the Scripture, that what was here granted to Noah, was not granted to his sons in common with him. His words are; 'as for the general community between Noah and his sons, which Mr Selden will have to be granted to them, *Genesis* 9:2, the text doth not warrant it' [217]. What warrant our author would have, when the plain express words of Scripture, not capable of another meaning, will not satisfy him, who pretends to build wholly on Scripture, is not easy to imagine. The text says, 'God blessed Noah and his sons, and said unto them', i.e. as our author would have it, 'unto him': for, saith he, 'although the sons are there mentioned with Noah in the blessing, yet it may best be understood, with a subordination or benediction in succession' [217]. That indeed is best, for our author to be understood, which best serves to his purpose, but that truly 'may best be understood' by anybody else, which best agrees with the plain construction of the words, and arises from the obvious meaning of the place, and then with subordination and in succession, will not 'be best understood', in a grant of God, where he himself put them not, nor mentions any such limitation. But yet, our author has reasons, why it 'may best be understood so'. 'The blessing', says he in the following words, 'might truly be fulfilled, if the sons either under or after their father, enjoyed a private dominion' [217], which is to say, that a grant, whose express words give a joint title in present (for the text says, 'into your hands they are delivered') 'may best be understood with a subordination or in succession': because 'tis possible, that in subordination, or succession it may be enjoyed. Which is all one as to say, that a grant of anything in present possession, 'may best be understood' of reversion: because 'tis possible one may live to enjoy it in reversion. If the grant be indeed to a father, and to his sons after him, who is so kind as to let his children enjoy it presently in common with him, one may truly say, as to the event one will be as good as the other: but it can never be true, that what the express words grant in possession, and in common, 'may best be understood', to be in reversion. The sum of all his reasoning amounts to this: God did not give to the sons of Noah the world in common with their father, because 'twas possible they might enjoy it under, or after him. A very good sort of argument, against an express text of Scripture: but God

must not be believed, though he speaks it himself, when he says he does anything, which will not consist with Sir Robert's hypothesis.

33. For 'tis plain, however he would exclude them, that part of this benediction, as he would have it in succession, must needs be meant to the sons, and not to Noah himself at all. 'Be fruitful, and multiply, and replenish the earth', says God, in this blessing [*Genesis* 9:1]. This part of the benediction, as appears by the sequel, concerned not Noah himself at all: for we read not of any children he had after the Flood, and in the following chapter, where his posterity is reckoned up, there is no mention of any, and so this 'benediction in succession', was not to take place till 350 years after, and to save our author's imaginary monarchy, the peopling of the world must be deferred 350 years; for this part of the benediction cannot be understood with subordination, unless our author will say, that they must ask leave of their father Noah to lie with their wives. But in this one point our author is constant to himself in all his discourses, he takes great care there should be monarchs in the world, but very little that there should be people: and indeed his way of government is not the way to people the world. For how much absolute monarchy helps to fulfil this great and primary blessing of God Almighty, 'be fruitful, and multiply, and replenish the earth', which contains in it the improvement too of arts and sciences, and the conveniences of life, may be seen in those large and rich countries, which are happy under the Turkish government, where are not now to be found one third, nay in many, if not most parts of them one thirtieth, perhaps I might say not one hundredth of the people, that were formerly, as will easily appear to anyone, who will compare the accounts we have of it at this time, with ancient history. But this by the by.

34. The other parts of this benediction or grant are so expressed, that they must needs be understood to belong to Noah and his sons, to them as much as to him, and not to his sons 'with a subordination or in succession'. 'The fear of you, and the dread of you', says God, 'shall be upon every beast', etc. [*Genesis* 9:2]. Will anybody but our author say, that the creatures feared and stood in awe of Noah only, and not of his sons without his leave, or till after his death? And the following words, 'into your hands they are delivered', are they to be understood as our author says,

if your father please, or they shall be delivered into your hands hereafter. If this be to argue from Scripture, I know not what may not be proved by it, and I can scarce see how much this differs from that 'fiction and fancy', or how much a surer foundation it will prove than the opinions of 'philosophers and poets', which our author so much condemns in his preface [236].

35. But our author goes on to prove, that 'it may best be understood with a subordination or a benediction in succession', for, says he, 'it is not probable, that the private dominion which God gave to Adam, and by his donation, assignation or cession to his children, was abrogated, and a community of all things instituted between Noah and his sons. Noah was left the sole heir of the world, why should it be thought that God would disinherit him of his birthright, and make him of all men in the world the only tenant in common with his children' [217].

36. The prejudices of our own ill grounded opinions, however by us called probable, cannot authorize us to understand Scripture contrary to the direct and plain meaning of the words. I grant, 'tis not probable that 'Adam's private dominion was here abrogated'; because it is more than improbable (for it will never be proved) that ever Adam had any such private dominion: and since parallel places of Scripture are most probable to make us know, how they may be best understood, there needs but the comparing this blessing here to Noah and his sons after the Flood, with that to Adam after the Creation, *Genesis* 1:28, to assure anyone that God gave Adam no such private dominion. 'Tis probable, I confess, that Noah should have the same title, the same property and dominion after the Flood, that Adam had before it. But since private dominion cannot consist with the blessing and grant God gave to him and his sons in common, 'tis a sufficient reason to conclude that Adam had none, especially since in the donation made to him, there is no words that express it, or do in the least favour it; and then let my reader judge whether 'it may best be understood', when in the one place there is not one word for it, not to say, what has been above proved, that the text itself proves the contrary, and in the other, the words and sense are directly against it.

37. But our author says, 'Noah was the sole heir of the world, why should it be thought that God would disinherit him of his birthright?' Heir, indeed, in England, signifies the eldest son, who

is by the law of England to have all his father's land, but where
God ever appointed any such heir of the world, our author would
have done well to have showed us, and how 'God disinherited
him of his birthright', or what harm was done him if God gave
his sons a right to make use of a part of the earth for the support
of themselves and families, when the whole was not only more
than Noah himself, but infinitely more than they all could make
use of, and the possessions of one could not at all prejudice, or as
to any use straiten that of the other.

38. Our author probably foreseeing he might not be very
successful in persuading people out of their senses, and, say what
he could, men would be apt to believe the plain words of Scripture,
and think, as they saw, that the grant was spoken to Noah and
his sons jointly. He endeavours to insinuate, as if this grant to
Noah, conveyed no property, no dominion; because, 'subduing
the earth and dominion over the creatures are therein omitted,
nor the earth once named'. And therefore, says he, 'there is a
considerable difference between these two texts [Genesis 1:28,
9:2], the first blessing gave Adam a dominion over the earth and
all creatures, the latter allows Noah liberty to use the living
creatures for food, here is no alteration or diminishing of his title,
to a property of all things, but an enlargement only of his
commons' [217–18]. So that in our author's sense, all that was said
here to Noah and his sons, gave them no dominion, no property,
but only 'enlarged the commons'; their commons, I should say since,
God says, 'to you are they given', though our author says 'his',
for as for Noah's sons, they it seems by Sir Robert's appointment
during their father's lifetime, were to keep fasting days.

39. Anyone but our author would be mightily suspected, to be
blinded with prejudice, that in all this blessing to Noah and his
sons, could see nothing but only an enlargement of commons. For
as to dominion which our author thinks omitted, 'the fear of you,
and the dread of you', says God, 'shall be upon every beast'
[Genesis 9:2], which I suppose, expresses the dominion, or superiority [which] was designed [for] man over the living creatures,
as fully as may be, for in that fear and dread, seems chiefly to
consist what was given to Adam, over the inferior animals; who
as absolute a monarch as he was, could not make bold with a lark
or a rabbit to satisfy his hunger, and had the herbs but in common

with the beasts, as is plain from *Genesis* 1:29 and 30. In the next place, 'tis manifest that in this blessing to Noah and his sons, property is not only given in clear words, but in a larger extent than it was to Adam. 'Into your hands they are given', says God, to Noah and his sons, which words, if they give not property, nay, property in possession, 'twill be hard to find words that can, since there is not a way to express a man's being possessed of anything more natural, nor more certain, than to say, 'it is delivered into his hands'. And, [*Genesis* 9] verse 3, to show, that they had then given them the utmost property man is capable of, which is to have a right to destroy anything by using it; 'every moving thing that liveth', saith God, 'shall be meat for you', which was not allowed to Adam in his charter. This our author calls, 'a liberty of using them for food, and only an enlargement of commons', but 'no alteration of property' [217–18]. What other property man can have in the creatures, but the liberty of using them, is hard to be understood: so that, if the first blessing, as our author says, gave 'Adam dominion over the creatures', and the blessing to Noah and his sons, gave them 'such a liberty to use them', as Adam had not; it must needs give them something that Adam with all his sovereignty wanted, something that one would be apt to take for a greater property; for certainly he has no absolute dominion over even the brutal part of the creatures, and the property he has in them is very narrow and scanty, who cannot make that use of them, which is permitted to another. Should anyone, who is absolute lord of a country, have bidden our author 'subdue the earth', and given him dominion over the creatures in it, but not have permitted him to have taken a kid or a lamb out of the flock, to satisfy his hunger, I guess he would scarce have thought himself lord or proprietor of that land, or the cattle on it: but would have found the difference between having dominion, which a shepherd may have, and having full property as an owner. So that, had it been his own case, Sir Robert I believe, would have thought here was an alteration, nay, an enlarging of property, and that Noah and his children had by this grant, not only property given them, but such a property given them in the creatures, as Adam had not; for however, in respect of one another, men may be allowed to have propriety in their distinct portions of the creatures; yet in respect of God the Maker of heaven and earth, who is sole lord and proprietor of the whole world, man's propriety in the creatures is nothing but that 'liberty to use them', which God has permitted, and so man's property may be altered and enlarged, as we see it was here, after the Flood, when other uses of them are allowed, which before were not. From all which I suppose, it is clear, that neither Adam nor Noah, had any private dominion, any property in the creatures, exclusive of his posterity, as they should successively grow up into need of them, and come to be able to make use of them.

40. Thus we have examined our author's argument for Adam's monarchy, founded on the blessing pronounced, *Genesis* 1:28. Wherein I think 'tis impossible for any sober reader, to find any other but the setting of mankind above the other kinds of creatures, in this habitable earth of ours. 'Tis nothing but the giving to man, the whole species of man, as the chief inhabitant, who is the image of his Maker, the dominion over the other creatures. This lies so obvious in the plain words, that anyone but our author would have thought it necessary to have shown, how these words that seemed to say the quite contrary, gave Adam monarchical absolute power over other men, or the sole property in all the creatures, and methinks in a business of this moment, and that whereon he builds all that follows, he should have done something more than barely cite words which apparently make against him; for I confess, I cannot see anything in them, tending to Adam's monarchy, or private dominion, but quite the contrary. And I the less deplore the dullness of my apprehension herein, since I find the apostle [St Paul] seems to have as little notion of any such private dominion of Adam as I, when he says, 'God gives us all things richly to enjoy' [1 Timothy 6:17], which he could not do, if it were all given away already, to monarch Adam, and the monarchs his heirs and successors. To conclude, this text is so far from proving Adam sole proprietor, that on the contrary, it is a confirmation of the original community of all things amongst the sons of men, which appearing from this donation of God, as well as other places of Scripture; the sovereignty of Adam, built upon his private dominion, must fall, not having any foundation to support it.

41. But yet, if after all, anyone will needs have it so, that by this donation of God, Adam was made sole proprietor of the whole earth, what will this be to his sovereignty? And how will it

appear, that property in land gives a man power over the life of another? Or how will the possession even of the whole earth, give anyone a sovereign arbitrary authority over the persons of men? The most specious thing to be said, is, that he that is proprietor of the whole world, may deny all the rest of mankind food, and so at his pleasure starve them, if they will not acknowledge his sovereignty, and obey his will. If this were true, it would be a good argument to prove, that there was never any such property, that God never gave any such private dominion; since it is more reasonable to think, that God who bid mankind increase and multiply, should rather himself give them all a right, to make use of the food and raiment, and other conveniences of life, the materials whereof he had so plentifully provided for them; than to make them depend upon the will of a man for their subsistence, who should have power to destroy them all when he pleased, and who being no better than other men, was in succession likelier by want and the dependence of a scanty fortune, to tie them to hard service, than by liberal allowance of the conveniences of life, to promote the great design of God, 'increase and multiply' [*Genesis* 1:28]: he that doubts this, let him look into the absolute monarchies of the world, and see what becomes of the conveniences of life, and the multitudes of people.

42. But we know God hath not left one man so to the mercy of another, that he may starve him if he please: God the Lord and Father of all, has given no one of his children such a property, in his peculiar portion of the things of this world, but that he has given his needy brother a right to the surplusage of his goods; so that it cannot justly be denied him, when his pressing wants call for it. And therefore no man could ever have a just power over the life of another, by right of property in land or possessions; since 'twould always be a sin in any man of estate, to let his brother perish for want of affording him relief out of his plenty. As justice gives every man a title to the product of his honest industry, and the fair acquisitions of his ancestors descended to him; so charity gives every man a title to so much out of another's plenty, as will keep him from extreme want, where he has no means to subsist otherwise; and a man can no more justly make use of another's necessity, to force him to become his vassal, by withholding that relief, God requires him to afford to the wants

of his brother, than he that has more strength can seize upon a weaker, master him to his obedience, and with a dagger at his throat offer him death or slavery.

43. Should anyone make so perverse a use of God's blessings poured on him with a liberal hand; should anyone be cruel and uncharitable to that extremity, yet all this would not prove that propriety in land, even in this case, gave any authority over the persons of men, but only that compact might; since the authority of the rich proprietor, and the subjection of the needy beggar began not from the possession of the lord, but the consent of the poor man, who preferred being his subject to starving. And the man he thus submits to, can pretend to no more power over him, than he has consented to, upon compact. Upon this ground a man's having his stores filled in a time of scarcity, having money in his pocket, being in a vessel at sea, being able to swim, etc., may as well be the foundation of rule and dominion, as being possessor of all the land in the world, any of these being sufficient to enable me to save a man's life who would perish if such assistance were denied him; and anything by this rule that may be an occasion of working upon another's necessity, to save his life, or anything dear to him, at the rate of his freedom, may be made a foundation of sovereignty, as well as property. From all which it is clear, that though God should have given Adam private dominion, yet that private dominion could give him no sovereignty; but we have already sufficiently proved, that God gave him no private dominion.

Chapter 5
OF ADAM'S TITLE TO SOVEREIGNTY
BY THE SUBJECTION OF EVE

44. The next place of Scripture we find our author builds his monarchy of Adam on, is *Genesis* 3:16, 'and thy desire shall be to thy husband, and he shall rule over thee'. 'Here we have' (says he) 'the original grant of government', from when he concludes, in the following part of the page [138], 'that the supreme power is settled in the fatherhood, and limited to one kind of government, that is to monarchy': for let his premises be what they will, this is

always the conclusion, let 'rule' in any text, be but once named, and presently absolute monarchy is by divine right established. If anyone will but carefully read our author's own reasoning from these words [138], and consider among other things, 'the line and posterity of Adam', as he there brings them in, he will find some difficulty, to make sense of what he says; but we will allow this at present, to his peculiar way of writing, and consider the force of the text in hand. The words are the curse of God upon the woman, for having been the first and forwardest in the disobedi- ence, and if we will consider the occasion of what God says here to our first parents, that he was denouncing judgment, and declaring his wrath against them both, for their disobedience, we cannot suppose that this was the time, wherein God was granting Adam prerogatives and privileges, investing him with dignity and authority, elevating him to dominion and monarchy: for though as a helper in the temptation, as well as a partner in the transgres- sion, Eve was laid below him, and so he had accidentally a superiority over her, for her greater punishment, yet he too had his share in the Fall, as well as the sin, and was laid lower, as may be seen in the following verses, and 'twould be hard to imagine, that God, in the same breath, should make him universal monarch over all mankind, and a day labourer for his life; turn him out of paradise, 'to till the ground', verse 23, and at the same time, advance him to a throne, and all the privileges and ease of absolute power.

45. This was not a time, when Adam could expect any favours, any grant of privileges, from his offended Maker. If this be 'the original grant of government', as our author tells us, and Adam was now made monarch, whatever Sir Robert would have him, 'tis plain, God made him but a very poor monarch, such a one, as our author himself would have counted it no great privilege to be. God sets him to work for his living, and seems rather to give him a spade into his hand, to subdue the earth, than a sceptre to rule over its inhabitants. 'In the sweat of thy face thou shalt eat thy bread', says God to him, verse 19. This was unavoidable, may it perhaps be answered, because he was yet without subjects, and had nobody to work for him, but afterwards living as he did above nine hundred years, he might have people enough, whom he might command, to work for him; 'no', says God, 'not only whilst thou

art without other help, save thy wife, but as long as thou livest, shalt thou live by thy labour'. 'In the sweat of thy face, shalt thou eat thy bread, till thou return unto the ground, for out of it wast thou taken, for dust thou art, and unto dust shalt thou return', verse 19. It will perhaps be answered again, in favour of our author, that these words are not spoken personally to Adam, but in him, as their representative, to all mankind, this being a curse upon mankind, because of the Fall.

46. God, I believe, speaks differently from men, because he speaks with more truth, more certainty: but when he vouchsafes to speak to men, I do not think, he speaks differently from them, in crossing the rules of language in use amongst them. This would not be to condescend to their capacities, when he humbles himself to speak to them, but to lose his design in speaking, what thus spoken, they could not understand. And yet thus must we think of God, if the interpretations of Scripture, necessary to maintain our author's doctrine, must be received for good. For by the ordinary rules of language, it will be very hard to understand, what God says; if what he speaks here, in the singular number to Adam, must be understood to be spoken to all mankind, and what he says in the plural number, *Genesis* 1:26 and 28, must be understood of Adam alone, exclusive of all others, and what he says to Noah and his sons jointly, must be understood to be meant to Noah alone, *Genesis* 9[:1].

47. Further it is to be noted, that these words here of *Genesis* 3:16, which our author calls 'the original grant of government' were not spoken to Adam, neither indeed was there any grant in them made to Adam, but a punishment laid upon Eve: and if we will take them as they were directed in particular to her, or in her, as their representative to all other women, they will at most concern the female sex only, and import no more but that subjection they should ordinarily be in to their husbands: but there is here no more law to oblige a woman to such a subjection, if the circumstances either of her condition or contract with her husband should exempt her from it, than there is, that she should bring forth her children in sorrow and pain, if there could be found a remedy for it, which is also a part of the same curse upon her: for the whole verse runs thus, 'unto the woman he said, I will greatly multiply thy sorrow and thy conception; in sorrow thou

shalt bring forth children, and thy desire shall be to thy husband, and he shall rule over thee'. 'Twould, I think, have been a hard matter for anybody, but our author to have found out a grant of 'monarchical government to Adam' in these words, which were neither spoke to, nor of him: neither will anyone, I suppose, by these words, think the weaker sex, as by a law so subjected to the curse contained in them, that 'tis their duty not to endeavour to avoid it. And will anyone say, that Eve, or any other woman, sinned, if she were brought to bed without those multiplied pains God threatens her here with? Or that either of our Queens Mary or Elizabeth, had they married any of their subjects, had been by this text put into a political subjection to him? Or that he thereby should have had monarchical rule over her? God, in this text, gives not, that I see, any authority to Adam over Eve, or to men over their wives, but only foretells what should be the woman's lot, how by his providence he would order it so, that she should be subject to her husband, as we see that generally the laws of mankind and customs of nations have ordered it so; and there is, I grant, a foundation in nature for it.

48. Thus when God says of Jacob and Esau, that 'the elder should serve the younger' (*Genesis* 25:23), nobody supposes that God hereby made Jacob Esau's sovereign, but foretold what should *de facto* come to pass.

But if these words here spoke to Eve must needs be understood as a law to bind her and all other women to subjection, it can be no other subjection than what every wife owes her husband, and then if this be the 'original grant of government' and the 'foundation of monarchical power', there will be as many monarchs as there are husbands. If therefore these words give any power to Adam, it can be only a conjugal power, not political, the power that every husband hath to order the things of private concernment in his family, as proprietor of the goods and land there, and to have his will take place before that of his wife in all things of their common concernment; but not a political power of life and death over her, much less over anybody else.

49. This I am sure: if our author will have this text to be a 'grant, the original grant of government', political government, he ought to have proved it by some better arguments than by barely saying, that 'thy desire shall be unto thy husband', was a

law whereby Eve and 'all that should come of her', were subjected to the absolute monarchical power of Adam and his heirs. 'Thy desire shall be to thy husband', is too doubtful an expression, of whose signification interpreters are not agreed, to build so confidently on, and in a matter of such moment, and so great and general concernment: but our author according to his way of writing, having once named the text, concludes presently without any more ado, that the meaning is, as he would have it. Let the words 'rule' and 'subject' be but found in the text or margin, and it immediately signifies the duty of a subject to his prince, the relation is changed, and though God says 'husband', Sir Robert will have it 'king'; Adam has presently 'absolute monarchical power' over Eve, and not only over Eve, but 'all that should come of her', though the Scripture says not a word of it, nor our author a word to prove it. But Adam must for all that be an absolute monarch, and so down to the end of the chapter. And here I leave my reader to consider, whether my bare saying, without offering any reasons to evince it, that this text gave not Adam that 'absolute monarchical power', our author supposes, be not as sufficient to destroy that power, as his bare assertion is to establish it, since the text mentions neither 'prince' nor 'people', speaks nothing of 'absolute' or 'monarchical' power, but the subjection of Eve to Adam, a wife to her husband. And he that would trace our author so all through, would make a short and sufficient answer to the greatest part of the grounds he proceeds on, and abundantly confute them by barely denying; it being a sufficient answer to assertions without proof, to deny them without giving a reason. And therefore should I have said nothing but barely denied that by this text 'the supreme power was settled and founded by God himself, in the fatherhood, limited to monarchy, and that to Adam's person and heirs', all which our author notably concludes from these words, as may be seen in the same page [138], it had been a sufficient answer; should I have desired any sober man only to have read the text, and considered to whom, and on what occasion it was spoken, he would no doubt have wondered how our author found out 'monarchical absolute power' in it, had he not had an exceeding good faculty to find it himself, where he could not show it others. And thus we have examined the two places of Scripture, all that I remember our author brings to prove 'Adam's sovereignty', that 'supremacy', which he says, 'it was God's ordinance should be unlimited in Adam, and as large as all the acts of his will' [138], *viz.* Genesis 1:28 and *Genesis* 3:16, one whereof signifies only the subjection of the inferior ranks of creatures to mankind, and the other the subjection that is due from a wife to her husband, both far enough from that which subjects owe the governors of political societies.

Chapter 6
OF ADAM'S TITLE TO SOVEREIGNTY
BY FATHERHOOD

50. There is one thing more, and then I think I have given you all that our author brings for proof of Adam's sovereignty, and that is a supposition of a natural right of dominion over his children, by being their father, and this title of fatherhood he is so pleased with, that you will find it brought in almost in every page, particularly, he says, 'not only Adam, but the succeeding patriarchs had by right of fatherhood royal authority over their children' [6]. And in the same page, 'this subjection of children being the fountain of all regal authority', etc. This being, as one would think by his so frequent mentioning it, the main basis of all his frame, we may well expect clear and evident reason for it, since he lays it down as a position necessary to his purpose, that 'every man that is born is so far from being free, that by his very birth he becomes a subject of him that begets him' [282]. So that Adam being the only man created, and all ever since being begotten, nobody has been born free. If we ask how Adam comes by this power over his children, he tells us here 'tis by begetting them: and so again, 'this natural dominion of Adam', says he, 'may be proved out of Grotius himself, who teacheth, that *generatione jus acquiritur parentibus in liberos* [by generation parents acquire a right over their children]' [226]. And indeed the act of begetting being that which makes a man a father, his right of father over his children can naturally arise from nothing else.

51. Grotius tells us not here how far this *jus in liberos* [right over children], this power of parents over their children extends; but our author always very clear in the point, assures us, 'tis supreme

power, and like that of absolute monarchs over their slaves, absolute power of life and death. He that should demand of him, how, or for what reason it is, that begetting a child gives the father such an absolute power over him, will find him answer nothing: we are to take his word for this as well as several other things, and by that the laws of nature and the constitutions of government must stand or fall. Had he been an absolute monarch, this way of talking might have suited well enough; *pro ratione voluntas* [his will standing for reason], might have been of force in his mouth, but in the way of proof or argument is very unbecoming and will little advantage his plea for absolute monarchy. Sir Robert has too much lessened a subject's authority to leave himself the hopes of establishing anything by his bare saying it. One slave's opinion without proof is not of weight enough to dispose of the liberty and fortunes of all mankind: if all men are not, as I think they are, naturally equal, I'm sure all slaves are; and then I may without presumption oppose my single opinion to his, and be confident that my saying, that begetting of children makes them not slaves to their fathers, as certainly sets all mankind free; as his affirming the contrary makes them all slaves. But that this position, which is the foundation of all their doctrine, who would have monarchy to be *jure divino* [by divine right], may have all fair play, let us hear what reasons others give for it, since our author offers none.

52. The argument, I have heard others make use of, to prove that fathers, by begetting them, come by an absolute power over their children, is this; that 'fathers have a power over the lives of their children, because they give them life and being', which is the only proof it is capable of, since there can be no reason, why naturally one man should have any claim or pretence of right over that in another, which was never his, which he bestowed not, but was received from the bounty of another. First, I answer, that everyone who gives another anything, has not always thereby a right to take it away again. But, secondly, they who say the father gives life to his children, are so dazzled with the thoughts of monarchy, that they do not, as they ought, remember God, who is the author and giver of life: ' 'tis in him alone we live, move, and have our being' [*Acts* 17:28]. How can he be thought to give life to another, that knows not wherein his own life consists? Philosophers are at a loss about it after their most diligent enquiries; and

anatomists, after their whole lives and studies spent in dissections, and diligent examining the bodies of men, confess their ignorance in the structure and use of many parts of man's body, and in that operation wherein life consists in the whole. And doth the rude ploughman, or the more ignorant voluptuary, frame or fashion such an admirable engine as this is, and then put life and sense into it? Can any man say, he formed the parts that are necessary to the life of his child? Or can he suppose himself to give the life, and yet not know what subject is fit to receive it, nor what actions or organs are necessary for its reception or preservation?

53. To give life to that which has yet no being, is to frame and make a living creature, fashion the parts, and mould and suit them to their uses, and having proportioned and fitted them together, to put into them a living soul. He that could do this, might indeed have some pretence to destroy his own workmanship. But is there anyone so bold, that dares thus far arrogate to himself the incomprehensible works of the Almighty? Who alone did at first, and continues still to make a living soul, he alone can breathe in the breath of life. If anyone thinks himself an artist at this, let him number up the parts of his child's body which he hath made, tell me their uses and operations, and when the living and rational soul began to inhabit this curious structure, when sense began, and how this engine which he has framed thinks and reasons; if he made it, let him, when it is out of order, mend it, at least tell wherein the defects lie. 'Shall he that made the eye not see?' says the Psalmist (Psalm 94:9). See these men's vanities: the structure of that one part is sufficient to convince us of an all wise contriver, and he has so visible a claim to us as his workmanship, that one of the ordinary appellations of God in Scripture is, 'God our Maker', and 'the Lord our Maker'. And therefore though our author for the magnifying his 'fatherhood', be pleased to say, 'that even the power which God himself exerciseth over mankind is by right of fatherhood' [284], yet this fatherhood is such a one as utterly excludes all pretence of title in earthly parents; for he is king because he is indeed Maker of us all, which no parents can pretend to be of their children.

54. But had men skill and power to make their children, 'tis not so slight a piece of workmanship, that it can be imagined they could make them without designing it. What father of a thousand,

when he begets a child, thinks further than the satisfying of his present appetite? God in his infinite wisdom has put strong desires of copulation into the constitution of men, thereby to continue the race of mankind, which he doth most commonly without the intention, and often against the consent and will of the begetter. And indeed those who desire and design children, are but the occasions of their being, and when they design and wish to beget them, do little more towards their making, than Deucalion and his wife in the fable did towards the making of mankind, by throwing pebbles over their heads.

55. But grant that the parents made their children, gave them life and being, and that hence there followed an absolute power. This would give the father but a joint dominion with the mother over them. For nobody can deny but that the woman hath an equal share, if not the greater, as nourishing the child a long time in her own body out of her own substance. There it is fashioned, and from her it receives the materials and principles of its constitution; and it is so hard to imagine the rational soul should presently inhabit the yet unformed embryo, as soon as the father has done his part in the act of generation, that if it must be supposed to derive anything from the parents, it must certainly owe most to the mother: but be that as it will, the mother cannot be denied an equal share in begetting of the child, and so the absolute authority of the father will not arise from hence. Our author indeed is of another mind; for he says, 'we know that God at the Creation gave the sovereignty to the man over the woman, as being the nobler and principal agent in generation' [192]. I remember not this in my Bible, and when the place is brought where God at the Creation gave the sovereignty to man over the woman, and that for this reason, because 'he is the nobler and principal agent in generation', it will be time enough to consider and answer it: but it is no new thing for our author to tell us his own fancies for certain and divine truths, though there be often a great deal of difference between his and divine revelation: for God in the Scripture says, 'his father and his mother that begot him' [*Zechariah* 13:3].

56. They who allege the practice of mankind, for exposing or selling their children [18, 282], as a proof of their power over them, are with Sir Robert happy arguers, and cannot but recommend their opinion by founding it on the most shameful action, and

most unnatural murder, human nature is capable of. The dens of
lions and nurseries of wolves know no such cruelty as this: these
savage inhabitants of the desert obey God and nature in being
tender and careful of their offspring: they will hunt, watch, fight,
and almost starve for the preservation of their young, never part
with them, never forsake them till they are able to shift for
themselves; and is it the privilege of man alone to act more
contrary to nature than the wild and most untamed part of the
creation? Doth God forbid us under the severest penalty, that of
death, to take away the life of any man, a stranger, and upon
provocation?, and does he permit us to destroy those he has given
us the charge and care of, and by the dictates of nature and reason,
as well as his revealed command, requires us to preserve? He has
in all the parts of the creation taken a peculiar care to propagate
and continue the several species of creatures, and makes the
individuals act so strongly to this end, that they sometimes neglect
their own private good for it, and seem to forget that general rule
which nature teaches all things of self-preservation, and the
preservation of their young, as the strongest principle in them
overrules the constitution of their particular natures. Thus we see
when their young stand in need of it, the timorous become
valiant, the fierce and savage kind, and the ravenous tender and
liberal.

57. But if the example of what hath been done, be the rule of
what ought to be, history would have furnished our author with
instances of this absolute fatherly power in its height and perfection, and he might have showed us in Peru, people that begot
children on purpose to fatten and eat them. The story is so
remarkable, that I cannot but set it down in the author's words.
'In some provinces', says he, 'they were so liquorish after man's
flesh, that they would not have the patience to stay till the breath
was out of the body, but would suck the blood as it ran from the
wounds of the dying man; they had public shambles of man's
flesh, and their madness herein was to that degree, that they
spared not their own children which they had begot on strangers
taken in war: for they made their captives their mistresses and
choicely nourished the children they had by them, till about
thirteen years old they butchered and eat them, and they served
the mothers after the same fashion, when they grew past child-

bearing, and ceased to bring them any more roasters' (Garcilaso de la Vega, *L'Histoire des Yncas de Peru*, 1.1.12).

58. Thus far can the busy mind of man carry him to a brutality below the level of beasts, when he quits his reason, which places him almost equal to angels. Nor can it be otherwise in a creature, whose thoughts are more than the sands, and wider than the ocean, where fancy and passion must needs run him into strange courses, if reason, which is his only star and compass, be not that [which] he steers by. The imagination is always restless and suggests variety of thoughts, and the will, reason being laid aside, is ready for every extravagant project; and in this state, he that goes furthest out of the way, is thought fittest to lead, and is sure of most followers: and when fashion hath once established, what folly or craft began, custom makes it sacred, and 'twill be thought impudence or madness, to contradict or question it. He that will impartially survey the nations of the world, will find so much of their governments, religions, and manners brought in and continued amongst them by these means, that he will have but little reverence for the practices which are in use and credit amongst men, and will have reason to think, that the woods and forests, where the irrational untaught inhabitants keep right by following nature, are fitter to give us rules, than cities and palaces, where those that call themselves civil and rational, go out of their way, by the authority of example. If precedents are sufficient to establish a rule in the case, our author might have found in holy writ children sacrificed by their parents and this amongst the people of God themselves. The Psalmist tells us (*Psalms* 106:38), 'they shed innocent blood even the blood of their sons and of their daughters whom they sacrificed unto the idols of Canaan'. But God judged not of this by our author's rule, nor allowed of the authority of practice against his righteous law, but as it follows there, 'the land was polluted with blood, therefore was the wrath of the Lord kindled against his people in so much that he abhorred his own inheritance'. The killing of their children, though it were fashionable, was charged on them as innocent blood, and so had, in the account of God, the guilt of murder, as the offering them to idols had the guilt of idolatry.

59. Be it then as Sir Robert says, that 'anciently, it was usual for men to sell and castrate their children' [282]. Let it be, that they exposed them; add to it, if you please, for this is still greater

power, that they begat them for their tables to fat and eat them: if this proves a right to do so, we may, by the same argument, justify adultery, incest and sodomy, for there are examples of these too, both ancient and modern; sins, which I suppose, have their principal aggravation from this, that they cross the main intention of nature, which willeth the increase of mankind, and the continuation of the species in the highest perfection, and the distinction of families, with the security of the marriage bed, as necessary thereunto.

60. In confirmation of this natural authority of the father, our author brings a lame proof, from the positive command of God in Scripture; his words are, 'to confirm the natural right of regal power, we find in the Decalogue, that the law which enjoins obedience to kings, is delivered in the terms, "honour thy father" ' [11] [*Exodus* 20:12]. 'Whereas many confess, that government only in the abstract, is the ordinance of God, they are not able to prove any such ordinance in the Scripture, but only in the fatherly power, and therefore we find the commandment, that enjoins obedience to superiors, given in the terms, "honour thy father"; so that not only the power and right of government, but the form of the power governing, and the person having the power, are all the ordinances of God. The first father had not only simply power, but power monarchical, as he was father immediately from God' [144]. To the same purpose, the same law is cited by our author in several other places, and just after the same fashion, that is, 'and mother', as apocryphal words, are always left out; a great argument of our author's ingenuity, and the goodness of his cause, which required in its defender zeal to a degree of warmth, able to warp the sacred rule of the word of God, to make it comply with his present occasion; a way of proceeding, not unusual to those, who embrace not truths, because reason and revelation offer them; but espouse tenets and parties, for ends different from truth, and then resolve at any rate to defend them; and so do with the words and sense of authors, they would fit to their purpose, just as Procrustes did with his guests, lop or stretch them, as may best fit them to the size of their notions: and they always prove like those, so served, deformed, lame, and useless.

61. For had our author set down this command without garbling, as God gave it, and joined mother to father, every reader would have seen that it had made directly against him, and that

it was so far from establishing the 'monarchical power of the father', that it set up the mother equal with him, and enjoined nothing but what was due in common, to both father and mother: for that is the constant tenor of the Scripture, 'honour thy father and thy mother' (*Exodus* 20[:12]); 'he that smiteth his father or mother, shall surely be put to death' (21:15); 'he that curseth his father or mother, shall surely be put to death' (verse 17); repeated *Leviticus* 20:9, and by our Saviour (*Matthew* 15:4); 'ye shall fear every man his mother and his father' (*Leviticus* 19:3); 'if a man have a rebellious son, which will not obey the voice of his father, or the voice of his mother; then shall his father and his mother, lay hold on him, and say, this our son is stubborn and rebellious, he will not obey our voice' (*Deuteronomy* 21:18–21); 'cursed be he that setteth light by his father or his mother' (27:16); 'my son, hear the instructions of thy father, and forsake not the law of thy mother', are the words of Solomon a king, who was not ignorant of what belonged to him, as a father or a king, and yet he joins father and mother together, in all the instructions he gives children quite through his book of *Proverbs*, 'woe unto him, that sayeth unto his father, what begettest thou, or to the woman, what hast thou brought forth' (*Isaiah* 45:10); 'in thee have they set light by father or mother' (*Ezekiel* 22:7); 'and it shall come to pass, that when any shall yet prophesy, then his father and his mother that begat him, shall say unto him, thou shalt not live, and his father and his mother that begat him, shall thrust him through when he prophesieth', (*Zechariah* 13:3). Here not the father only, but father and mother jointly, had power in this case of life and death. Thus ran the law of the Old Testament, and in the New they are likewise joined, in the obedience of their children (*Ephesians* 6:1). The rule is, 'children obey your parents', and I do not remember, that I anywhere read, 'children obey your father' and no more. The Scripture joins mother too in that homage, which is due from children, and had there been any text, where the honour or obedience of children had been directed to the father alone, 'tis not likely that our author, who pretends to build all upon Scripture, would have omitted it. Nay, the Scripture makes the authority of father and mother, in respect of those they have begot, so equal, that in some places it neglects, even the priority of order, which is thought due to the father, and the mother is put

first, as *Leviticus* 19:3. From which so constantly joining father
and mother together, as is found quite through the Scripture, we
may conclude that the honour they have a title to from their
children, is one common right belonging so equally to them both,
that neither can claim it wholly, neither can be excluded.

62. One would wonder then how our author infers from the
Fifth Commandment, that 'all power was originally in the father'.
How he finds monarchical power of government, settled and fixed
by the commandment, 'honour thy father and thy mother'. If all
the honour due by the commandment, be it what it will, be the
only right of the father, because he, as our author says, 'has the
sovereignty over the woman, as being the nobler and principal
agent in generation' [192], why did God afterwards all along join
the mother with him, to share in his honour? Can the father, by
this sovereignty of his, discharge the child from paying this honour
to his mother? The Scripture gave no such licence to the Jews, and
yet there were often breaches wide enough betwixt husband and
wife, even to divorce and separation, and, I think, nobody will say
a child may withhold honour from his mother, or, as the Scripture
terms it, 'set light by her', though his father should command him
to do so, no more than the mother could dispense with him, for
neglecting to honour his father, whereby 'tis plain, that this
command of God, gives the father no sovereignty, no supremacy.

63. I agree with our author, that the title to this honour is
vested in the parents by nature, and is a right which accrues to
them, by their having begotten their children, and God by many
positive declarations has confirmed it to them: I also allow our
author's rule, 'that in grants and gifts, that have their original from
God and nature, as the power of the father' (let me add 'and
mother', for whom God hath joined together, let no man put
asunder) 'no inferior power of men can limit, nor make any law
of prescription against them' [283], so that the mother having by
this law of God, a right to honour from her children, which is not
subject to the will of her husband, we see this 'absolute monarchical power of the father', can neither be founded on it, nor
consist with it; and he has a power very far from monarchical,
very far from that absoluteness our author contends for, when
another has over his subjects the same power he hath, and by the
same title: and therefore he cannot forbear saying himself that 'he

cannot see how any man's children can be free from subjection to
their parents' [7], which, in common speech, I think, signifies
'mother' as well as 'father', or if 'parents' here signifies only
'father', 'tis the first time I ever yet knew it to do so, and by such
a use of words, one may say anything.

64. By our author's doctrine, the father having absolute jurisdiction over his children, has also the same over their issue, and
the consequence is good, were it true, that the father had such a
power: and yet I ask our author whether the grandfather, by his
sovereignty, could discharge the grandchild from paying to his
father the honour due to him by the Fifth Commandment. If the
grandfather hath by right of fatherhood, sole sovereign power in
him, and that obedience which is due to the supreme magistrate,
be commanded in these words, 'honour thy father', 'tis certain the
grandfather might dispense with the grandson's honouring his
father, which, since 'tis evident in common sense, he cannot, it
follows from hence that, 'honour thy father and mother', cannot
mean an absolute subjection to a sovereign power, but something
else. The right therefore which parents have by nature, and which
is confirmed to them by the Fifth Commandment, cannot be that
political dominion, which our author would derive from it: for
that being in every civil society supreme somewhere, can discharge
any subject from any political obedience to anyone of his fellow
subjects. But what law of the magistrate, can give a child liberty,
not to honour his father and mother? 'Tis an eternal law annexed
purely to the relation of parents and children, and so contains
nothing of the magistrate's power in it, nor is subjected to it.

65. Our author says, 'God hath given to a father, a right or
liberty to alien his power over his children to any other' [282]. I
doubt whether he can alien wholly the right of honour that is due
from them; but be that as it will, this I am sure, he cannot alien,
and retain the same power, if therefore the magistrate's sovereignty be as our author would have it, 'nothing but the authority
of a supreme father' [11], 'tis unavoidable, that if the magistrate
hath all this paternal right as he must have if fatherhood be the
fountain of all authority, then the subjects though fathers, can
have no power over their children, no right to honour from them:
for it cannot be all in another's hands, and a part remain with the
parents. So that according to our author's own doctrine, 'honour

thy father and mother' cannot possibly be understood of political subjection and obedience; since the laws both in the Old and New Testament, that commanded children to 'honour and obey their parents', were given to such, whose fathers were under civil government, and fellow subjects with them in political societies; and to have bid them 'honour and obey their parents' in our author's sense, had been to bid them be subjects to those who had no title to it, the right to obedience from subjects, being all vested in another: and instead of teaching obedience, this had been to foment sedition, by setting up powers that were not. If therefore this command, 'honour thy father and mother', concern political dominion, it directly overthrows our author's monarchy; since it being to be paid by every child to his father, even in society, every father must necessarily have political dominion, and there will be as many sovereigns as there are fathers: besides that the mother too hath her title, which destroys the sovereignty of one supreme monarch. But if 'honour thy father and mother' mean something distinct from political power, as necessarily it must, it is besides our author's business, and serves nothing to his purpose.

66. 'The law that enjoins obedience to kings is delivered', says our author, 'in the terms, "honour thy father", as if all power were originally in the father' [11-12]. And that law is also delivered, say I, in the terms, 'honour thy mother', as if all power were originally in the mother. I appeal whether the argument be not as good on one side as the other, father and mother being joined all along in the Old and New Testament wherever honour or obedience is enjoined [upon] children. Again our author tells us, 'that this command, "honour thy father" gives the right to govern, and makes the form of government, monarchical' [144]. To which I answer, that, if by 'honour thy father' be meant obedience to the political power of the magistrate, it concerns not any duty we owe to our natural fathers who are subjects: because they, by our author's doctrine, are divested of all that power, it being placed wholly in the prince, and so being equally subjects and slaves with their children, can have no right by that title, to any such honour or obedience, as contains in it political subjection: if 'honour thy father and mother' signifies the duty we owe our natural parents, as by our Saviour's interpretation (*Matthew* 15:4), and all the other mentioned places, 'tis plain it does, then it cannot concern

political obedience, but a duty that is owing to persons, who have
no title to sovereignty, nor any political authority as magistrates
over subjects. For the person of a private father, and a title to
obedience, due to the supreme magistrate, are things inconsistent;
and therefore this command, which must necessarily comprehend
the persons of our natural fathers, must mean a duty we owe them
distinct from our obedience to the magistrate, and from which the
most absolute power of princes cannot absolve us: what this duty
is, we shall in its due place examine.

67. And thus we have at last got through all that in our author
looks like an argument for that absolute unlimited sovereignty
described, section 8, which he supposes in Adam, so that mankind
ever since have been all born slaves, without any title to freedom.
But if creation which gave nothing but a being, made not Adam
prince of his posterity: if Adam, *Genesis* 1:28, was not constituted
lord of mankind, nor had a private dominion given him exclusive
of his children, but only a right and power over the earth, and inferior
creatures in common with the children of men: if also, *Genesis* 3:16,
God gave not any political power to Adam over his wife and
children, but only subjected Eve to Adam, as a punishment, or
foretold the subjection of the weaker sex, in the ordering the
common concernments of their families, but gave not thereby to
Adam, as to the husband, power of life and death, which necessarily
belongs to the magistrate: if fathers by begetting their children
acquire no such power over them: and if the command, 'honour
thy father and mother', give it not, but only enjoins a duty owing
to parents equally, whether subjects or not, and to the mother as
well as the father; if all this be so, as I think, by what has been
said, is very evident, then man has a natural freedom, notwithstanding all our author confidently says to the contrary, since all
that share in the same common nature, faculties and powers, are
in nature equal, and ought to partake in the same common rights
and privileges, till the manifest appointment of God, 'who is Lord
over all, blessed for ever' [*Romans* 9:5], can be produced to show
any particular person's supremacy, or a man's own consent
subjects him to a superior. This is so plain, that our author confesses,
that 'Sir John Hayward, Blackwood and Barclay, the great vindi-
cators of the rights of kings, could not deny it, but admit with one
consent the natural liberty and equality of mankind', for a truth

unquestionable. And our author hath been so far from producing anything, that may make good his great position, that 'Adam was absolute monarch', and so 'men are not naturally free', that even his own proofs make against him; so that to use his own way of arguing, 'this first erroneous principle failing, the whole fabric of this vast engine of absolute power and tyranny, drops down of itself' [3], and there needs no more to be said in answer to all that he builds upon so false and frail a foundation.

68. But to save others the pains, were there any need, he is not sparing himself to show, by his own contradictions, the weakness of his own doctrine. Adam's absolute and sole dominion is that which he is everywhere full of, and all along builds on, and yet he tells us, page [6], 'that as Adam was lord of his children, so his children under him had a command and power over their own children'. The unlimited and undivided sovereignty of Adam's fatherhood, by our author's computation, stood but a little while, only during the first generation, but as soon as he had grandchildren, Sir Robert could give but a very ill account of it. 'Adam, as father of his children', saith he, 'hath an absolute, unlimited royal power over them, and by virtue thereof over those that they begot, and so to all generations' [7]; and yet his children, *viz*. Cain and Seth, have a paternal power over their children at the same time: so that they are at the same time 'absolute lords', and yet 'vassals and slaves': Adam has all the authority, as grandfather of the people, and they have a part of it as fathers of a part of them: he is absolute over them and their posterity, by having begotten them, and yet they are absolute over their children by the same title. 'No', says our author, 'Adam's children under him, had power over their own children, but still with subordination to the first parent' [6]. A good distinction that sounds well, and 'tis [a] pity it signifies nothing, nor can be reconciled with our author's words. I readily grant, that supposing Adam's absolute power over his posterity, any of his children might have from him a delegated, and so a subordinate power over a part, or all the rest: but that cannot be the power our author speaks of here, it is not a power by grant and commission, but the natural paternal power he supposes a father to have over his children. For first, he says, 'as Adam was lord of his children, so his children under him had a power over their own children': they were then lords over their

own children after the same manner, and by the same title, that Adam was, i.e. by right of generation, by right of fatherhood. Secondly, 'tis plain he means the natural power of fathers, because he limits it to be only over their own children; a delegated power has no such limitation, as only over their own children, it might be over others, as well as their own children. Thirdly, if it were a delegated power, it must appear in Scripture: but there is no ground in Scripture to affirm, that Adam's children had any other power over theirs, than what they naturally had as fathers.

69. But that he means here paternal power, and no other, is past doubt from the inference he makes in these words immediately following, 'I see not then how the children of Adam, or of any man else can be free from subjection to their parents' [7]: whereby it appears, that the power on one side, and the subjection on the other, our author here speaks of, is that natural power and subjection between parents and children. For that which every man's children owed, could be no other: and that our author always affirms to be absolute and unlimited. This natural power of parents over their children, Adam had over his posterity, says our author, and this power of parents over their children, his children had over theirs in his lifetime, says our author also: so that Adam, by a natural right of father, had an absolute, unlimited power over all his posterity, and at the same time his children had by the same right absolute unlimited power over theirs. Here then are two absolute unlimited powers existing together, which I would have anybody reconcile one to another, or to common sense. For the salvo he has put in of subordination, makes it more absurd: to have one absolute, unlimited, nay unlimitable power in subordination to another, is so manifest a contradiction, that nothing can be more. Adam is 'absolute prince with the unlimited authority of fatherhood over all his posterity'; all his posterity are then absolutely his subjects, and, as our author says, his slaves, children and grandchildren, are equally in this state of subjection and slavery, and yet, says our author, 'the children of Adam have paternal', i.e. absolute, unlimited 'power over their own children': which in plain English is, they are slaves and absolute princes at the same time, and in the same government, and one part of the subjects have an absolute unlimited power over the other by the natural right of parentage.

70. If anyone will suppose in favour of our author that he here meant, that parents, who are in subjection themselves to the absolute authority of their father, have yet some power over their children: I confess he is something nearer the truth: but he will not at all hereby help our author. For he nowhere speaking of the paternal power, but as an absolute unlimited authority, cannot be supposed to understand anything else here, unless he himself had limited it, and showed how far it reached. And that he means here paternal authority in that large extent, is plain from the immediate following words; 'this subjection of children being', says he, 'the fountain of all regal authority' [7]. The subjection, then that in the former line he says, every man is in to his parents, and consequently what Adam's grandchildren were in to their parents, was that which was the fountain of all regal authority, i.e. according to our author, absolute, unlimitable authority. And thus Adam's children had regal authority over their children, whilst they themselves were subjects to their father, and fellow subjects with their children. But let him mean as he pleases, 'tis plain he allows 'Adam's children to have paternal power' [6], as also all other fathers to have 'paternal power over their children' [282]. From whence one of these two things will necessarily follow, that either Adam's children, even in his lifetime, had, and so all other fathers have, as he phrases it, 'by right of fatherhood royal authority over their children' [6], or else, that Adam, by right of fatherhood, had not royal authority: for it cannot be but that paternal power does, or does not, give royal authority to them that have it: if it does not, then Adam could not be sovereign by this title, nor anybody else, and then there is an end of all our author's politics at once; if it does give royal authority, then everyone that has paternal power has royal authority, and then by our author's patriarchal government, there will be as many kings as there are fathers.

71. And thus what a monarchy he hath set up, let him and his disciples consider. Princes certainly will have great reason to thank him for these new politics, which set up as many absolute kings in every country as there are fathers of children. And yet who can blame our author for it, it lying unavoidably in the way of one discoursing upon our author's principles? For having placed an absolute power in fathers by right of begetting, he could

not easily resolve how much of this power belonged to a son over the children he had begotten; and so it fell out to be a very hard matter to give all the power, as he does, to Adam, and yet allow a part in his lifetime to his children, when they were parents, and which he knew not well how to deny them. This makes him so doubtful in his expressions, and so uncertain where to place this absolute natural power, which he calls fatherhood; sometimes Adam alone has it all, as pages [7, 138, 236]. Sometimes 'parents' have it, which word scarce signifies the father alone [7, 10]. Sometimes 'children' during their father's lifetime, as page [6]. Sometimes 'fathers of families', as page [35]. Sometimes 'fathers' indefinitely [282]. Sometimes 'the heir to Adam' [144]. Sometimes 'the posterity of Adam' [71]. Sometimes 'prime fathers, all sons or grandchildren of Noah' [138]. Sometimes 'the eldest parents' [7]. Sometimes all kings [10]. Sometimes all that have supreme power [138]. Sometimes 'heirs to those first progenitors, who were at first the natural parents of the whole people' [10]. Sometimes an elective king [11]. Sometimes those whether a few or a multitude that govern the commonwealth [11]. Sometimes he that can catch it, a usurper [11, 282].

72. Thus this new nothing, that is to carry with it all power, authority, and government; this fatherhood which is to design the person, and establish the throne of monarchs, whom the people are to obey, may, according to Sir Robert, come into any hands, anyhow, and so by his politics give to democracy royal authority, and make a usurper a lawful prince. And if it will do all these fine feats, much good do our author and all his followers with their omnipotent fatherhood, which can serve for nothing but to unsettle and destroy all the lawful governments in the world, and to establish in their room disorder, tyranny, and usurpation.

Chapter 7

OF FATHERHOOD AND PROPERTY CONSIDERED
TOGETHER AS FOUNTAINS OF SOVEREIGNTY

73. In the foregoing chapters we have seen what Adam's monarchy was, in our author's opinion, and upon what titles he founded it. The foundations which he lays the chief stress on, as

those from which he thinks he may best derive monarchical power to future princes, are two, *viz.* 'fatherhood and property', and therefore the way he proposes to 'remove the absurdities and inconveniences of the doctrine of natural freedom', is, 'to maintain the natural and private dominion of Adam' [225]. Conformable hereunto, he tells us, the 'grounds and principles of government necessarily depend upon the original of property' [252]. 'The subjection of children to their parents is the fountain of all regal authority' [7]. And 'all power on earth is either derived or usurped from the fatherly power, there being no other original to be found of any power whatsoever' [284]. I will not stand here to examine how it can be said without a contradiction, that the 'first grounds and principles of government necessarily depend upon the original of property', and yet, 'that there is no other original of any power whatsoever, but that of the father': it being hard to understand how there can be no other original but fatherhood, and yet that the 'grounds and principles of government depend upon the original of property'; property and fatherhood being as far different as lord of a manor and father of children. Nor do I see how they will either of them agree with what our author says, of God's sentence against Eve (*Genesis* 3:16), 'that it is the original grant of government' [138]: so that if that were the original, government had not its original by our author's own confession, either from property or fatherhood; and this text which he brings as a proof of Adam's power over Eve, necessarily contradicts what he says of the fatherhood, that it is the 'sole fountain of all power'. For if Adam had any such regal power over Eve, as our author contends for, it must be by some other title than that of begetting.

74. But I leave him to reconcile these contradictions as well as many others, which may plentifully be found in him by anyone, who will but read him with a little attention, and shall come now to consider how these two originals of government, 'Adam's natural and private dominion', will consist, and serve to make out and establish the titles of succeeding monarchs, who, as our author obliges them, must all derive their power from these fountains. Let us then suppose Adam made by God's donation lord and sole proprietor of the whole earth, in as large and ample a manner as Sir Robert could wish; let us suppose him also by right of fatherhood absolute ruler over his children with an

unlimited supremacy, I ask then upon Adam's death what becomes of both his natural and private dominion, and I doubt not 'twill be answered, that they descended to his next heir, as our author tells us in several places; but this way 'tis plain, cannot possibly convey both his natural and private dominion to the same person. For should we allow that all the property, all the estate of the father ought to descend to the eldest son, (which will need some proof to establish it) and so he has by that title all the private dominion of the father, yet the father's natural dominion, the paternal power cannot descend to him by inheritance. For it being a right that accrues to a man only by begetting, no man can have this natural dominion over anyone he does not beget: unless it can be supposed, that a man can have a right to anything, without doing that upon which that right is solely founded. For if a father by begetting, and no other title, has natural dominion over his children, he that does not beget them, cannot have this natural dominion over them: and therefore be it true or false that our author says, that 'every man that is born, by his very birth becomes a subject to him that begets him' [282], this necessarily follows, *viz.* that a man by his birth cannot become a subject to his brother, who did not beget him: unless it can be supposed that a man by the very same title can come to be under the natural and absolute dominion of two different men at once, or it be sense to say, that a man by birth is under the natural dominion of his father, only because he begat him, and a man by birth also is under the natural dominion of his eldest brother, though he did not beget him.

75. If then the private dominion of Adam, i.e. his property in the creatures, descended at his death all entirely to his eldest son, his heir; (for if it did not, there is presently an end of all Sir Robert's monarchy) and his natural dominion, the dominion a father has over his children by begetting them, belonged immediately upon Adam's decease equally to all his sons who had children, by the same title their father had it, the sovereignty founded upon property, and the sovereignty founded upon fatherhood, come to be divided: since Cain as heir had that of property alone, Seth and the other sons that of fatherhood equally with him. This is the best can be made of our author's doctrine, and of the two titles of sovereignty he sets up in Adam, one of them will either signify nothing, or if they both must stand, they can serve only to

confound the rights of princes, and disorder government in his posterity. For by building upon two titles to dominion, which cannot descend together, and which he allows may be separated (for he yields that 'Adam's children had their distinct territories by right of private dominion' [217, quoting Selden]) he makes it perpetually a doubt upon his principles where the sovereignty is, or to whom we owe our obedience, since fatherhood and property are distinct titles, and began presently upon Adam's death to be in distinct persons. And which then was to give way to the other?

76. Let us take the account of it, as he himself gives it us. He tells us out of Grotius [i.e. Selden], that 'Adam's children by donation, assignation, or some kind of cession before he was dead, had their distinct territories by right of private dominion; Abel had his flocks and pastures for them; Cain had his fields for corn, and the land of Nod where he built him a city' [217] [Genesis 4:16–17]. Here 'tis obvious to demand which of these two after Adam's death, was sovereign? 'Cain', says our author [10]. By what title? 'As heir; for heirs to progenitors, who were natural parents of their people, are not only lords of their own children, but also of their brethren', says our author [10] [Genesis 27:29]. What was Cain heir to? Not the entire possessions, not all that which Adam had private dominion in, for our author allows that Abel by a title derived from his father, 'had his distinct territory for pasture by right of private dominion'. What then Abel had by private dominion, was exempt from Cain's dominion [217]. For he could not have private dominion over that, which was under the private dominion of another, and therefore his sovereignty over his brother is gone with this private dominion, and so there are presently two sovereigns, and his imaginary title of fatherhood is out of doors, and Cain is no prince over his brother: or else if Cain retain his sovereignty over Abel, notwithstanding his private dominion, it will follow that the first grounds and principles of government have nothing to do with property, whatever our author says to the contrary. 'Tis true, Abel did not outlive his father Adam, but that makes nothing to the argument, which will hold good against Sir Robert in Abel's issue, or in Seth, or any of the posterity of Adam, not descended from Cain.

77. The same inconvenience he runs into about the three sons of Noah, who, as he says, 'had the whole world divided amongst

them by their father' [7]. I ask then in which of the three shall we find the establishment of regal power after Noah's death? If in all three, as our author there seems to say; then it will follow, that regal power is founded in property of land, and follows private dominion, and not in paternal power or natural dominion, and so there is an end of paternal power as the fountain of regal authority, and the so much magnified fatherhood quite vanishes. If the regal power descended to Shem as eldest, and heir to his father, then 'Noah's division of the world by lot to his sons, or his ten years sailing about the Mediterranean to appoint each son his part' [8], which our author tells of, was labour lost, his division of the world to them, was to ill, or to no purpose. For his grant to Cham and Japhet was little worth if Shem, notwithstanding this grant, as soon as Noah was dead, was to be lord over them. Or, if this grant of private dominion to them over their assigned territories, were good, here were set up two distinct sorts of power, not subordinate one to the other, with all those inconveniences which he musters up against the power of the people, which I shall set down in his own words, only changing 'property' for 'people'. 'All power on earth is either derived or usurped from the fatherly power, there being no other original to be found of any power whatsoever: for if there should be granted two sorts of power, without any subordination of one to the other, they would be in perpetual strife which should be supreme, for two supremes cannot agree: if the fatherly power be supreme, then the power grounded on private dominion must be subordinate, and depend on it; and if the power grounded on property be supreme, then the fatherly power must submit to it, and cannot be exercised without the licence of the proprietors, which must quite destroy the frame and course of nature' [284]. This is his own arguing against two distinct independent powers, which I have set down in his own words, only putting power rising from 'property', for power of the 'people'; and when he has answered what he himself has urged here against two distinct powers, we shall be better able to see how, with any tolerable sense, he can derive all regal authority from the natural and private dominion of Adam, from fatherhood and property together, which are distinct titles that do not always meet in the same person; and 'tis plain, by his own confession, presently separated as soon both as Adam's and

Noah's death made way for succession: though our author frequently in his writings jumbles them together, and omits not to make use of either, where he thinks it will sound best to his purpose. But the absurdities of this will more fully appear in the next chapter, where we shall examine the ways of conveyance of the sovereignty of Adam, to princes that were to reign after him.

Chapter 8
OF THE CONVEYANCE OF ADAM'S SOVEREIGN
MONARCHICAL POWER

78. Sir Robert, having not been very happy in any proof he brings for the sovereignty of Adam, is not much more fortunate in conveying it to future princes, who, if his politics be true, must all derive their titles from that first monarch. The ways he has assigned, as they lie scattered up and down in his writings, I will set down in his own words: in his preface he tells us, that 'Adam being monarch of the whole world, none of his posterity had any right to possess anything, but by his grant or permission, or by succession from him' [236]: here he makes two ways of conveyance of anything Adam stood possessed of, and those are grant or succession. Again he says, 'all kings either are, or are to be reputed, the next heirs to those first progenitors, who were at first the natural parents of the whole people' [10]. 'There cannot be any multitude of men whatsoever, but that in it, considered by itself, there is one man amongst them, that in nature hath a right to be the king of all the rest, as being the next heir to Adam' [144]. Here in these places inheritance is the only way he allows of conveying monarchical power to princes. In other places he tells us, 'all power on earth is either derived or usurped from the fatherly power' [284]. 'All kings that now are, or ever were, are or were either fathers of their people, or the heirs of such fathers or usurpers of the right of such fathers' [143–4]. And here he makes inheritance or usurpation the only ways whereby kings come by this original power: but yet he tells us, 'this fatherly empire, as it was of itself hereditary, so it was alienable by patent, and seizable by a usurper' [203]. So then here inheritance, grant or usurpation will convey it. And last of all, which is most

admirable, he tell us, 'it skills not which way kings come by their power, whether by election, donation, succession, or by any other means, for it is still the manner of the government by supreme power, that makes them properly kings, and not the means of obtaining their crowns' [44]. Which I think is a full answer to all his whole hypothesis, and discourse about Adam's royal authority, as the fountain from which all princes were to derive theirs: and he might have spared the trouble of speaking so much, as he does, up and down of heirs and inheritance, if to make anyone properly a king, needs no more but governing by supreme power, and it matters not by what means he came by it.

79. By this notable way, our author may make Oliver [Cromwell] as properly king, as anyone else he could think of: and had he had the happiness to live under Masaniello's government, he could not by this his own rule have forborne to have done homage to him, with 'O king live for ever', since the manner of his government by supreme power, made him properly king, who was but the day before properly a fisherman. And if Don Quixote had taught his squire to govern with supreme authority, our author no doubt could have made a most loyal subject in Sancho Pancha's island: and he must needs have deserved some preferment in such governments, since I think he is the first politician, who, pretending to settle government upon its true basis, and to establish the thrones of lawful princes, ever told the world, that he was 'properly a king, whose manner of government was by supreme power', by what means soever he obtained it' [44]; which in plain English is to say, that regal and supreme power is properly and truly his, who can by any means seize upon it: and if this be, to be properly a king, I wonder how he came to think of, or where he will find, a usurper.

80. This is so strange a doctrine, that the surprise of it hath made me pass by, without their due reflection, the contradictions he runs into, by making sometimes inheritance alone, sometimes only grant or inheritance, sometimes only inheritance or usurpation, sometimes all these three, and at last election, or any other means, added to them, the ways whereby Adam's royal authority, that is, his right to supreme rule, could be conveyed down to future kings and governors, so as to give them a title to the obedience and subjection of the people. But these contradictions

lie so open, that the very reading of our author's own words, will discover them to any ordinary understanding: and though what I have quoted out of him (with abundance more of the same strain and coherence which might be found in him) might well excuse me from any further trouble in this argument, yet having proposed to myself, to examine the main parts of his doctrine, I shall a little more particularly consider how inheritance, grant, usurpation or election, can any way make out government in the world upon his principles; or derive to anyone a right of empire, from this regal authority of Adam, had it been never so well proved, that he had been absolute monarch, and lord of the whole world.

Chapter 9
OF MONARCHY, BY INHERITANCE FROM ADAM

81. Though it be never so plain that there ought to be government in the world, nay should all men be of our author's mind, that divine appointment had ordained it to be monarchical, yet since men cannot obey anything, that cannot command, and ideas of government in the fancy, though never so perfect, though never so right, cannot give laws, nor prescribe rules to the actions of men; it would be of no behoof for the settling of order, and establishment of government in its exercise and use amongst men, unless there were a way also taught how to know the person, to whom it belonged to have this power, and exercise this dominion over others. 'Tis in vain then to talk of subjection and obedience, without telling us whom we are to obey. For were I never so fully persuaded, that there ought to be magistracy and rule in the world, yet I am nevertheless at liberty still, till it appears who is the person that hath right to my obedience: since if there be no marks to know him by, and distinguish him, that hath right to rule from other men, it may be myself, as well as any other. And therefore though submission to government be everyone's duty, yet since that signifies nothing but submitting to the direction and laws of such men, as have authority to command, 'tis not enough to make a man a subject, to convince him that there is regal power in the world, but there must be ways of designing, and knowing the person to whom this regal power of right belongs, and a man

can never be obliged in conscience to submit to any power, unless
he can be satisfied who is the person, who has a right to exercise
that power over him. If this were not so, there would be no
distinction between pirates and lawful princes, he that has force
is without any more ado to be obeyed, and crowns and sceptres
would become the inheritance only of violence and rapine. Men
too might as often and as innocently change their governors, as
they do their physicians, if the person cannot be known, who has
a right to direct me, and whose prescriptions I am bound to follow.
To settle therefore men's consciences under an obligation to
obedience, 'tis necessary that they know not only that there is a
power somewhere in the world, but the person who by right is
vested with this power over them.

82. How successful our author has been in his attempts, to set
up a monarchical absolute power in Adam, the reader may judge
by what has been already said: but were that absolute monarchy
as clear as our author would desire it, as I presume it is the
contrary, yet it could be of no use to the government of mankind
now in the world, unless he also make out these two things.

First, that this power of Adam was not to end with him, but
was upon his decease conveyed entire to some other person, and
so on to posterity.

Secondly, that the princes and rulers now on earth, are possessed of this power of Adam, by a right way of conveyance
derived to them.

83. If the first of these fail, the power of Adam, were it never
so great, never so certain, will signify nothing to the present
governments and societies in the world, but we must seek out
some other original of power for the government of polities than
this of Adam, or else there will be none at all in the world. If the
latter fail, it will destroy the authority of the present governors,
and absolve the people from subjection to them, since they having
no better claim than others to that power, which is alone the
fountain of all authority, can have no title to rule over them.

84. Our author having fancied an absolute sovereignty in
Adam, mentions several ways of its conveyance to princes, that
were to be his successors, but that which he chiefly insists on, is,
that of inheritance, which occurs so often in his several discourses,
and I having in the foregoing chapter quoted several of these

passages, I shall not need here again to repeat them. This sovereignty he erects, as has been said upon a double foundation, *viz.* that of property, and that of fatherhood. One was the right he was supposed to have in all creatures, a right to possess the earth with the beasts, and other inferior ranks of things in it for his private use, exclusive of all other men. The other was the right he was supposed to have, to rule and govern men, all the rest of mankind.

85. In both these rights, there being supposed an exclusion of all other men, it must be upon some reason peculiar to Adam, that they must both be founded.

That of his property our author supposes to arise from God's immediate donation, *Genesis* 1:28, and that of fatherhood from the act of begetting: now in all inheritance, if the heir succeed not to the reason, upon which his father's right was founded, he cannot succeed to the right which followeth from it: for example, Adam had a right of property in the creatures, upon the donation and grant of God Almighty, who was Lord and proprietor of them all, let this be so as our author tells us, yet upon his death his heir can have no title to them, no such right of property in them, unless the same reason, *viz.* God's donation, vested a right in the heir too. For if Adam could have had no property in, nor use of, the creatures without this positive donation from God, and this donation, were only personally to Adam, his heir could have no right by it, but upon his death, it must revert to God the Lord and owner again: for positive grants give no title further than the express words convey it, and by which only it is held. And thus, if as our author himself contends, that donation, *Genesis* 1:28, were made only to Adam personally his heir could not succeed to his property in the creatures; and if it were a donation to any but Adam, let it be shown, that it was to his heir in our author's sense, i.e. to one of his children exclusive of all the rest.

86. But not to follow our author too far out of the way, the plain of the case is this. God having made man, and planted in him, as in all other animals, a strong desire of self-preservation, and furnished the world with things fit for food and raiment and other necessaries of life, subservient to his design, that man should live and abide for some time upon the face of the earth, and not that so curious and wonderful a piece of workmanship by its own negligence, or want of necessaries, should perish again, presently

after a few moments continuance: God, I say, having made man and the world thus, spoke to him, (that is) directed him by his senses and reason, as he did the inferior animals by their sense, and instinct, which he had placed in them to that purpose, to the use of those things, which were serviceable for his subsistence, and given him as means of his preservation. And therefore I doubt not, but before these words were pronounced, *Genesis* 1:28-29 (if they must be understood literally to have been spoken) and without any such verbal donation, man had a right to a use of the creatures, by the will and grant of God. For the desire, strong desire of preserving his life and being having been planted in him, as a principle of action by God himself, reason, which was the voice of God in him, could not but teach him and assure him, that pursuing that natural inclination he had to preserve his being, he followed the will of his Maker, and therefore had a right to make use of those creatures, which by his reason or senses he could discover would be serviceable thereunto. And thus man's property in the creatures, was founded upon the right he had, to make use of those things, that were necessary or useful to his being.

87. This being the reason and foundation of Adam's property gave the same title, on the same ground, to all his children, not only after his death, but in his lifetime: so that here was no privilege of his heir above his other children, which could exclude them from an equal right to the use of the inferior creatures, for the comfortable preservation of their beings, which is all the property man hath in them: and so Adam's sovereignty built on property, or as our author calls it, 'private dominion' comes to nothing. Every man had a right to the creatures, by the same title Adam had, *viz.* by the right everyone had to take care of, and provide for their subsistence: and thus men had a right in common, Adam's children in common with him. But if anyone had began, and made himself a property in any particular thing, (which how he, or anyone else, could do, shall be shown in another place) that thing, that possession, if he disposed not otherwise of it by his positive grant, descended naturally to his children, and they had a right to succeed to it, and possess it.

88. It might reasonably be asked here, how come children by this right of possessing, before any other, the properties of their parents upon their decease. For it being personally the parents,

when they die, without actually transferring their right to another, why does it not return again to the common stock of mankind? 'Twill perhaps be answered, that common consent hath disposed of it, to the children. Common practice, we see indeed does so dispose of it but we cannot say, that it is the common consent of mankind; for that hath never been asked, nor actually given: and if common tacit consent hath established it, it would make but a positive and not natural right of children to inherit the goods of their parents: but where the practice is universal, 'tis reasonable to think the cause is natural. The ground then, I think, to be this. The first and strongest desire God planted in men, and wrought into the very principles of their nature being that of self-preservation, that is the foundation of a right to the creatures, for the particular support and use of each individual person himself. But next to this, God planted in men a strong desire also of propagating their kind, and continuing themselves in their posterity, and this gives children a title, to share in the property of their parents, and a right to inherit their possessions. Men are not proprietors of what they have merely for themselves, their children have a title to part of it, and have their kind of right joined with their parents, in the possession which comes to be wholly theirs, when death having put an end to their parents' use of it, hath taken them from their possessions, and this we call inheritance. Men being by a like obligation bound to preserve what they have begotten, as to preserve themselves, their issue come to have a right in the goods they are possessed of. That children have such a right is plain from the laws of God, and that men are convinced, that children have such a right, is evident from the law of the land, both which laws require parents to provide for their children.

89. For children being by the course of nature, born weak, and unable to provide for themselves, they have by the appointment of God himself, who hath thus ordered the course of nature, a right to be nourished and maintained by their parents, nay a right not only to a bare subsistence but to the conveniences and comforts of life, as far as the conditions of their parents can afford it. Hence it comes, that when their parents leave the world, and so the care due to their children ceases, the effects of it are to extend as far as possibly they can, and the provisions they have made in their lifetime, are understood to be intended as nature

requires they should, for their children, whom after themselves, they are bound to provide for, though the dying parents, by express words, declare nothing about them, nature appoints the descent of their property to their children, who thus come to have a title, and natural right of inheritance to their father's goods, which the rest of mankind cannot pretend to.

90. Were it not for this right of being nourished, and maintained by their parents, which God and nature has given to children, and obliged parents to, as a duty, it would be reasonable, that the father should inherit the estate of his son, and be preferred in the inheritance before his grandchild. For to the grandfather, there is due a long score of care and expenses laid out upon the breeding and education of his son, which one would think in justice ought to be paid. But that having been done in obedience to the same law, whereby he received nourishment and education from his own parents, this score of education received from a man's father, is paid by taking care, and providing for his own children; is paid, I say, as much as is required of payment by alteration of property, unless present necessity of the parents require a return of goods for their necessary support and subsistence. For we are not now speaking of that reverence, acknowledgement, respect and honour that is always due from children to their parents, but of possessions and commodities of life valuable by money. But though it be incumbent on parents to bring up and provide for their children, yet this debt to the children does not quite cancel the score due to their parents, but only is made by nature preferable to it. For the debt a man owes his father, takes place, and gives the father a right to inherit the son's goods, where for want of issue, the right of children doth not exclude the title. And therefore a man having a right to be maintained by his children where he needs it, and to enjoy also the comforts of life from them, when the necessary provision due to them, and their children will afford it, if his son die without issue, the father has a right in nature to possess his goods, and inherit his estate (whatever the municipal laws of some countries, may absurdly direct otherwise,) and so again his children and their issue from him, or for want of such, his father and his issue. But where no such are to be found, i.e. no kindred, there we see the possessions of a private man revert to the community, and so in politic

societies come into the hands of the public magistrate: but in the state of nature become again perfectly common, nobody having a right to inherit them: nor can anyone have a property in them, otherwise than in other things common by nature, of which I shall speak in its due place.

91. I have been the larger in showing upon what ground children have a right to succeed to the possession of their father's properties, not only because by it, it will appear, that if Adam had a property (a titular insignificant useless property; for it could be no better, for he was bound to nourish and maintain his children and posterity out of it) in the whole earth and its product, yet all his children coming to have by the law of nature and right of inheritance a joint title, and right of property in it after his death, it could convey no right of sovereignty to any one of his posterity over the rest: since everyone having a right of inheritance to his portion, they might enjoy their inheritance, or any part of it in common, or share it, or some parts of it by division, as it best liked them. But no one could pretend to the whole inheritance, or any sovereignty supposed to accompany it, since a right of inheritance gave every one of the rest, as well as any one, a title to share in the goods of his father. Not only upon this account, I say, have I been so particular in examining the reason of children's inheriting the property of their fathers, but also because it will give us further light in the inheritance of rule and power, which in countries where their particular municipal laws give the whole possession of land entirely to the first-born, and descent of power has gone so to men by this custom, some have been apt to be deceived into an opinion, that there was a natural or divine right of primogeniture, to both estate and power; and that the inheritance of both rule over men and property in things, sprang from the same original, and were to descend by the same rules.

92. Property, whose original is from the right a man has to use any of the inferior creatures, for the subsistence and comfort of his life, is for the benefit and sole advantage of the proprietor, so that he may even destroy the thing, that he has property in by his use of it, where need requires: but government being for the preservation of every man's right and property, by preserving him from the violence or injury of others, is for the good of the governed. For the magistrate's sword being for a 'terror to evil doers' [*Romans*

13:3], and by that terror to enforce men to observe the positive laws of the society, made conformable to the laws of nature, for the public good, i.e. the good of every particular member of that society, as far as by common rules, it can be provided for; the sword is not given the magistrate for his own good alone.

93. Children therefore, as has been showed, by the dependence they have on their parents for subsistence, have a right of inheritance to their father's property, as that which belongs to them for their proper good and behoof, and therefore are fitly termed goods, wherein the first-born has not a sole or peculiar right by any law of God and nature, the younger children having an equal title with him founded on that right they all have to maintenance, support and comfort from their parents, and nothing else. But government being for the benefit of the governed, and not the sole advantage of the governors (but only for theirs with the rest, as they make a part of that politic body, each of whose parts and members are taken care of, and directed in its peculiar functions for the good of the whole, by the laws of the society) cannot be inherited by the same title that children have the goods of their father. The right a son has to be maintained and provided with the necessaries and conveniences of life out of his father's stock, gives him a right to succeed to his father's property for his own good, but this can give him no right to succeed also to the rule, which his father had over other men. All that a child has right to claim from his father is nourishment and education, and the things nature furnishes for the support of life: but he has no right to demand rule or dominion from him: he can subsist and receive from him the portion of good things, and advantages of education naturally due to him, without empire and dominion. That (if his father hath any) 'twas vested in him, for the good and behoof of others, and therefore the son cannot claim or inherit it by a title, which is founded wholly on his own private good and advantage.

94. We must know how the first ruler, from whom anyone claims, came by his authority, upon what ground anyone has empire, what his title is to it, before we can know who has a right to succeed him in it, and inherit it from him. If the agreement and consent of men first gave a sceptre into anyone's hand, or put a crown on his head, that also must direct its descent and conveyance. For the same authority, that made the first a lawful ruler,

must make the second too, and so give right of succession: in this case inheritance or primogeniture, can in itself have no right, no pretence to it, any further than that consent, which established the form of the government, hath so settled the succession. And thus we see the succession of crowns, in several countries places it on different heads, and he comes by right of succession, to be a prince in one place, who would be a subject in another.

95. If God by his positive grant and revealed declaration, first gave rule and dominion to any man, he that will claim by that title, must have the same positive grant of God for his succession. For if that has not directed the course of its descent and conveyance down to others, nobody can succeed to this title of the first ruler; children have no right of inheritance to this; and primogeniture can lay no claim to it, unless God the author of this constitution hath so ordained it. Thus we see the pretensions of Saul's family, who received his crown from the immediate appointment of God, ended with his reign; and David by the same title that Saul reigned, *viz.* God's appointment, succeeded in his throne, to the exclusion of Jonathan, and all pretensions of paternal inheritance. And if Solomon had a right to succeed his father, it must be by some other title, than that of primogeniture. A cadet, or sister's son, must have the preference in succession, if he has the same title the first lawful prince had: and in dominion that has its foundation only in the positive appointment of God himself, Benjamin the youngest, must have the inheritance of the crown, if God so direct as well as one of that tribe had the first possession.

96. If paternal right, the act of begetting, give a man rule and dominion, inheritance or primogeniture can give no title. For he that cannot succeed to his father's title, which was begetting, cannot succeed to that power over his brethren, which his father had by paternal right over them. But of this I shall have occasion to say more in another place. This is plain in the meantime, that any government, whether supposed to be at first founded in paternal right, consent of the people, or the positive appointment of God himself, which can supersede either of the other, and so begin a new government upon a new foundation, I say, any government began upon either of these, can by right of succession come to those only, who have the title of him, they succeed to. Power founded on contract, can descend only to him, who has

right by that contract: power founded on begetting, he only can have that begets: and power founded on the positive grant or donation of God, he only can have by right of succession, to whom that grant directs it.

97. From what I have said, I think this is clear, that a right to the use of the creatures, being founded originally in the right a man has to subsist and enjoy the conveniences of life, and the natural right children have to inherit the goods of their parents, being founded in the right they have to the same subsistence and commodities of life, out of the stock of their parents, who are therefore taught by natural love and tenderness to provide for them, as a part of themselves: and all this being only for the good of the proprietor, or heir; it can be no reason for children's inheriting of rule and dominion, which has another original and a different end. Nor can primogeniture have any pretence to a right of solely inheriting either property or power, as we shall, in its due place, see more fully. 'Tis enough to have showed here, that Adam's property, or private dominion, could not convey any sovereignty or rule to his heir, who not having a right to inherit all his father's possessions, could not thereby come to have any sovereignty over his brethren: and therefore if any sovereignty on account of his property, had been vested in Adam, which in truth there was not; yet it would have died with him.

98. As Adam's sovereignty, if by virtue of being proprietor of the whole world, he had any authority over men, could not have been inherited by any of his children over the rest, because they had the same title to divide the inheritance, and everyone had a right to a portion of his father's possessions: so neither could Adam's sovereignty by right of fatherhood, if any such he had, descend to any one of his children. For it being in our author's account, a right acquired by begetting to rule over those he had begotten, it was not a power possible to be inherited, because the right being consequent to, and built on, an act perfectly personal, made that power so too, and impossible to be inherited. For paternal power, being a natural right rising only from the relation of father and son, is as impossible to be inherited as the relation itself, and a man may pretend as well to inherit the conjugal power the husband, whose heir he is, had over his wife, as he can to inherit the paternal power of a father over his children. For the

power of the husband being founded on contract, and the power of the father on begetting, he may as well inherit the power obtained by the conjugal contract, which was only personal, as he may the power obtained by begetting, which could reach no further than the person of the begetter, unless begetting can be a title to power in him, that does not beget.

99. Which makes it a reasonable question to ask, whether Adam, dying before Eve, his heir (suppose Cain or Seth) should have had, by right of inheriting Adam's fatherhood, sovereign power over Eve his mother. For Adam's fatherhood being nothing but a right he had to govern his children, because he begot them, he that inherits Adam's fatherhood, inherits nothing, even in our author's sense, but the right Adam had to govern his children, because he begot them: so that the monarchy of the heir would not have taken in Eve, or if it did, it being nothing but the fatherhood of Adam descended by inheritance, the heir must have right to govern Eve, because Adam begot her; for fatherhood is nothing else.

100. Perhaps it will be said with our author [282], that a man can alien his power over his child, and what may be transferred by compact, may be possessed by inheritance. I answer, a father cannot alien the power he has over his child, he may perhaps to some degrees forfeit it, but cannot transfer it: and if any other man acquire it, 'tis not by the father's grant, but by some act of his own. For example, a father, unnaturally careless of his child, sells or gives him to another man; and he again exposes him: a third man finding him, breeds up, cherishes and provides for him as his own. I think in this case, nobody will doubt but that the greatest part of filial duty and subjection was here owing, and to be paid to this foster-father: and if anything could be demanded from the child, by either of the other, it could be only due to his natural father: who perhaps might have forfeited his right to much of that duty comprehended in the command, 'honour your parents', but could transfer none of it to another. He that purchased, and neglected, the child, got by his purchase and grant of the father, no title to duty or honour from the child, but only he acquired it, who by his own authority, performing the office and care of a father, to the forlorn and perishing infant, made himself by paternal care, a title to proportionable degrees of paternal power.

This will be more easily admitted upon consideration of the nature of paternal power, for which I refer my reader to the Second Book.

101. To return to the argument in hand: this is evident, that paternal power arising only from begetting, for in that our author places it alone, can neither be transferred, nor inherited: and he that does not beget, can no more have paternal power which arises from thence, than he can have a right to anything who performs not the condition, to which only it is annexed. If one should ask, by what law has a father power over his children? It will be answered, no doubt, by the law of nature, which gives such a power over them, to him that begets them. If one should ask likewise, by what law does our author's heir come by a right to inherit? I think it would be answered, by the law of nature too. For I find not that our author brings one word of Scripture to prove the right of such an heir he speaks of: why then the law of nature gives fathers paternal power over their children, because they did beget them, and the same law of nature gives the same paternal power to the heir over his brethren, who did not beget them: whence it follows, that either the father has not his paternal power by begetting, or else that the heir has it not at all: for 'tis hard to understand how the law of nature, which is the law of reason, can give the paternal power to the father over his children, for the only reason of begetting, and to the first-born over his brethren without this only reason, i.e. for no reason at all: and if the eldest, by the law of nature, can inherit this paternal power, without the only reason that gives a title to it, so may the youngest as well as he, and a stranger as well as either; for where there is no reason for anyone, as there is not, but for him that begets, all have an equal title. I am sure our author offers no reason, and when anybody does, we shall see whether it will hold or no.

102. In the mean time 'tis as good sense to say, that by the law of nature a man has right to inherit the property of another, because he is of kin to him, and is known to be of his blood, and therefore by the same law of nature, an utter stranger to his blood, has right to inherit his estate: as to say that by the law of nature he that begets them, has paternal power over his children, and therefore by the law of nature the heir that begets them not, has this paternal power over them: or supposing the law of the land gave absolute power over their children, to such only who nursed

them, and fed their children themselves, could anybody pretend that this law gave anyone, who did no such thing, absolute power over those, who were not his children?

103. When therefore it can be showed, that conjugal power can belong to him that is not a husband, it will also I believe be proved, that our author's paternal power acquired by begetting, may be inherited by a son, and that a brother as heir to his father's power, may have paternal power over his brethren, and by the same rule conjugal power too, but till then, I think we may rest satisfied, that the paternal power of Adam, this sovereign authority of fatherhood, were there any such, could not descend to, nor be inherited by, his next heir. Fatherly power I easily grant our author if it will do him any good, can never be lost, because it will be as long in the world as there are fathers: but none of them will have Adam's paternal power, or derive theirs from him, but everyone will have his own, by the same title Adam had his, *viz.* by begetting, but not by inheritance or succession, no more than husbands have their conjugal power by inheritance from Adam. And thus we see as Adam had no such property, no such paternal power, as gave him sovereign jurisdiction over mankind; so likewise his sovereignty built upon either of these titles, if he had any such, could not have descended to his heir, but must have ended with him. Adam therefore, as has been proved, being neither monarch, nor his imaginary monarchy hereditable, the power which is now in the world, is not that which was Adam's, since all that Adam could have upon our author's grounds, either of property or fatherhood, necessarily died with him, and could not be conveyed to posterity by inheritance. In the next place we will consider whether Adam had any such heir, to inherit his power, as our author talks of.

Chapter 10
OF THE HEIR TO ADAM'S
MONARCHICAL POWER

104. Our author tells us, 'that it is a truth undeniable, that there cannot be any multitude of men whatsoever, either great or small, though gathered together from the several corners and

remotest regions of the world, but that in the same multitude considered by itself, there is one man amongst them, that in nature hath a right to be king of all the rest, as being the next heir to Adam, and all the other subject to him, every man by nature is a king or a subject' [144]. And again, 'if Adam himself were still living, and now ready to die, it is certain that there is one man, and but one in the world who is next heir' [10]. Let this multitude of men be, if our author pleases, all the princes upon the earth, there will then be by our author's rule, one amongst them, that in nature hath a right to be king of all the rest, as being the right heir to Adam; an excellent way to establish the thrones of princes, and settle the obedience of their subjects, by setting up a hundred, or perhaps a thousand titles (if there be so many princes in the world) against any king now reigning, each as good upon our author's grounds, as his who wears the crown. If this right of heir carry any weight with it, if it be the ordinance of God, as our author seems to tell us [138], must not all be subject to it, from the highest to the lowest? Can those who wear the name of princes, without having the right of being heirs to Adam, demand obedience from their subjects by this title, and not be bound to pay it by the same law? Either governments in the world are not to be claimed and held by this title of Adam's heir, and then the starting of it is to no purpose, the being or not being Adam's heir signifies nothing as to the title of dominion; or if it really be, as our author says, the true title to government and sovereignty, the first thing to be done, is to find out this true heir of Adam, seat him in his throne, and then all the kings and princes of the world ought [to] come and resign up their crowns and sceptres to him, as things that belong no more to them, than to any of their subjects.

105. For either this right in nature, of Adam's heir, to be king over all the race of men, (for altogether they make one multitude) is a right not necessary to the making of a lawful king, and so there may be lawful kings without it, and then kings' titles and power depend not on it, or else all the kings in the world but one are not lawful kings, and so have no right to obedience: either this title of heir to Adam is that whereby kings hold their crowns, and have a right to subjection from their subjects, and then one only can have it, and the rest being subjects can require no obedience from other men, who are but their fellow subjects, or else it is not

the title whereby kings rule, and have a right to obedience from their subjects, and then kings are kings without it, and this dream of the natural sovereignty of Adam's heir is of no use to obedience and government. For if kings have a right to dominion, and the obedience of their subjects, who are not, nor can possibly be, heirs to Adam, what use is there of such a title, when we are obliged to obey without it? If kings, who are not heirs to Adam, have no right to sovereignty, we are all free till our author or anybody for him, will show us Adam's right heir. If there be but one heir of Adam, there can be but one lawful king in the world, and nobody in conscience can be obliged to obedience till it be resolved who that is; for it may be anyone who is not known to be of a younger house, and all others have equal titles. If there be more than one heir of Adam, everyone is his heir, and so everyone has regal power. For if two sons can be heirs together, then all the sons are equally heirs, and so all are heirs, being all sons, or sons' sons of Adam. Betwixt these two the right of heir cannot stand: for by it either but one only man, or all men are kings. Take which you please, it dissolves the bonds of government and obedience: since if all men are heirs, they can owe obedience to nobody; if only one, nobody can be obliged to pay obedience to him, till he be known and his title made out.

Chapter 11
WHO HEIR?

106. The great question which in all ages has disturbed mankind, and brought on them the greatest part of those mischiefs which have ruined cities, depopulated countries, and disordered the peace of the world, has been, not whether there be power in the world, nor whence it came, but who should have it. The settling of this point being of no smaller moment than the security of princes, and the peace and welfare of their estates and kingdoms, a reformer of politics, one would think, should lay this sure, and be very clear in it. For if this remain disputable, all the rest will be to very little purpose; and the skill used in dressing up power with all the splendour and temptation absoluteness can add to it, without showing who has a right to have it, will serve only

to give a greater edge to man's natural ambition, which of itself is but too keen. What can this do but set men on the more eagerly to scramble, and so lay a sure and lasting foundation of endless contention and disorder, instead of that peace and tranquillity, which is the business of government, and the end of human society?

107. This designation of the person our author is more than ordinarily obliged to take care of, because he, affirming that 'the assignment of civil power is by divine institution' [7], hath made the conveyance as well as the power itself sacred: so that no consideration, no act or art of man can divert it from that person, to whom by this divine right, it is assigned, no necessity or contrivance can substitute another person in his room. For if 'the assignment of civil power be by divine institution'; and Adam's heir be he, to whom it is thus assigned, as in the foregoing chapter our author tells us, it would be as much sacrilege for anyone to be king, who was not Adam's heir, as it would have been amongst the Jews, for anyone to have been priest, who had not been of Aaron's posterity: for not only the priesthood in general being by divine institution, but the assignment of it to the sole line and posterity of Aaron, made it impossible to be enjoyed or exercised by anyone, but those persons, who are the offspring of Aaron: whose succession therefore was carefully observed, and by that the persons who had a right to the priesthood certainly known.

108. Let us see then what care our author has taken, to make us know who is this heir, who by divine institution, has a right to be king over all men. The first account of him we meet with is page [7], in these words: 'this subjection of children, being the fountain of all regal authority, by the ordination of God himself; it follows, that civil power not only in general, is by divine institution, but even the assignment of it specifically to the eldest parents'. Matters of such consequence as this is, should be in plain words, as little liable as might be to doubt or equivocation; and I think if language be capable of expressing anything distinctly and clearly, that of kindred, and the several degrees of nearness of blood, is one. It were therefore to be wished, that our author had used a little more intelligible expressions here, that we might have better known who it is, to whom the assignment of civil power is made by divine institution, or at least would have told us what he

meant by 'eldest parents'. For I believe if land had been assigned or granted to him, and the eldest parents of his family, he would have thought it had needed an interpreter, and 'twould scarce have been known to whom next it belonged.

109. In propriety of speech, and certainly propriety of speech is necessary in a discourse of this nature, 'eldest parents' signifies either the eldest men and women that have had children, or those who have longest had issue: and then our author's assertion will be, that those fathers and mothers who have been longest in the world, or longest fruitful, have by divine institution a right to civil power. If there be any absurdity in this, our author must answer for it: and if his meaning be different from my explication, he is to be blamed, that he would not speak it plainly. This I am sure, 'parents' cannot signify heirs male, nor 'eldest parents' an infant child: who yet may sometimes be the true heir, if there can be but one. And we are hereby still as much at a loss, who civil power belongs to, notwithstanding this 'assignment by divine institution', as if there had been no such assignment at all, or our author had said nothing of it. This of 'eldest parents' leaving us more in the dark, who by divine institution has a right to civil power, than those who never heard anything at all of heir, or descent, of which our author is so full. And though the chief matter of his writings be to teach obedience to those who have a right to it, which he tells us is conveyed by descent, yet who those are to whom this right by descent belongs, he leaves like the philosopher's stone in politics, out of the reach of anyone to discover from his writings.

110. This obscurity cannot be imputed to want of language in so great a master of style as Sir Robert is, when he is resolved with himself what he would say: and therefore, I fear, finding how hard it would be to settle rules of descent by divine institution, and how little it would be to his purpose, or conduce to the clearing and establishing the titles of princes, if such rules of descent were settled, he chose rather to content himself with doubtful and general terms, which might make no ill sound in men's ears, who were willing to be pleased with them, rather than offer any clear rules of descent of this fatherhood of Adam, by which men's consciences might be satisfied to whom it descended, and know the persons who had a right to regal power, and with it to their obedience.

111. How else is it possible, that laying so much stress as he does upon 'descent', and 'Adam's heir', 'next heir', 'true heir', he should never tell us what 'heir' means, nor the way to know who the next or true heir is. This I do not remember he does anywhere expressly handle, but where it comes in his way very warily and doubtfully touches: though it be so necessary that without it all discourses of government and obedience upon his principles would be to no purpose, and fatherly power, never so well made out, will be of no use to anybody. Hence he tells us, 'that not only the constitution of power in general, but the limitation of it to one kind, (i.e.) monarchy and the determination of it to the individual person and line of Adam, are all three ordinances of God, neither Eve nor her children could either limit Adam's power, or join others with him; and what was given unto Adam was given in his person to his posterity' [138]. Here again our author informs us, that the divine ordinance hath limited the descent of Adam's monarchical power. To whom? 'To Adam's line and posterity', says our author. A notable limitation, a limitation to all mankind. For if our author can find anyone amongst mankind that is not of the line and posterity of Adam, he may perhaps tell him who this next heir of Adam is: but for us, I despair how this limitation of Adam's empire to his line and posterity will help us to find out one heir. This limitation indeed of our author will save those the labour who would look for him amongst the race of brutes, if any such there were; but will very little contribute to the discovery of 'one next heir' amongst men, though it make a short and easy determination of the question about the descent of Adam's regal power, by telling us, that the line and posterity of Adam is to have it, that is in plain English, anyone may have it, since there is no person living that hath not the title of being of the line and posterity of Adam, and while it keeps there, it keeps within our author's limitation by God's ordinance. Indeed, he tells us, that 'such heirs are not only lords of their own children, but of their brethren' [10], whereby, and by the words following, which we shall consider anon, he seems to insinuate that the eldest son is heir: but he nowhere, that I know, says it in direct words, but by the instances of Cain and Jacob that there follow, we may allow this to be so far his opinion concerning heirs, that where there are divers children, the eldest son has the right to be heir. That

primogeniture cannot give any title to paternal power we have already showed. That a father may have a natural right to some kind of power over his children, is easily granted, but that an elder brother has so over his brethren remains to be proved. God or nature has not anywhere, that I know, placed such jurisdiction in the first-born, nor can reason find any such natural superiority amongst brethren. The law of Moses gave a double portion of the goods and possessions to the eldest, but we find not anywhere that naturally, or by God's institution, superiority or dominion belonged to him, and the instances there brought by our author are but slender proofs of a right to civil power and dominion in the first-born, and do rather show the contrary.

112. His words are in the forecited place: 'and therefore we find God told Cain of his brother Abel; his desire shall be subject unto thee, and thou shalt rule over him' [10] [*Genesis* 4:7]. To which I answer,

(1) These words of God to Cain, are by many interpreters with great reason, understood in a quite different sense than what our author uses them in.

(2) Whatever was meant by them, it could not be, that Cain as elder, had a natural dominion over Abel; for the words are conditional: 'if thou dost well' and so personal to Cain, and whatever was signified by them, did depend on his carriage and not follow his birthright, and therefore could by no means be an establishment of dominion in the first-born in general. For before this Abel had his 'distinct territories by right of private dominion', as our author himself confesses [217], which he could not have had to the prejudice of the heir's title, if by divine institution, Cain as heir were to inherit all his father's dominion.

(3) If this were intended by God as the charter of primogeniture, and the grant of dominion to elder brothers in general as such, by right of inheritance, we might expect it should have included all his brethren. For we may well suppose, Adam, from whom the world was to be peopled, had by this time, that these were grown up to be men, more sons than these two: whereas Abel himself is not so much as named; and the words in the original, can scarce, with any good construction, be applied to him.

(4) It is too much to build a doctrine of so mighty consequence upon so doubtful and obscure a place of Scripture, which may be

well, nay better, understood in a quite different sense, and so can be but an ill proof, being as doubtful as the thing to be proved by it, especially when there is nothing else in Scripture or reason to be found, that favours or supports it.

113. It follows, 'accordingly when Jacob bought his brother's birthright, Isaac blessed him thus; be lord over thy brethren, and let the sons of thy mother bow before thee' [10] [*Genesis* 27:29]. Another instance I take it, brought by our author to evince dominion due to birthright, and an admirable one it is. For it must be no ordinary way of reasoning in a man, that is pleading for the natural power of kings, and against all compact to bring for proof of it, an example where his own account of it founds all the right upon compact, and settles empire in the younger brother, unless buying and selling be no compact; for he tells us, 'when Jacob bought his brother's birthright'. But passing by that, let us consider the history itself, with what use our author makes of it, and we shall find these following mistakes about it.

(1) That our author reports this, as if Isaac had given Jacob this blessing, immediately upon his purchasing the birthright; for he says, 'when Jacob bought Isaac blessed him', which is plainly otherwise in the Scripture. For it appears there was a distance of time between, and if we will take the story in the order it lies, it must be no small distance; all Isaac's sojourning in Gerar, and transactions with Abimelech, *Genesis* 26, coming between, Rebecca being then beautiful and consequently young, but Isaac when he blessed Jacob, was old and decrepit; and Esau also complains of Jacob, *Genesis* 27:36, that two times he had supplanted him, 'he took away my birthright', says he, 'and behold now he hath taken away my blessing'; words, that I think signify distance of time and difference of action.

(2) Another mistake of our author's, is, that he supposes Isaac gave Jacob the blessing, and bid him be lord over his brethren, because he had the birthright: for our author brings this example to prove, that he, that has the birthright, has thereby a right to be lord over his brethren. But it is also manifest by the text, that Isaac had no consideration of Jacob's having bought the birthright, for when he blessed him, he considered him not as Jacob, but took him for Esau. Nor did Esau understand any such connection between birthright and the blessing, for he says, 'he hath supplanted

me these two times, he took away my birthright, and behold now he hath taken away my blessing': whereas had the blessing, which was to be lord over his brethren, belonged to the birthright, Esau could not have complained of this second as a cheat, Jacob having got nothing but what Esau had sold him, when he sold him his birthright: so that it is plain, dominion, if these words signify it, was not understood to belong to the birthright.

114. And that in those days of the patriarchs, dominion was not understood to be right of the heir, but only a greater portion of goods, is plain from *Genesis* 21:10, for Sarah taking Isaac to be heir, says, 'cast out this bondwoman and her son, for the son of this bondwoman shall not be heir with my son': whereby could be meant nothing, but that he should not have a pretence to an equal share of his father's estate after his death, but should have his portion presently and be gone. Accordingly we read, *Genesis* 25:5-6, that 'Abraham gave all that he had unto Isaac, but unto the sons of the concubines which Abraham had, Abraham gave gifts and sent them away from Isaac his son, while he yet lived': that is, Abraham having given portions to all his other sons, and sent them away, that which he had reserved, being the greatest part of his substance, Isaac as heir possessed after his death, but by being heir, he had no right to be lord over his brethren; for if he had, why should Sarah endeavour to rob him of one of his subjects, or lessen the number of his slaves, by desiring to have Ishmael sent away.

115. Thus, as under the law, the privilege of birthright was nothing but a double portion, so we see that before Moses in the patriarchs' time, from when our author pretends to take his model, there was no knowledge, no thought, that birthright gave rule or empire, paternal or kingly authority, to anyone over his brethren. If this be not plain enough in the story of Isaac and Ishmael, he that will look into *1 Chronicles* 5:1-2, may there read these words, 'Reuben was the first-born, but forasmuch as he defiled his father's bed, his birthright was given unto the sons of Joseph, the son of Israel, and the genealogy is not to be reckoned after the birthright; for Judah prevailed above his brethren, and of him came the chief ruler, but the birthright was Joseph's': what this birthright was, Jacob blessing Joseph, *Genesis* 48:22 telleth us in these words, 'moreover I have given thee one portion above

thy brethren, which I took out of the hand of the Amorite, with my sword and with my bow'. Whereby it is not only plain, that the birthright was nothing but a double portion, but the text in *Chronicles* is express against our author's doctrine, and shows that dominion was no part of the birthright. For it tells us that Joseph had the birthright, but Judah the dominion. One would think our author were very fond of the very name of birthright when he brings this instance of Jacob and Esau, to prove that dominion belongs to the heir over his brethren.

116. (1) Because it will be but an ill example to prove, that dominion by God's ordination belonged to the eldest son, because Jacob the youngest here had it, let him come by it how he would. For if it prove anything, it can only prove against our author that the assignment of dominion to the eldest, is not by divine institution, which would then be unalterable. For if by the law of God, or nature, absolute power and empire belongs to the eldest son and his heirs, so that they are supreme monarchs, and all the rest of their brethren slaves, our author gives us reason to doubt whether the eldest son has a power to part with it, to the prejudice of his posterity, since he tells us that 'in grants and gifts that have their original from God or nature, no inferior power of man can limit, or make any law of prescription against them' [283].

117. (2) Because this place, *Genesis* 27:29, brought by our author concerns not at all the dominion of one brother over the other, nor the subjection of Esau to Jacob. For 'tis plain in the history, that Esau was never subject to Jacob, but lived apart in Mount Seir, where he founded a distinct people and government, and was himself prince over them, as much as Jacob was in his own family. This text if considered, can never be understood of Esau himself, or the personal dominion of Jacob over him: for the words 'brethren' and 'sons of thy mother', could not be used literally by Isaac, who knew Jacob had only one brother; and these words are so far from being true in a literal sense, or establishing any dominion in Jacob over Esau, that in the story we find the quite contrary, for *Genesis* 32, Jacob several times calls Esau lord and himself his servant, and *Genesis* 33 [:3], 'he bowed himself seven times to the ground to Esau'. Whether Esau then were a subject and vassal, nay (as our author tells us, all subjects are) slave to Jacob, and Jacob his sovereign prince by birthright, I leave

the reader to judge; and to believe if he can, that these words of Isaac, 'be lord over thy brethren, and let thy mother's sons bow down to thee', confirmed Jacob in a sovereignty over Esau, upon the account of the birthright he had got from him.

118. He that reads the story of Jacob and Esau, will find there was never any jurisdiction or authority, that either of them had over the other after their father's death: they lived with the friendship and equality of brethren, neither lord, neither slave to his brother, but independent of each other, were both heads of their distinct families, where they received no laws from one another, but lived separately, and were the roots out of which sprang two distinct peoples, under two distinct governments. This blessing then of Isaac, whereon our author would build the dominion of the elder brother, signifies no more but what Rebecca had been told from God (*Genesis* 25:23), 'two nations are in thy womb, and two manner of people, shall be separated from thy bowels, and the one people shall be stronger than the other people, and the elder shall serve the younger'; and so Jacob blessed Judah, *Genesis* 49[:8–10], and gave him the sceptre and dominion, from whence our author might have argued as well, that jurisdiction and dominion belongs to the third son over his brethren, as well as from this blessing of Isaac, that it belonged to Jacob: both these places contain only predictions of what should long after happen to their posterities, and not any declaration of the right of inheritance to dominion in either. And thus we have our author's two great and only arguments to prove, that heirs are lords over their brethren.

(1) Because God tells Cain, *Genesis* 4[:7], that however sin might set upon him, he ought or might be master of it: for the most learned interpreters understand the words of sin, and not of Abel, and give so strong reasons for it, that nothing can convincingly be inferred from so doubtful a text, to our author's purpose.

(2) Because in this of *Genesis* 27 [:29] Isaac foretells that the Israelites, the posterity of Jacob, should have dominion over the Edomites, and posterity of Esau; therefore says our author, heirs are lords of their brethren: I leave anyone to judge of the conclusion.

119. And now we see how our author has provided for the descending and conveyance down of Adam's monarchical power, or paternal dominion to posterity, by the inheritance of his heir,

succeeding to all his father's authority, and becoming upon his death as much lord as his father was, 'not only over his own children, but over his brethren', and all descended from his father, and so *in infinitum*. But yet who this heir is, he does not once tell us; and all the light we have from him in this so fundamental a point, is only that in his instance of Jacob, by using the word birthright, as that which passed from Esau to Jacob, he leaves us to guess, that by heir, he means the eldest son, though I do not remember he anywhere mentions expressly the title of the first-born, but all along keeps himself under the shelter of the indefinite term 'heir'. But taking it to be his meaning, that the eldest son is heir, (for if the eldest be not, there will be no pretence why the sons should not be all heirs alike) and so by right of primogeniture has dominion over his brethren; this is but one step towards the settlement of succession, and the difficulties remain still as much as ever, till he can show us who is meant by right heir, in all those cases which may happen where the present possessor hath no son. This he silently passes over, and perhaps wisely too: for what can be wiser after one has affirmed, that 'the person having that power, as well as the power and form of government, is the ordinance of God, and by divine institution', *vide* [7, 144], than to be careful, not to start any question concerning the person, the resolution whereof will certainly lead him into a confession, that God and nature hath determined nothing about him. And if our author cannot show who by right of nature, or a clear positive law of God, has the next right to inherit the dominion of this natural monarch, he has been at such pains about, when he died without a son, he might have spared his pains in all the rest, it being more necessary for the settling men's consciences, and determining their subjection and allegiance, to show them who by original right, superior and antecedent to the will, or any act of men, hath a title to this paternal jurisdiction, than it is to show that by nature there was such a jurisdiction: it being to no purpose for me to know there is such a paternal power, which I ought, and am disposed to obey, unless where there are many pretenders, I also know the person that is rightly invested and endowed with it.

120. For the main matter in question being concerning the duty of my obedience, and the obligation of conscience I am under to pay it to him that is of right my lord and ruler, I must know

the person that this right of paternal power resides in, and so empowers him to claim obedience from me. For let it be true what he says, that 'civil power not only in general is by divine institution, but even the assignment of it specifically to the eldest parents' [7]; and, 'that not only the power or right of government, but the form of the power of governing, and the person having that power, are all the ordinance of God' [144]; yet unless he show us in all cases who is this person, ordained by God, who is this eldest parent, all his abstract notions of monarchical power will signify just nothing, when they are to be reduced to practice, and men are conscientiously to pay their obedience. For paternal jurisdiction being not the thing to be obeyed, because it cannot command, but is only that which gives one man a right, which another hath not, and if it come by inheritance, another man cannot have, to command and be obeyed; it is ridiculous to say, I pay obedience to the paternal power, when I obey him, to whom paternal power gives no right to my obedience; for he can have no divine right to my obedience, who cannot show his divine right to the power of ruling over me, as well as that by divine right, there is such a power in the world.

121. And hence not being able to make out any prince's title to government, as heir to Adam, which therefore is of no use, and had been better let alone, he is fain to resolve all into present possession, and makes civil obedience as due to a usurper as to a lawful king; and thereby the usurper's title as good. His words are, and they deserve to be remembered: 'if a usurper dispossess the true heir, the subject's obedience to the fatherly power must go along and wait upon God's providence' [144]. But I shall leave his title of usurpers to be examined in its due place, and desire my sober reader to consider what thanks princes owe such politics as this, which can suppose paternal power (i.e.) a right to government in the hands of a Cade, or a Cromwell, and so all obedience being due to paternal power, the obedience of subjects will be due to them by the same right, and upon as good grounds as it is to lawful princes; and yet this, as dangerous a doctrine as it is, must necessarily follow from making all political power to be nothing else but Adam's paternal power by right and divine institution, descending from him, without being able to show to whom it descended, or who is heir to it.

122. To settle government in the world, and to lay obligations to obedience on any man's conscience, it is as necessary (supposing with our author that all power be nothing but the being possessed of Adam's fatherhood) to satisfy him, who has a right to this power, this fatherhood, when the possessor dies without sons to succeed immediately to it, as it was to tell him that upon the death of the father, the eldest son had a right to it: for it is still to be remembered, that the great question is, (and that which our author would be thought to contend for, if he did not sometimes forget it) what persons have a right to be obeyed, and not whether there be a power in the world, which is to be called paternal, without knowing in whom it resides: for so it be a power, i.e. right to govern, it matters not, whether it be termed paternal, or regal; natural, or acquired; whether you call it supreme fatherhood, or supreme brotherhood, will be all one provided we know who has it.

123. I go on then to ask whether in the inheriting of this paternal power, this supreme fatherhood, the grandson by a daughter, hath a right before a nephew by a brother? Whether the grandson by the eldest son, being an infant, before the younger son a man and able? Whether the daughter before the uncle? Or any other man, descended by a male line? Whether a grandson by a younger daughter, before a granddaughter by an elder daughter? Whether the elder son by a concubine, before a younger son by a wife? From whence also will arise many questions of legitimation, and what in nature is the difference betwixt a wife and a concubine? For as to the municipal or positive laws of men, they can signify nothing here. It may further be asked, whether the eldest son being a fool, shall inherit this paternal power, before the younger a wise man? And what degree of folly it must be, that shall exclude him? And who shall be judge of it? Whether the son of a fool excluded for his folly, before the son of his wise brother who reigned? Who has the paternal power, whilst the widow queen is with child by the deceased king, and nobody knows whether it will be a son or a daughter? Which shall be heir of two male twins, who by the dissection of the mother, were laid open to the world? Whether a sister by the half blood, before a brother's daughter by the whole blood?

124. These, and many more such doubts, might be proposed about the titles of succession, and the right of inheritance; and

that not as idle speculations, but such as in history we shall find, have concerned the inheritance of crowns and kingdoms; and if ours want them, we need not go further for famous examples of it, than the other kingdom in this very island, which having been fully related by the ingenious and learned author of *Patriarcha non Monarcha* [James Tyrrell], I need say no more of. Till our author hath resolved all the doubts that may arise about the next heir, and showed that they are plainly determined by the law of nature, or the revealed law of God, all his suppositions of a monarchical, absolute, supreme, paternal power in Adam, and the descent of that power to his heirs, would not be of the least use to establish the authority, or make out the title of any one prince now on earth, but would rather unsettle and bring all into question: for let our author tell us as long as he please, and let all men believe it too, that Adam had a paternal, and thereby a monarchical power; that this (the only power in the world) descended to his heirs, and that there is no other power in the world but this: let this be all as clear demonstration, as it is manifest error, yet if it be not past doubt, to whom this paternal power descends, and whose now it is, nobody can be under any obligation of obedience, unless anyone will say, that I am bound to pay obedience to paternal power in a man, who has no more paternal power than I myself; which is all one as to say, I obey a man, because he has a right to govern, and if I be asked, how I know he has a right to govern, I should answer, it cannot be known, that he has any at all. For that cannot be the reason of my obedience, which I know not to be so; much less can that be a reason of my obedience, which nobody at all can know to be so.

125. And therefore all this ado about Adam's fatherhood, the greatness of its power, and the necessity of its supposal, helps nothing to establish the power of those that govern, or to determine the obedience of subjects, who are to obey, if they cannot tell whom they are to obey, or it cannot be known who are to govern, and who to obey. In the state the world now is, irrecoverably ignorant who is Adam's heir, this fatherhood, this monarchical power of Adam descending to his heirs, would be of no more use to the government of mankind, than it would be to the quieting of men's consciences, or securing their healths, if our author had assured them, that Adam had a power to forgive

sins or cure diseases, which by divine institution descended to his heir, whilst this heir is impossible to be known. And should not he do as rationally, who upon this assurance of our author went and confessed his sins, and expected a good absolution, or took physic with expectation of health from anyone who had taken on himself the name of priest or physician, or thrust himself into those employments, saying, I acquiesce in the absolving power descending from Adam, or I shall be cured by the medicinal power descending from Adam; as he who says, I submit to, and obey the paternal power descending from Adam, when 'tis confessed all these powers descend only to his single heir, that heir is unknown.

126. 'Tis true, the civil lawyers have pretended to determine some of these cases concerning the succession of princes; but by our author's principles, they have meddled in a matter that belongs not to them: for if all political power be derived only from Adam, and be to descend only to his successive heirs, by the ordinance of God and divine institution, this is a right antecedent and paramount to all government; and therefore the positive laws of men, cannot determine that which is itself the foundation of all law and government, and is to receive its rule only from the law of God and nature. And that being silent in the case, I am apt to think there is no such right to be conveyed this way: I am sure it would be to no purpose if there were, and men would be more at a loss concerning government and obedience to governors, than if there were no such right: since by positive laws and compact, which divine institution (if there be any) shuts out, all these endless inextricable doubts, can be safely provided against; but it can never be understood, how a divine natural right, and that of such moment as is all order and peace in the world, should be conveyed down to posterity, without any plain natural or divine rule concerning it. And there would be an end of all civil government, if the assignment of civil power were by divine institution to the heir, and yet by that divine institution, the person of the heir could not be known. This paternal regal power, being by divine right only his, it leaves no room for human prudence, or consent to place it anywhere else: for if only one man hath a divine right to the obedience of mankind, nobody can claim that obedience, but he that can show that right; nor can men's consciences by any

other pretence be obliged to it. And thus this doctrine cuts up all government by the roots.

127. Thus we see how our author laying it for a sure foundation, that the very person that is to rule, is the ordinance of God, and by divine institution, tells us at large, only that this person is the heir, but who this heir is, he leaves us to guess; and so this divine institution which assigns it to a person, whom we have no rule to know, is just as good as an assignment to nobody at all. But whatever our author does, divine institution makes no such ridiculous assignments: nor can God be supposed to make it a sacred law, that one certain person should have a right to something, and yet not to give rules to mark out, and know that person by, or give an heir a divine right to power, and yet not point out who that heir is. 'Tis rather to be thought, that an heir, had no such right by divine institution, than that God should give such a right to the heir, but yet leave it doubtful, and undeterminable who such heir is.

128. If God had given the land of Canaan to Abraham, and in general terms to somebody after him, without naming his seed, whereby it might be known, who that somebody was, it would have been as good and useful an assignment, to determine the right to the land of Canaan, as it would to the determining the right of crowns, to give empire to Adam and his successive heirs after him, without telling who his heir is: for the word heir, without a rule to know who it is, signifies no more than somebody, I know not whom. God making it a divine institution, that men should not marry those who were near of kin, thinks it not enough to say, 'none of you shall approach to any that is near of kin to him, to uncover their nakedness' [*Leviticus* 18:6]: but moreover, gives rules to know who are those near of kin, forbidden by divine institution, or else that law would have been of no use: it being to no purpose to lay restraint, or give privileges, to men, in such general terms, as the particular person concerned cannot be known by. But God not having anywhere said, the next heir shall inherit all his father's estate or dominion, we are not to wonder that he hath nowhere appointed who that heir should be, for never having intended any such thing, never designed any heir in that sense, we cannot expect he should anywhere nominate, or appoint any person to it, as we might, had it been otherwise. And therefore

in Scripture, though the word heir occur, yet there is no such thing as heir in our author's sense, one that was by right of nature to inherit all that his father had, exclusive of his brethren. Hence Sarah supposes, that if Ishmael stayed in the house, to share in Abraham's estate after his death, this son of a bondwoman might be heir with Isaac: and therefore, says she, 'cast out this bondwoman and her son, for the son of this bondwoman shall not be heir with my son' [*Genesis* 21:10]; but this cannot excuse our author, who telling us there is in every number of men, one who is right and next heir to Adam, ought to have told us what the laws of descent are. He having been so sparing to instruct us by rules, how to know who is heir, let us see in the next place, what his history out of Scripture, on which he pretends wholly to build his government, gives us in this necessary and fundamental point.

129. Our author to make good the title of his book, begins the history of the descent of Adam's regal power, in these words: 'this lordship which Adam by command had over the whole world, and by right descending from him, the patriarchs did enjoy was as large', etc. [7]. How does he prove that the patriarchs by descent did enjoy it? for 'dominion of life and death', says he, 'we find Judah the father pronounced sentence of death against Tamar his daughter-in-law for playing the harlot' [7] [*Genesis* 38:24]. How does this prove that Judah had absolute and sovereign authority, 'he pronounced sentence of death'? The pronouncing of sentence of death is not a certain mark of sovereignty, but usually the office of inferior magistrates. The power of making laws of life and death, is indeed a mark of sovereignty, but pronouncing the sentence according to those laws may be done by others, and therefore this will but ill prove that he had sovereign authority: as if one should say, Judge Jeffreys, pronounced sentence of death in the late times, therefore Judge Jeffreys, had sovereign authority: but it will be said, Judah did it not by commission from another, and therefore did it in his own right. Who knows whether he had any right at all? heat of passion might carry him to do that which he had no authority to do. 'Judah had dominion of life and death', how does that appear? he exercised it, he pronounced sentence of death against Tamar, our author thinks it is very good proof, that because he did it, therefore he had a right to do it; he lay with her also: by the same

way of proof, he had a right to do that too: if the consequence be good from doing to a right of doing. Absalom too may be reckoned amongst our author's sovereigns, for he pronounced such a sentence of death against his brother Amnon, and much upon a like occasion, and had it executed too; if that be sufficient to prove a dominion of life and death [2 *Samuel* 13].

But allowing this all to be clear demonstration of sovereign power, who was it that had this 'lordship by right descending to him from Adam, as large and ample as the absolutest dominion of any monarch'? [7]. Judah, says our author, Judah a younger son of Jacob, his father and elder brethren living: so that if our author's own proof be to be taken, a younger brother may in the life of his father and elder brothers, by right of descent, enjoy Adam's monarchical power; and if one so qualified may be monarch by descent, why may not every man? if Judah, his father and elder brother living were one of Adam's heirs, I know not who can be excluded from this inheritance; all men by inheritance may be monarchs as well as Judah.

130. 'Touching war, we see that Abraham commanded an army of three hundred and eighteen soldiers of his own family [*Genesis* 14:14], and Esau met his brother Jacob with four hundred men at arms [*Genesis* 33:1]; for matter of peace; Abraham made a league with Abimelech' [*Genesis* 21:23-4], etc. [7]. Is it not possible for a man to have three hundred and eighteen men in his family, without being heir to Adam? A planter in the West Indies has more, and might, if he pleased (who doubts) muster them up and lead them out against the Indians, to seek reparation upon any injury received from them, and all this without the 'absolute dominion of a monarch, descending to him from Adam'. Would it not be an admirable argument to prove, that all power by God's institution descended from Adam by inheritance, and that the very person and power of this planter were the ordinance of God, because he had power in his family over servants, born in his house, and bought with his money? For this was just Abraham's case: those who were rich in the patriarch's days, as in the West Indies now, bought men and maidservants, and by their increase as well as purchasing of new, came to have large and numerous families, which though they made use of in war or peace, can it be thought the power they had over them was an inheritance

descended from Adam, when 'twas the purchase of their money? A man's riding in an expedition against an enemy, his horse bought in a fair, would be as good a proof that the owner 'enjoyed the lordship which Adam by command had over the whole world, by right descending to him', as Abraham's leading out the servants of his family is, that the patriarchs enjoyed this lordship by descent from Adam: since the title to the power, the master had in both cases, whether over slaves or horses, was only from his purchase; and the getting a dominion over anything by bargain and money, is a new way of proving one had it by descent and inheritance.

131. 'But making war and peace are marks of sovereignty' [7]. Let it be so in politic societies. May not therefore a man in the West Indies, who hath with him sons of his own, friends, or companions, soldiers under pay, or slaves bought with money, or perhaps a band made up of all these, make war and peace, if there should be occasion, and 'ratify the articles too with an oath' [7], without being a sovereign, an absolute king over those who went with him? he that says he cannot, must then allow many masters of ships, many private planters to be absolute monarchs, for as much as this they have done. War and peace cannot be made for politic societies, but by the supreme power of such societies; because war and peace, giving a different motion to the force of such a politic body, none can make war or peace, but that which has the direction of the force of the whole body, and that in politic societies is only the supreme power. In voluntary societies for the time, he that has such a power by consent, may make war and peace, and so may a single man for himself, the state of war not consisting in the number of partisans, but the enmity of the parties, where they have no superior to appeal to.

132. The actual making of war or peace is no proof of any other power, but only of disposing those to exercise or cease acts of enmity for whom he makes it, and this power in many cases anyone may have without any politic supremacy: and therefore the making of war or peace will not prove that everyone that does so is a politic ruler, much less a king; for then commonwealths must be kings too, for they do as certainly make war and peace as monarchical government.

133. But granting this a mark of sovereignty in Abraham, is it a proof of the descent to him, of Adam's sovereignty over the

whole world? If it be, it will surely be as good a proof of the descent of Adam's lordship to others too. And then commonwealths, as well as Abraham, will be heirs of Adam, for they make war and peace, as well as he. If you say, that the lordship of Adam doth not by right descend to commonwealths, though they make war and peace, the same say I of Abraham, and then there is an end of your argument; if you stand to your argument, and say those that do make war and peace, as commonwealths do without doubt, do inherit Adam's lordship, there is an end of your monarchy, unless you will say, that commonwealths by descent enjoying Adam's lordship are monarchies, and that indeed would be a new way of making all the governments in the world monarchical.

134. To give our author the honour of this new invention, for I confess it is not I [who] have first found it out by tracing his principles, and so charged it on him, 'tis fit my readers know that (as absurd as it may seem) he teaches it himself [11], where he ingeniously says, 'in all kingdoms and commonwealths in the world, whether the prince be the supreme father of the people, or but the true heir to such a father, or come to the crown by usurpation or election, or whether some few or a multitude govern the commonwealth: yet still the authority that is in any one, or in many, or in all these is the only right, and natural authority of a supreme father', which right of fatherhood he often tells us, is 'regal and royal authority'; as particularly, [6–7], the page immediately preceding this instance of Abraham. This regal authority, he says, those that govern commonwealths have: and if it be true, that regal and royal authority be in those that govern commonwealths, it is as true, that commonwealths are governed by kings: for if regal authority be in him that governs, he that governs must needs be a king, and so all commonwealths are nothing but downright monarchies, and then what need any more ado about the matter? The governments of the world are as they should be, there is nothing but monarchy in it. This without doubt, was the surest way our author could have found, to turn all other governments, but monarchical, out of the world.

135. But all this scarce proves Abraham, to have been a king as heir to Adam. If by inheritance he had been king, Lot, who was of the same family, must needs have been his subject, by that title before the servants in his family: but we see they lived as friends

and equals, and when their herdsmen could not agree, there was no pretence of jurisdiction or superiority between them, but they parted by consent, *Genesis* 13[:8], hence he is called both by Abraham, and by the text Abraham's 'brother', the name of friendship and equality, and not of jurisdiction and authority, though he were really but his nephew. And if our author knows that Abraham was Adam's heir, and a king, 'twas more it seems than Abraham himself knew, or his servant whom he sent a-wooing for his son; for when he sets out the advantages of the match, *Genesis* 24:35, thereby to prevail with the young woman [Rebecca] and her friends, he says, 'I am Abraham's servant, and the Lord hath blessed my master greatly, and he is become great, and he hath given him flocks and herds and silver and gold, and menservants and maidservants, and camels and asses, and Sarah my master's wife, bare a son to my master when she was old, and unto him he hath given all he hath'. Can one think that a discreet servant, that was thus particular to set out his master's greatness, would have omitted the crown Isaac was to have, if he had known of any such? Can it be imagined he should have neglected to have told them on such an occasion as this that Abraham was a king, a name well known at that time, for he had nine of them his neighbours, if he or his master had thought any such thing, the likeliest matter of all the rest, to make his errand successful?

136. But this discovery it seems was reserved for our author to make two or three thousand years after, and let him enjoy the credit of it, only he should have taken care that some of Adam's land should have descended to this his heir, as well as all Adam's lordship, for though this lordship which Abraham, (if we may believe our author) as well as the other patriarchs, 'by right descending to him did enjoy, was as large and ample as the absolutest dominion of any monarch which hath been since the Creation' [7]. Yet his estate, his territories, his dominions were very narrow and scanty, for he had not the possession of a foot of land, till he bought a field and a cave of the sons of Heth to bury Sarah in [*Genesis* 23].

137. The instance of Esau joined with this of Abraham, to prove that the 'lordship which Adam had over the whole world, by right descending from him, the patriarchs did enjoy', is yet more pleasant than the former: 'Esau met his brother Jacob with

four hundred men at arms' [7] [*Genesis* 33:1]; he therefore was a king by right of heir to Adam. Four hundred armed men then however got together are enough to prove him that leads them to be a king and Adam's heir. There have been Tories in Ireland, (whatever there are in other countries) who would have thanked our author for so honourable an opinion of them, especially if there had been nobody near with a better title of five hundred armed men, to question their royal authority of four hundred. 'Tis a shame for men to trifle so, to say no worse of it, in so serious an argument. Here Esau is brought as a proof that Adam's lordship, 'Adam's absolute dominion, as large as that of any monarch descended by right to the patriarchs', and in this very chapter, Jacob is brought as an instance of one, that 'by birthright was lord over his brethren' [10] [*Genesis* 27:29]. So we have here two brothers absolute monarchs by the same title, and at the same time heirs to Adam: the eldest heir to Adam, because he met his brother with four hundred men, and the youngest heir to Adam by birthright: 'Esau enjoyed the lordship which Adam had over the whole world by right descending to him, in as large and ample manner, as the absolutest dominion of any monarch', and at the same time, 'Jacob lord over him, by the right heirs have to be lords over their brethren'. *Risum teneatis?* [can you help laughing?] I never, I confess, met with any man of parts so dexterous as Sir Robert at this way of arguing: but 'twas his misfortune to light upon a hypothesis that could not be accommodated to the nature of things, and human affairs, his principles could not be made to agree with that constitution and order which God had settled in the world, and therefore must needs often clash with common sense and experience.

138. In the next section, he tells us, 'this patriarchal power continued not only till the Flood, but after it, as the name patriarchs doth in part prove' [7]. The word patriarch doth more than 'in part prove', that patriarchal power continued in the world as long as there were patriarchs, for 'tis necessary that patriarchal power should be whilst there are patriarchs, as it is necessary there should be paternal or conjugal power whilst there are fathers or husbands: but this is but playing with names. That which he would fallaciously insinuate is the thing in question to be proved, *viz.* that the lordship which Adam had over the world, the

supposed absolute universal dominion of Adam by right descending from him the patriarchs did enjoy. If he affirms such an absolute monarchy continued to the Flood, in the world, I would be glad to know what records he has it from; for I confess I cannot find a word of it in my Bible: if by patriarchal power, he means anything else, it is nothing to the matter in hand: and how the name patriarch in 'some part proves', that those, who are called by that name, had absolute monarchical power, I confess, I do not see, and therefore I think needs no answer, till the argument from it be made out a little clearer.

139. 'The three sons of Noah had the world', says our author, 'divided amongst them by their father, for of them was the whole world overspread' [7]. The world might be overspread by the offspring of Noah's sons, though he never divided the world amongst them; for the earth might be replenished without being divided, so that all our author's arguments here, proves no such division. However I allow it to him, and then ask, the world being divided amongst them, which of the three was Adam's heir? If Adam's lordship, Adam's monarchy, by right descended only to the eldest, then the other two could be but his subjects, his slaves; if by right it descended to all three brothers, by the same right, it will descend to all mankind, and then it will be impossible what he says that 'heirs are lords of their brethren' [10], should be true, but all brothers, and consequently all men will be equal and independent, all heirs to Adam's monarchy, and consequently all monarchs too, one as much as another. But 'twill be said Noah their father divided the world amongst them, so that our author will allow more to Noah, than he will to God Almighty, for, he thought it hard, that God himself should give the world to Noah and his sons, to the prejudice of Noah's birthright, his words are, 'Noah was left sole heir to the world, why should it be thought that God would disinherit him by his birthright, and make him of all men in the world, the only tenant in common with his children?' [217]. And yet here he thinks it fit, that Noah should disinherit Shem of his birthright, and divide the world betwixt him and his brethren, so that this birthright, when our author pleases, must, and when he pleases, must not, be sacred and inviolable.

140. If Noah did divide the world between his sons, and his assignment of dominions to them were good, there is an end of

divine institution; all our author's discourse of Adam's heir, with whatsoever he builds on it, is quite out of doors; and the natural power of kings falls to the ground; and then 'the form of the power governing, and the person having that power', will not be (as he says they are) 'the ordinance of God' [144], but they will be ordinances of man. For if the right of the heir be the ordinance of God, a divine right, no man, father, or not father, can alter it: if it be not a divine right, it is only human depending on the will of man: and so where human institution gives it not, the first-born has no right at all above his brethren; and men may put government into what hands, and under what form, they please.

141. He goes on, 'most of the civilest nations of the earth, labour to fetch their original from some of the sons or nephews of Noah' [7]. How many do most of the civilest nations amount to? and who are they? I fear the Chinese, a very great and civil people, as well as several other people of the east, west, north and south, trouble not themselves much about this matter. All that believe the Bible, which I believe are our author's 'most of the civilest nations', must necessarily derive themselves from Noah, but for the rest of the world, they think little of his sons or nephews. But if the heralds and antiquaries of all nations, for 'tis these men generally that labour to find out the originals of nations, or all the nations themselves should 'labour to fetch their original from some of the sons or nephews of Noah', what would this be to prove, that the 'lordship which Adam had over the whole world, by right descended to the patriarchs'? Whoever, nations, or races of men, labour to fetch their original from, may be concluded to be thought by them, men of renown, famous to posterity for the greatness of their virtues and actions; but beyond these they look not, nor consider who they were heirs to, but look on them as such as raised themselves by their own virtue to a degree that would give a lustre to those, who in future ages could pretend to derive themselves from them. But if it were Ogygis, Hercules, Brahma, Tamberlain, Pharamond; nay, if Jupiter and Saturn were the names, from whence divers races of man, both ancient and modern, have laboured to derive their original; will that prove that those men 'enjoyed the lordship of Adam, by right descending to them'? If not, this is but a flourish of our author's to mislead his reader, that in itself signifies nothing.

142. To as much purpose, is, what he tells us concerning this division of the world, 'that some say it was by lot, and others that Noah sailed round the Mediterranean in ten years, and divided the world into Asia, Africa and Europe, portions for his three sons' [8]. America then, it seems, was left to be his that could catch it. Why our author takes such pains to prove the division of the world by Noah to his sons, and will not leave out an imagination, though no better than a dream, that he can find anywhere to favour it, is hard to guess, since such a division, if it prove anything, must necessarily take away the title of Adam's heir: unless three brothers can altogether be heirs of Adam; and therefore the following words, 'howsoever the manner of this division be uncertain, yet it is most certain the division itself was by families from Noah and his children, over which the parents were heads and princes' [8], if allowed him to be true, and of any force to prove, that all the power in the world is nothing but the lordship of Adam's descending by right, they will only prove that the fathers of the children are all heirs to this lordship of Adam. For if in those days Cham and Japhet, and other parents besides the eldest son were heads and princes over their families, and had a right to divide the earth by families, what hinders younger brothers, being fathers of families, from have the same right? If Cham and Japhet were princes by right descending to them, notwithstanding any title of heir in their eldest brother, younger brothers by the same right descending to them are princes now, and so all our author's natural power of kings will reach no further than their own children, and no kingdom by this natural right, can be bigger than a family. For either this 'lordship of Adam over the whole world', by right descends only to the eldest son, and then there can be but one heir, as our author says [10]. Or else, it by right descends to all the sons equally, and then every father of a family will have it, as well as the three sons of Noah: take which you will, it destroys the present governments and kingdoms, that are now in the world, since whoever has this natural power of a king, by right descending to him, must have it either, as our author tells us, Cain had it, and be lord over his brethren, and so be alone king of the whole world, or else as he tells us here, Shem, Cham and Japhet had it, three brothers, and so be only prince of his own family, and all families independent one of another; all the world must be only

one empire by the right of the next heir, or else every family be a distinct government of itself, by the 'lordship of Adam's descending to parents of families'. And to this only tends all the proofs he here gives us of the descent of Adam's lordship: for continuing his story of this descent he says;

143. 'In the dispersion of Babel, we must certainly find the establishment of royal power, throughout the kingdoms of the world' [7]. If you must find it, pray do, and you will help us to a new piece of history: but you must show it us before we shall be bound to believe, that regal power was established in the world upon your principles. For, that regal power was established in the kingdoms of the world, I think nobody will dispute, but that there should be kingdoms in the world, whose several kings enjoyed their crowns, 'by right descending to them from Adam', that we think not only apocrypha, but also utterly impossible. If our author has no better foundation for his monarchy than a supposition of what was done at the dispersion of Babel, the monarchy he erects thereon, whose top is to reach to heaven to unite mankind, will serve only to divide and scatter them as that tower did; and instead of establishing civil government and order in the world will produce nothing but confusion.

144. For he tells us, the nations they were divided into, 'were distinct families, which had fathers for rulers over them; whereby it appears, that even in the confusion, God was careful to preserve the fatherly authority, by distributing the diversity of languages, according to the diversity of families' [8]. It would have been a hard matter for anyone but our author to have found out so plainly in the text, he here brings, that all the nations in that dispersion were governed by fathers, and that 'God was careful to preserve the fatherly authority'. The words of the text are; 'these are the sons of Shem after their families, after their tongues in their lands, after their nations' [*Genesis* 10:31]; and the same thing is said of Cham and Japhet, after an enumeration of their posterities: in all which there is not one word said of their governors, or forms of government; of fathers, or fatherly authority. But our author who is very quick sighted, to spy out fatherhood, where nobody else could see any the least glimpses of it, tells us positively their 'rulers were fathers, and God was careful to preserve the fatherly authority'; and why? Because those

of the same family spoke the same language, and so of necessity in the division kept together. Just as if one should argue thus; Hannibal in his army, consisting of divers nations, kept those of the same language together, therefore fathers were captains of each band, and Hannibal was careful of the fatherly authority. Or in peopling of Carolina, the English, French, Scotch, and Welsh that are there, plant themselves together, and by them the country is divided 'in their lands after their tongues, after their families, after their nations'; therefore care was taken of the fatherly authority. Or because in many parts of America, every little tribe was a distinct people, with a different language, one should infer, that therefore 'God was careful to preserve the fatherly authority', or that therefore their rulers 'enjoyed Adam's lordship by right descending to them', though we know not who were their governors, nor what their form of government, but only that they were divided into little independent societies, speaking different languages.

145. The Scripture says not a word of their rulers or forms of government, but only gives an account, how mankind came to be divided into distinct languages and nations; and therefore 'tis not to argue that the authority of Scripture, to tell us positively, fathers were their rulers, when the Scripture says no such thing, but to set up fancies of one's own brain, when we confidently aver matter of fact, where records are utterly silent. Upon a like ground, i.e. none at all he says, 'that they were not confused multitudes without heads and governors, and at liberty to choose what governors or governments they pleased' [7–8].

146. For I demand, when mankind were all yet of one language, all congregated in the plain of Shinar, were they then all under one monarch, 'who enjoyed the lordship of Adam by right descending to him'? If they were not, there was then no thoughts, 'tis plain, of Adam's heir, no right to government known then upon that title, no care taken by God or man, of Adam's fatherly authority. If when mankind were but one people, dwelt together, and were of one language, and were upon building a city together; and when 'twas plain, they could not but know the right heir, for Shem lived till Isaac's time, a long while after the division at Babel; if then, I say, they were not under the monarchical government of Adam's fatherhood, by right descending to the heir, 'tis plain

there was no regard had to the fatherhood, no monarchy acknowledged due to Adam's heir, no empire of Shem's in Asia, and consequently no such division of the world by Noah, as our author has talked of. As far as we can conclude anything from Scripture in this matter, it seems from this place, that if they had any government, it was rather a commonwealth than an absolute monarchy: for the Scripture tells us, *Genesis* 11[:4], 'they said'. 'Twas not a prince commanded the building of this city and tower, 'twas not by the command of one monarch, but by the consultation of many, a free people, 'let us build us a city'; they built it for themselves as free men, not as slaves for their lord and master: 'that we be not scattered abroad'; having a city once built, and fixed habitations to settle our abodes and families. This was the consultation and design of a people, that were at liberty to part asunder, but desired to keep in one body, and could not have been either necessary or likely in men tied together under the government of one monarch, who if they had been, as our author tells us, all slaves under the absolute dominion of a monarch, needed not have taken such care to hinder themselves from wandering out of the reach of his dominion. I demand whether this be not plainer in Scripture than anything of 'Adam's heir or fatherly authority'?

147. But if being, as God says, *Genesis* 11:6, one people, they had one ruler, one king by natural right, absolute and supreme over them, 'what care had God to preserve the paternal authority of the supreme fatherhood' [8], if on a sudden he suffers seventy-two (for so many our author talks of) 'distinct nations' [7], to be erected out of it, under distinct governors, and at once to withdraw themselves from the obedience of their sovereign. This is to entitle God's care how, and to what we please. Can it be sense to say, that God was careful to preserve the fatherly authority in those who had it not? For if these were subjects under a supreme prince, what authority had they? Was it an instance of God's care to preserve the fatherly authority, when he took away the true supreme fatherhood of the natural monarch? Can it be reason to say, that God, for the preservation of fatherly authority, lets several new governments with their governors start up, who could not all have fatherly authority? and is it not as much reason to say, that God is careful to destroy fatherly authority, when he suffers one who is in possession of it, to have his government torn

in pieces, and shared by several of his subjects? Would it not be an argument just like this, for monarchical government, to say, when any monarchy was shattered to pieces, and divided amongst revolted subjects, that God was careful to preserve monarchical power, by rending a settled empire into a multitude of little governments? If anyone will say, that what happens in providence to be preserved, God is careful to preserve as a thing therefore to be esteemed by men as necessary or useful, 'tis a peculiar propriety of speech, which everyone will not think fit to imitate: but this I am sure is impossible to be either proper, or true speaking, that Shem, for example (for he was then alive) should have fatherly authority, or sovereignty by right of fatherhood over that one people at Babel, and that the next moment Shem yet living, seventy-two others should have fatherly authority, or sovereignty by right of fatherhood over the same people, divided into so many distinct governments; either these seventy-two fathers actually were rulers, just before the confusion, and then they were not one people, but that God himself says they were; or else they were a commonwealth, and then where was monarchy? or else these seventy-two fathers had fatherly authority, but knew it not. Strange! that fatherly authority should be the only original of government amongst men, and yet all mankind not know it; and stranger yet, that the confusion of tongues should reveal it to them all of a sudden, that in an instant these seventy-two should know that they had fatherly power, and all others know that they were to obey it in them, and everyone know that particular fatherly authority to which he was a subject. He that can think this arguing from Scripture, may from hence make out what model of a utopia will best suit with his fancy or interest, and this fatherhood thus disposed of, will justify both a prince who claims a universal monarchy, and his subjects, who being fathers of families, shall quit all subjection to him, and canton his empire into less governments for themselves: for it will always remain a doubt in which of these the fatherly authority resided, till our author resolves us, whether Shem, who was then alive, or these seventy-two new princes, beginning so many new empires in his dominions, and over his subjects, had right to govern, since our author tells us, that both one and t'other had fatherly, which is supreme, authority, and are brought in by him as instances of those, who did 'enjoy the lordship of Adam by right descending to them, which was as large and ample as the absolutest dominion of any monarch' [7]. This at least is unavoidable, that if 'God was careful to preserve the fatherly authority, in the seventy-two new erected nations' [7], it necessarily follows, that he was as careful to destroy all pretences of Adam's heir; since he took care, and therefore did preserve the fatherly authority in so many, at least seventy-one, that could not possibly be Adam's heirs, when the right heir (if God had ever ordained any such inheritance) could not but be known, Shem then living, and they being all one people.

148. Nimrod [*Genesis* 10:8–9] is his next instance of enjoying this patriarchal power, but I know not for what reason our author seems a little unkind to him, and says, that he 'against right enlarged his empire, by seizing violently on the rights of other lords of families' [8]: these 'lords of families' here were called 'fathers of families', in his account of the dispersion at Babel: but it matters not how they were called, so we know who they are; for this fatherly authority must be in them, either as heirs to Adam, and so there could not be seventy-two, nor above one at once, or else as natural parents over their children, and so every father will have paternal authority over his children by the same right, and in as large extent as those seventy-two had, and so be independent princes over their own offspring. Taking his lords of families, in this latter sense (as 'tis hard to give those words any other sense in this place) he gives us a very pretty account of the original of monarchy in these following words, 'and in this sense he may be said to be the author and founder of monarchy' [8], *viz.*, as against right seizing violently on the rights of fathers over their children, which paternal authority, if it be in them by right of nature; (for else how could those seventy-two come by it) nobody can take from them without their own consents, and then I desire our author and his friends to consider how far this will concern other princes, and whether it will not according to his conclusion of that paragraph, resolve all regal power of those, whose dominions extend beyond their families, either into tyranny and usurpation, or election and consent of fathers of families, which will differ very little from consent of the people.

149. All his instances, in the next section [8–9], of the twelve dukes of Edom [*Genesis* 36], the nine kings in a little corner of

Asia in Abraham's days [*Genesis* 14], the thirty-one kings in
Canaan destroyed by Joshua [*Joshua* 12:24], and the care he
takes to prove that these were all sovereign princes, and that every
town in those days had a king, are so many direct proofs against
him, that it was not the lordship of Adam by right descending to
them that made kings: for if they had held their royalties by that
title, either there must have been but one sovereign over them all,
or else every father of a family had been as good a prince, and had
as good a claim to royalty as these: for if all the sons of Esau, had
each of them, the younger as well as the eldest, the right of
fatherhood, and so were sovereign princes after their father's
death, the same right had their sons after them, and so on to all
posterity, which will limit all the natural power of fatherhood,
only to be over the issue of their own bodies, and their descendants, which power of fatherhood dies with the head of each
family, and makes way for the like power of fatherhood to take
place, in each of his sons, over their respective posterities, whereby
the power of fatherhood will be preserved indeed, and is intelligible, but will not be at all to our author's purpose: none of the
instances he brings, are proofs of any power they had, as heirs of
Adam's paternal authority, by the title of his fatherhood descending to them, no, nor of any power they had by virtue of their own:
for Adam's fatherhood being over all mankind, it could descend
but to one at once, and from him to his right heir only, and so
there could by that title be but one king in the world at a time;
and by right of fatherhood, not descending from Adam, it must
be only as they themselves were fathers, and so could be over none
but their own posterity: so that if those twelve dukes of Edom; if
Abraham and the nine kings his neighbours; if Jacob and Esau
and the thirty-one kings in Canaan, the seventy-two kings muti-
lated by Adonibezek [*Judges* 1:7], the thirty-two kings that came
to Benhadad [1 Kings 20:16], the seventy kings of Greece making
war at Troy, were as our author contends [9], all of them
sovereign princes; 'tis evident that kings derived their power from
some other original than fatherhood, since some of these had
power over more than their own posterity, and 'tis demonstration,
they could not be all heirs to Adam: for I challenge any man to
make any pretence to power by right of fatherhood, either intelligible or possible in anyone, otherwise, than either as Adam's

heir, or as progenitor over his own descendants, naturally sprung from him. And if our author could show that any one of these princes, of which he gives us here so large a catalogue, had his authority by either of these titles, I think I might yield him the cause: though 'tis manifest they are all impertinent and directly contrary to what he brings them to prove, *viz.* that the 'lordship which Adam had over the world by right descended to the patriarchs'.

150. Having told us 'that the patriarchal government continued in Abraham, Isaac, and Jacob, until the Egyptian bondage' [8], he tells us, 'by manifest footsteps we may trace this paternal government unto the Israelites coming into Egypt, where the exercise of supreme patriarchal government was intermitted, because they were in subjection to a stronger prince' [9]. What these footsteps are of paternal government, in our author's sense, i.e. of absolute monarchical power descending from Adam, and exercised by right of fatherhood we have seen, that is for 2290 years no footsteps at all: since in all that time he cannot produce any one example of any person who claimed or exercised regal authority by right of fatherhood; or show anyone who being a king was Adam's heir. All that his proofs amount to, is only this, that there were fathers, patriarchs and kings in that age of the world; but that the fathers and patriarchs had any absolute arbitrary power, or by what title those kings had theirs, and of what extent it was, the Scripture is wholly silent; 'tis manifest by right of fatherhood they neither did, nor could claim any title to dominion and empire.

151. To say, that 'the exercise of supreme patriarchal government was intermitted, because they were in subjection to a stronger prince', proves nothing but what I before suspected, *viz.* that patriarchal jurisdiction or government is a fallacious expression, and does not in our author signify (what he would yet insinuate by it) paternal and regal power; such an absolute sovereignty, as he supposes was in Adam.

152. For how can he say that 'patriarchal jurisdiction was intermitted in Egypt', where there was a king, under whose regal government the Israelites were, if patriarchal were absolute monarchical jurisdiction? And if it were not, but something else, why does he make such ado about a power not in question, and

nothing to the purpose? The exercise of patriarchal jurisdiction, if patriarchal be regal, was not intermitted whilst the Israelites were in Egypt. 'Tis true, the exercise of regal power was not then in the hands of any of the promised seed of Abraham, nor before neither that I know, but what is that to the intermission of regal authority, as descending from Adam, unless our author will have it, that this chosen line of Abraham, had the right of inheritance to Adam's lordship? And then to what purpose are his instances of the seventy-two rulers, in whom the fatherly authority was preserved in the confusion at Babel? Why does he bring the twelve princes sons of Ishmael; and the dukes of Edom, and join them with Abraham, Isaac, and Jacob, as examples of the exercise of true patriarchal government, if the exercise of patriarchal jurisdiction were intermitted in the world, whenever the heirs of Jacob had not supreme power? I fear supreme patriarchal jurisdiction was not only intermitted, but from the time of the Egyptian bondage quite lost in the world, since 'twill be hard to find from that time downwards, anyone who exercised it as an inheritance descending to him from the patriarchs Abraham, Isaac, and Jacob. I imagined monarchical government would have served his turn in the hands of Pharaoh or anybody. But one cannot easily discover in all places what his discourse tends to, as particularly in this place, it is not obvious to guess what he drives at, when he says, 'the exercise of supreme patriarchal jurisdiction in Egypt', or how this serves to make out the descent of Adam's lordship to the patriarchs or anybody else.

153. For I thought he had been giving us out of Scripture, proofs and examples of monarchical government, founded on paternal authority, descending from Adam; and not a history of the Jews: amongst whom yet we find no kings, till many years after they were a people: and when kings were their rulers, there is not the least mention or room for a pretence that they were heirs to Adam or kings by paternal authority. I expected, talking so much as he does of Scripture, that he would have produced thence a series of monarchs, whose titles were clear to Adam's father-hood, and who, as heirs to him, owned and exercised paternal jurisdiction over their subjects, and that this was the true patriar-chal government: whereas he neither proves, that the patriarchs were kings, nor that either kings or patriarchs were heirs to Adam,

or so much as pretended to it: and one may as well prove, that the patriarchs were all absolute monarchs; that the power both of patriarchs and kings was only paternal; and that this power descended to them from Adam; I say all these propositions may be as well proved by a confused account of a multitude of little kings in the West Indies, out of Ferdinand Soto, or any of our late histories of the Northern America, or by our author's seventy kings of Greece, out of Homer, as by anything he brings out of Scripture, in that multitude of kings he has reckoned up.

154. And methinks he should have let Homer and his wars of Troy alone, since his great zeal to truth or monarchy carried him to such a pitch of transport against philosophers and poets, that he tells us in his preface, that there 'are too many in these days, who please themselves in running after the opinions of philosophers and poets, to find out such an original of government, as might promise them some title to liberty, to the great scandal of Christianity, and bringing in of atheism' [236-7]. And yet these heathens, philosopher Aristotle, and poet Homer, are not rejected by our zealous Christian politician, whenever they offer anything that seems to serve his turn, whether to the great scandal of Christianity, and bringing in of atheism; let him look. This I cannot but observe in authors who ('tis visible) write not for truth, how ready zeal for interest and party is to entitle Christianity to their design, and to charge atheism on those who will not without examining, submit to their doctrines, and blindly swallow their nonsense.

But to return to his Scripture history, our author further tells us, that 'after the return of the Israelites out of bondage, God out of a special care of them, chose Moses and Joshua successively to govern as princes in the place and stead of the supreme fathers' [9]. If it be true, that they 'returned out of bondage', it must be into a state of freedom, and must imply, that both before and after this bondage they were free, unless our author will say, that changing of masters, is returning out of bondage, or that a slave returns out of bondage, when he is removed from one galley to another. If then they 'returned out of bondage', 'tis plain that in those days, whatever our author in his preface says to the contrary [237], there was difference between a son, a subject, and a slave; and that neither the patriarchs before, nor their rulers after this Egyptian bondage, numbered their sons or subjects amongst their possessions, and disposed of them with as absolute a dominion, as they did their other goods.

155. This is evident in Jacob, to whom Reuben offered his two sons as pledges, and Judah was at last surety for Benjamin's safe return out of Egypt: which all had been vain, superfluous, and but a sort of mockery, if Jacob had had the same power over every one of his family as he had over his ox or his ass, as an owner over his substance; and the offers that Reuben or Judah made had been such a security for returning of Benjamin, as if a man should take two lambs out of his lord's flock, and offer one as security, that he will safely restore the other [*Genesis* 42–3].

156. When they were out of this bondage, what then? 'God out of a special care of them, the Israelites' [9]. 'Tis well that once in his book, he will allow God to have any care of the people, for in other places he speaks of mankind, as if God had no care of any part of them, but only of their monarchs, and that the rest of the people, the societies of men, were made as so many herds of cattle, only for the service, use, and pleasure of their princes.

157. 'Chose Moses and Joshua successively to govern as princes' [9]; a shrewd argument our author has found out to prove God's care of the fatherly authority, and Adam's heirs, that here as an expression of his care of his own people, he chooses those for princes over them, that had not the least pretence to either. The persons chosen were, Moses of the tribe of Levi, and Joshua of the tribe of Ephraim, neither of which had any title of fatherhood: but says our author they were in the place and stead of the supreme fathers: if God had anywhere, as plainly declared his choice of such fathers to be rulers, as he did of Moses and Joshua, we might believe Moses and Joshua were in their place and stead, but that being the question in debate, till that be better proved, Moses being chosen by God to be ruler of his people, will no more prove that government belonged to Adam's heir or to the fatherhood, than God's choosing Aaron of the tribe of Levi to be priest, will prove that the priesthood belonged to Adam's heir or the prime fathers, since God could choose Aaron to be priest, and Moses ruler in Israel, though neither of those offices, were settled on Adam's heir or the fatherhood.

158. Our author goes on. 'And after them likewise for a time he raised up judges, to defend his people in time of peril' [9]. This

proves fatherly authority to be the original of government, and that it descended from Adam to his heirs, just as well as what went before: only here our author seems to confess, that these judges, who were all the governors, they then had, were only men of valour, whom they made their generals to defend them in time of peril; and cannot God raise up such men, unless fatherhood have a title to government?

159. But says our author, 'when God gave the Israelites kings, he re-established the ancient and prime right of lineal succession to paternal government' [9].

160. How did God re-establish it? By a law, a positive command? We find no such thing. Our author means then, that when God gave them a king, in giving them a king, he re-established the right, etc. To re-establish *de facto* the right of lineal succession to paternal government, is to put a man in possession of that government which his fathers did enjoy, and he by lineal succession had a right to. For, first, if it were another government, than what his ancestors had, it was not succeeding to an ancient right, but beginning a new one. For if a prince should give a man, besides his ancient patrimony, which for some ages his family had been disseised of, an additional estate, never before in the possession of his ancestors, he could not be said to 're-establish the right of lineal succession' to any more, than what had been formerly enjoyed by his ancestors. If therefore the power the kings of Israel had, were anything more than Isaac or Jacob had, it was not the re-establishing in them the right of succession to a power, but giving them a new power, however you please to call it paternal or not: and whether Isaac and Jacob had the same power, that the kings of Israel had, I desire anyone, by what has been above said, to consider, and I do not think they will find that either Abraham, Isaac, or Jacob had any regal power at all.

161. Next, there can be no 're-establishment of the prime and ancient right of lineal succession' to anything, unless he, that is put in possession of it has the right to succeed, and be the true and next heir to him he succeeds to. Can that be a re-establishment, which begins in a new family? or that the 're-establishment of an ancient right of lineal succession', when a crown is given to one, who has no right of succession to it, and who, if the lineal succession had gone on, had been out of all possibility of pretence

to it? Saul the first king that God gave the Israelites, was of the tribe of Benjamin. Was the 'ancient and prime right of lineal succession re-established' in him? The next was David the youngest son of Jesse, of the posterity of Judah, Jacob's third son. Was the 'ancient and prime right of lineal succession to paternal government re-established' in him? Or in Solomon his younger son and successor in the throne? Or in Jeroboam over the ten tribes? Or in Athaliah a woman, who reigned six years an utter stranger to the royal blood? If the 'ancient and prime right of lineal succession to paternal government', were 're-established' in any of these or their posterity, 'the ancient and prime right of lineal succession to paternal government' belongs to younger brothers as well as elder, and may be re-established in any man living: for whatever younger brothers, by 'ancient and prime right of lineal succession', may have as well as the elder, that every man living may have a right to, by lineal succession, and Sir Robert as well as any other. And so what a brave right of lineal succession, to his paternal or regal government, our author has 're-established' for the securing the rights and inheritances of crowns, where everyone may have it, let the world consider.

162. But says our author however, 'whensoever God made choice of any special person to be king, he intended that the issue also should have benefit thereof, as being comprehended sufficiently in the person of the father, although the father was only named in the grant' [9–10]. This yet will not help out succession; for if, as our author says, the benefit of the grant be intended to the issue of the grantee, this will not direct the succession; since if God give anything to a man and his issue in general, the claim cannot be to anyone of that issue in particular, everyone that is of his race will have an equal right. If it be said, our author meant heir, I believe our author was as willing as anybody to have used that word, if it would have served his turn; but Solomon who succeeded David in the throne, being no more his heir than Jeroboam, who succeeded him in the government of the ten tribes, was his issue; our author had reason to avoid saying, that God intended it to the heirs, when that would not hold in a succession, which our author could not except against, and so he has left his succession as undetermined, as if he had said nothing about it. For if the regal power be given by God to a man and his issue, as

the land of Canaan was to Abraham and his seed, must they not all have a title to it, all share in it? And one may as well say, that by God's grant to Abraham and his seed, the land of Canaan was to belong only to one of his seed exclusive of all others, as by God's grant of dominion to a man and his issue, this dominion was to belong in peculiar to one of his issue exclusive of all others.

163. But how will our author prove, that whensoever God made choice of any special person to be a king, he intended that 'the' (I suppose he means 'his') 'issue also should have benefit thereof' [10]. Has he so soon forgot Moses and Joshua whom in this very section, he says, 'God out of a special care chose to govern as princes', and the judges that God raised up? Had not these princes, having the authority of the supreme fatherhood, the same power that the kings had, and being specially chosen by God himself, should not their issue have the benefit of that choice, as well as David's or Solomon's? If these had the paternal authority put into their hands immediately by God, why had not their issue the benefit of this grant in a succession to his power? Or if they had it as Adam's heirs, why did not their heirs enjoy it after them by right descending to them? For they could not be heirs to one another. Was the power the same, and from the same original in Moses, Joshua and the judges, as it was in David and the kings, and was it inheritable in one and not in the other? If it was not paternal authority, then God's own people were governed by those that had not paternal authority, and those governors did well enough without it: if it were paternal authority and God chose the persons that were to exercise it, our author's rule fails, that 'whensoever God makes choice of any person to be supreme ruler' (for I suppose the name king has no spell in it, 'tis not the title, but the power makes the difference) 'he intends that the issue also should have the benefit of it', since from their coming out of Egypt to David's time, four hundred years, the issue was never 'so sufficiently comprehended in the person of the father' [10], as that any son after the death of his father, succeeded to the government amongst all those judges that judged Israel. If to avoid this, it be said, God always chose the person of the successor, and so transferring the fatherly authority to him, excluded his issue from succeeding to it, that is manifestly not so in the story of Jephtha,

where he articled with the people, and they made him judge over them, as is plain, *Judges* 11 [:11].

164. 'Tis in vain then to say [9–10], that 'whensoever God chooses any special person' to have the exercise of paternal authority (for if that be not to be king, I desire to know the difference between a king and one having the exercise of paternal authority,) 'he intends the issue also should have the benefit of it', since we find the authority, the judges had, ended with them, and descended not to their issue, and if the judges had not paternal authority, I fear it will trouble our author or any of the friends to his principles, to tell who had then the paternal authority, that is, the government and supreme power amongst the Israelites; and I suspect they must confess that the chosen people of God continued a people several hundreds of years, without any knowledge or thought of this paternal authority, or any appearance of monarchical government at all.

165. To be satisfied of this, he need but read the story of the Levite, and the war thereupon with the Benjamites, in the three last chapters of *Judges* [19–21]: and when he finds, that the Levite appeals to the people for justice; that it was the tribes and the congregation, that debated, resolved, and directed all that was done on that occasion, he must conclude, either that God was not 'careful to preserve the fatherly authority' amongst his own chosen people; or else that the fatherly authority may be preserved, where there is no monarchical government; if the latter, then it will follow that though fatherly authority be never so well proved, yet it will not infer a necessity of monarchical government; if the former, it will seem very strange and improbable that God should ordain fatherly authority to be so sacred amongst the sons of men, that there could be no power or government without it, and yet that amongst his own people, even whilst he is providing a government for them, and therein prescribes rules to the several states and relations of men, this great and fundamental one, this most material and necessary of all the rest should be concealed, and lie neglected for four hundred years after.

166. Before I leave this, I must ask how our author knows that 'whensoever God makes choice of any special person to be king, he intends that the issue should have the benefit thereof'? does God by the law of nature or revelation say so? [9–10]. By the same

law also he must say, which of his issue must enjoy the crown in succession, and so point out the heir, or else leave his issue to divide or scramble for the government: both alike absurd, and such as will destroy the benefit of such grant to the issue. When any such declaration of God's intention is produced, it will be our duty to believe God intends it so, but till that be done, our author must show us some better warrant, before we shall be obliged to receive him as the authentic revealer of God's intentions.

167. 'The issue', says our author 'is comprehended sufficiently in the person of the father, although the father only was named in the grant' [10]: and yet God, when he gave the land of Canaan to Abraham, *Genesis* 13:15, thought fit to put his seed into the grant too. So the priesthood was given to Aaron and his seed; and the crown God gave not only to David, but his seed also: and however our author assures us that 'God intends, that the issue should have the benefit of it, when he chooses any person to be king', yet we see that the kingdom which he gave to Saul, without mentioning his seed after him, never came to any of his issue; and why when God chose a person to be king, he should intend that his issue should have the benefit of it, more than when he chose one to be judge in Israel, I would fain know a reason; or why does a grant of fatherly authority to a king more comprehend the issue, than when a like grant is made to a judge? Is paternal authority by right to descend to the issue, of one and not of the other? There will need some reason to be shown of this difference, more than the name, when the thing given is the same fatherly authority, and the manner of giving it, God's choice of the person the same too; for I suppose our author, when he says, 'God raised up judges', will by no means allow, they were chosen by the people.

168. But since our author has so confidently assured us of the care of God to preserve the fatherhood, and pretends to build all, he says, upon the authority of the Scripture, we may well expect that the people whose law, constitution and history is chiefly contained in the Scripture, should furnish him with the clearest instances of God's care of preserving of the fatherly authority, in that people who 'tis agreed he had a most peculiar care of. Let us see then what state this paternal authority or government was in amongst the Jews, from their beginning to be a people. It was omitted by our author's confession, from their coming into Egypt,

till their return out of that bondage, above two hundred years. From thence till God gave the Israelites a king about four hundred years more, our author gives but a very slender account of it, nor indeed all that time are there the least footsteps of paternal or regal government amongst them. But then says our author, 'God re-established the ancient and prime right of lineal succession to paternal government' [9].

169. What a 'lineal succession to paternal government' was then established, we have already seen. I only now consider how long this lasted, and that was to their captivity about five hundred years: from thence to their destruction by the Romans, above six hundred and fifty years after, the 'ancient and prime right of lineal succession to paternal government' was again lost, and they continued a people in the promised land without it. So that of eleven hundred and fifty years that they were God's peculiar people, they had hereditary kingly government amongst them, not one third of the time, and of that time there is not the least footstep of one moment of 'paternal government', nor 'the re-establishment of the ancient and prime right of lineal succession to it', whether we suppose it to be derived, as from its fountain, from David, Saul, Abraham, or, which upon our author's principles is the only true; from Adam.

THE SECOND TREATISE OF GOVERNMENT

AN ESSAY
CONCERNING THE
TRUE ORIGINAL, EXTENT, AND END
OF
CIVIL GOVERNMENT

Chapter 1
THE INTRODUCTION

1. It having been shown in the foregoing discourse,

(1) That Adam had not either by natural right of fatherhood, or by positive donation from God, any such authority over his children, or dominion over the world as is pretended.

(2) That if he had, his heirs, yet, had no right to it.

(3) That if his heirs had, there being no law of nature nor positive law of God that determines, which is the right heir in all cases that may arise, the right of succession, and consequently of bearing rule, could not have been certainly determined.

(4) That if even that had been determined, yet the knowledge of which is the eldest line of Adam's posterity, being so long since utterly lost, that in the races of mankind and families of the world, there remains not to one above another, the least pretence to be the eldest house, and to have the right of inheritance.

All these premises having, as I think, been clearly made out, it is impossible that the rulers now on earth, should make any benefit, or derive any the least shadow of authority from that, which is held to be the fountain of all power, Adam's private dominion and paternal jurisdiction, so that, he that will not give just occasion, to think that all government in the world is the product only of force and violence, and that men live together by no other rules but that of beasts, where the strongest carries it, and so lay a foundation for perpetual disorder and mischief, tumult, sedition and rebellion, (things that the followers of that hypothesis so loudly cry out against) must of necessity find out another rise of government, another original of political power, and another way of designing and knowing the persons that have it, than what Sir Robert Filmer hath taught us.

2. To this purpose, I think it may not be amiss, to set down what I take to be political power. That the power of a magistrate over a subject, may be distinguished from that of a father over his children, a master over his servant, a husband over his wife, and a lord over his slave. All which distinct powers happening sometimes together in the same man, if he be considered under

these different relations, it may help us to distinguish these powers one from another, and show the difference betwixt a ruler of a commonwealth, a father of a family, and a captain of a galley.

3. Political power then I take to be a right of making laws with penalties of death, and consequently all less penalties, for the regulating and preserving of property, and of employing the force of the community, in the execution of such laws, and in the defence of the commonwealth from foreign injury, and all this only for the public good.

Chapter 2
OF THE STATE OF NATURE

4. To understand political power right, and derive it from its original, we must consider what state all men are naturally in, and that is, a state of perfect freedom to order their actions, and dispose of their possessions, and persons as they think fit, within the bounds of the law of nature, without asking leave, or depending upon the will of any other man.

A state also of equality, wherein all the power and jurisdiction is reciprocal, no one having more than another: there being nothing more evident, than that creatures of the same species and rank promiscuously born to all the same advantages of nature, and the use of the same faculties, should also be equal one amongst another without subordination or subjection, unless the lord and master of them all, should by any manifest declaration of his will set one above another, and confer on him by an evident and clear appointment an undoubted right to dominion and sovereignty.

5. This equality of men by nature, the judicious Hooker looks upon as so evident in itself, and beyond all question, that he makes it the foundation of that obligation to mutual love amongst men, on which he builds the duties they owe one another, and from whence he derives the great maxims of justice and charity. His words are;

'The like natural inducement, hath brought men to know that it is no less their duty, to love others than themselves, for seeing those things which are equal, must needs all have one measure; if

I cannot but wish to receive good, even as much at every man's hands, as any man can wish unto his own soul, how should I look to have any part of my desire herein satisfied, unless myself be careful to satisfy the like desire, which is undoubtedly in other men, being of one and the same nature? to have anything offered them repugnant to this desire, must needs in all respects grieve them as much as me, so that if I do harm, I must look to suffer, there being no reason that others should show greater measure of love to me, than they have by me, showed unto them; my desire therefore to be loved of my equals in nature, as much as possible may be, imposeth upon me a natural duty of bearing to themward, fully the like affection; from which relation of equality between ourselves and them, that are as ourselves, what several rules and canons, natural reason hath drawn for direction of life, no man is ignorant' (*Ecclesiastical Polity*, Bk I [Ch. 8, p. 80]).

6. But though this be a state of liberty, yet it is not a state of licence, though man in that state have an uncontrollable liberty, to dispose of his person or possessions, yet he has not liberty to destroy himself, or so much as any creature in his possession, but where some nobler use, than its bare preservation calls for it. The state of nature has a law of nature to govern it, which obliges everyone: and reason, which is that law, teaches all mankind, who will but consult it, that being all equal and independent, no one ought to harm another in his life, health, liberty, or possessions. For men being all the workmanship of one omnipotent, and infinitely wise Maker; all the servants of one sovereign master, sent into the world by his order and about his business, they are his property, whose workmanship they are, made to last during his, not one another's pleasure. And being furnished with like faculties, sharing all in one community of nature, there cannot be supposed any such subordination among us, that may authorize us to destroy one another, as if we were made for one another's uses, as the inferior ranks of creatures are for ours. Everyone as he is bound to preserve himself, and not to quit his station wilfully; so by the like reason when his own preservation comes not in competition, ought he, as much as he can, to preserve the rest of mankind, and may not unless it be to do justice on an offender, take away, or impair the life, or what tends to the preservation of the life, the liberty, health, limb or goods of another.

7. And that all men may be restrained from invading others' rights, and from doing hurt to one another, and the law of nature be observed, which willeth the peace and preservation of all mankind, the execution of the law of nature is in that state, put into every man's hands, whereby everyone has a right to punish the transgressors of that law to such a degree, as may hinder its violation. For the law of nature would, as all other laws that concern men in this world, be in vain, if there were nobody that in the state of nature, had a power to execute that law, and thereby preserve the innocent and restrain offenders, and if anyone in the state of nature may punish another, for any evil he has done, everyone may do so. For in that state of perfect equality, where naturally there is no superiority or jurisdiction of one, over another, what any may do in prosecution of that law, everyone must needs have a right to do.

8. And thus in the state of nature, one man comes by a power over another; but yet no absolute or arbitrary power, to use a criminal when he has got him in his hands, according to the passionate heats, or boundless extravagancy of his own will, but only to retribute to him, so far as calm reason and conscience dictates, what is proportionate to his transgression, which is so much as may serve for reparation and restraint. For these two are the only reasons, why one man may lawfully do harm to another, which is what we call punishment. In transgressing the law of nature, the offender declares himself to live by another rule, than that of reason and common equity, which is that measure God has set to the actions of men, for their mutual security: and so he becomes dangerous to mankind, the tie, which is to secure them from injury and violence, being slighted and broken by him. Which being a trespass against the whole species, and the peace and safety of it, provided for by the law of nature, every man upon this score, by the right he hath to preserve mankind in general, may restrain, or where it is necessary, destroy things noxious to them, and so may bring such evil on anyone, who hath transgressed that law, as may make him repent the doing of it, and thereby deter him, and by his example others, from doing the like mischief. And in this case, and upon this ground, every man hath a right to punish the offender, and be executioner of the law of nature.

9. I doubt not but this will seem a very strange doctrine to some men: but before they condemn it, I desire them to resolve me, by what right any prince or state can put to death, or punish an alien, for any crime he commits in their country. 'Tis certain their laws by virtue of any sanction they receive from the promulgated will of the legislative, reach not a stranger. They speak not to him, nor if they did, is he bound to hearken to them. The legislative authority, by which they are in force over the subjects of that commonwealth, hath no power over him. Those who have the supreme power of making laws in England, France or Holland, are to an Indian, but like the rest of the world, men without authority: and therefore if by the law of nature, every man hath not a power to punish offences against it, as he soberly judges the case to require, I see not how the magistrates of any community, can punish an alien of another country, since in reference to him, they can have no more power, than what every man naturally may have over another.

10. Besides the crime which consists in violating the law, and varying from the right rule of reason, whereby a man so far becomes degenerate, and declares himself to quit the principles of human nature, and to be a noxious creature, there is commonly injury done to some person or other, and some other man receives damage by his transgression, in which case he who hath received any damage, has besides the right of punishment common to him with other men, a particular right to seek reparation from him that has done it. And any other person who finds it just, may also join with him that is injured, and assist him in recovering from the offender, so much as may make satisfaction for the harm he has suffered.

11. From these two distinct rights, the one of punishing the crime for restraint, and preventing the like offence, which right of punishing is in everybody; the other of taking reparation, which belongs only to the injured party, comes it to pass that the magistrate, who by being magistrate, hath the common right of punishing put into his hands, can often, where the public good demands not the execution of the law, remit the punishment of criminal offences by his own authority, but yet cannot remit the satisfaction due to any private man, for the damage he has received. That, he who has suffered the damage has a right to

demand in his own name, and he alone can remit: the damnified person has this power of appropriating to himself, the goods or service of the offender, by right of self-preservation, as every man has a power to punish the crime, to prevent its being committed again, by the right he has of preserving all mankind, and doing all reasonable things he can in order to that end: and thus it is, that every man in the state of nature, has a power to kill a murderer, both to deter others from doing the like injury, which no reparation can compensate, by the example of the punishment that attends it from everybody, and also to secure men from the attempts of a criminal, who having renounced reason, the common rule and measure, God hath given to mankind, hath by the unjust violence and slaughter he hath committed upon one, declared war against all mankind, and therefore may be destroyed as a lion or a tiger, one of those wild savage beasts, with whom men can have no society nor security: and upon this is grounded the great law of nature, 'Whoso sheddeth man's blood, by man shall his blood be shed' [*Genesis* 9:6]. And Cain was so fully convinced, that everyone had a right to destroy such a criminal, that after the murder of his brother, he cries out, 'Everyone that findeth me, shall slay me' [*Genesis* 4:14]; so plain was it writ in the hearts of all mankind.

12. By the same reason, may a man in the state of nature punish the lesser breaches of that law. It will perhaps be demanded, with death? I answer, each transgression may be punished to that degree, and with so much severity as will suffice to make it an ill bargain to the offender, give him cause to repent, and terrify others from doing the like. Every offence that can be committed in the state of nature, may in the state of nature be also punished, equally, and as far forth as it may, in a commonwealth; for though it would be besides my present purpose, to enter here into the particulars of the law of nature, or its measures of punishment; yet, it is certain there is such a law, and that too, as intelligible and plain to a rational creature, and a studier of that law, as the positive laws of commonwealths, nay possibly plainer; as much as reason is easier to be understood, than the fancies and intricate contrivances of men, following contrary and hidden interests put into words; for so truly are a great part of the municipal laws of countries, which are only so far right, as they

are founded on the law of nature, by which they are to be regulated and interpreted.

13. To this strange doctrine, *viz.* that in the state of nature, everyone has the executive power of the law of nature, I doubt not but it will be objected, that it is unreasonable for men to be judges in their own cases, that self-love will make men partial to themselves and their friends. And on the other side, that ill nature, passion and revenge will carry them too far in punishing others. And hence nothing but confusion and disorder will follow, and that therefore God hath certainly appointed government to restrain the partiality and violence of men [*Romans* 13:4]. I easily grant, that civil government is the proper remedy for the inconveniences of the state of nature, which must certainly be great, where men may be judges in their own case, since 'tis easily to be imagined, that he who was so unjust as to do his brother an injury, will scarce be so just as to condemn himself for it: but I shall desire those who make this objection, to remember that absolute monarchs are but men, and if government is to be the remedy of those evils, which necessarily follow from men's being judges in their own cases, and the state of nature is therefore not [to] be endured, I desire to know what kind of government that is, and how much better it is than the state of nature, where one man commanding a multitude, has the liberty to be judge in his own case, and may do to all his subjects whatever he pleases, without the least liberty to anyone to question or control those who execute his pleasure? And in whatsoever he doth, whether led by reason, mistake or passion, must be submitted to? Much better it is in the state of nature wherein men are not bound to submit to the unjust will of another: and if he that judges, judges amiss in his own, or any other case, he is answerable for it to the rest of mankind.

14. 'Tis often asked as a mighty objection, where are, or ever were, there any men in such a state of nature? To which it may suffice as an answer at present; that since all princes and rulers of independent governments all through the world, are in a state of nature, 'tis plain the world never was, nor ever will be, without numbers of men in that state. I have named all governors of independent communities, whether they are, or are not, in league with others: for 'tis not every compact that puts an end to the state of nature between men, but only this one of agreeing together

mutually to enter into one community, and make one body politic; other promises and compacts, men may make one with another, and yet still be in the state of nature. The promises and bargains for truck, etc. between the two men in the desert island, mentioned by Garcilaso de la Vega, in his history of Peru, or between a Swiss and an Indian, in the woods of America, are binding to them, though they are perfectly in a state of nature, in reference to one another. For truth and keeping of faith belongs to men, as men, and not as members of society.

15. To those that say, there were never any men in the state of nature; I will not only oppose the authority of the judicious Hooker (*Ecclesiastical Polity*, Bk I, Ch. 10 [p. 87]) where he says, 'the laws which have been hitherto mentioned', i.e. the laws of nature, 'do bind men absolutely, even as they are men, although they have never any settled fellowship, never any solemn agreement amongst themselves what to do or not to do, but forasmuch as we are not by ourselves sufficient to furnish ourselves with competent store of things, needful for such a life, as our nature doth desire, a life, fit for the dignity of man; therefore to supply those defects and imperfections which are in us, as living singly and solely by ourselves, we are naturally induced to seek communion and fellowship with others, this was the cause of men's uniting themselves, at first in politic societies'. But I moreover affirm, that all men are naturally in that state, and remain so, till by their own consents they make themselves members of some politic society; and I doubt not in the sequel of this discourse, to make it very clear.

Chapter 3
OF THE STATE OF WAR

16. The state of war is a state of enmity and destruction; and therefore declaring by word or action, not a passionate and hasty, but a sedate settled design, upon another man's life, puts him in a state of war with him against whom he has declared such an intention, and so has exposed his life to the other's power to be taken away by him, or anyone that joins with him in his defence, and espouses his quarrel: it being reasonable and just I should have a right to destroy that which threatens me with destruction.

For by the fundamental law of nature, man being to be preserved, as much as possible, when all cannot be preserved, the safety of the innocent is to be preferred: and one may destroy a man who makes war upon him, or has discovered an enmity to his being, for the same reason, that he may kill a wolf or a lion; because such men are not under the ties of the common law of reason, have no other rule, but that of force and violence, and so may be treated as beasts of prey, those dangerous and noxious creatures, that will be sure to destroy him, whenever he falls into their power.

17. And hence it is, that he who attempts to get another man into his absolute power, does thereby put himself into a state of war with him; it being to be understood as a declaration of a design upon his life. For I have reason to conclude, that he who would get me into his power without my consent, would use me as he pleased, when he had got me there, and destroy me too when he had a fancy to it: for nobody can desire to have me in his absolute power, unless it be to compel me by force to that, which is against the right of my freedom, i.e. make me a slave. To be free from such force is the only security of my preservation: and reason bids me look on him, as an enemy to my preservation, who would take away that freedom, which is the fence to it: so that he who makes an attempt to enslave me, thereby puts himself into a state of war with me. He that in the state of nature, would take away the freedom, that belongs to anyone in that state, must necessarily be supposed to have a design to take away everything else, that freedom being the foundation of all the rest: as he that in the state of society, would take away the freedom belonging to those of that society or commonwealth, must be supposed to design to take away from them everything else, and so be looked on as in a state of war.

18. This makes it lawful for a man to kill a thief, who has not in the least hurt him, nor declared any design upon his life, any further than by the use of force, so to get him in his power, as to take away his money, or what he pleases from him: because using force, where he has no right, to get me into his power, let his pretence be what it will, I have no reason to suppose, that he, who would take away my liberty, would not when he had me in his power, take away everything else. And therefore it is lawful for me to treat him, as one who has put himself into a state of war with me, i.e. kill him if I can; for to that hazard does he justly expose

himself, whoever introduces a state of war, and is aggressor in it.

19. And here we have the plain difference between the state of nature, and the state of war, which however some men have confounded, [yet] are as far distant, as a state of peace, good will, mutual assistance, and preservation, and a state of enmity, malice, violence, and mutual destruction are one from another. Men living together according to reason, without a common superior on earth, with authority to judge between them, is properly the state of nature. But force, or a declared design of force upon the person of another, where there is no common superior on earth to appeal to for relief, is the state of war: and 'tis the want of such an appeal gives a man the right of war even against an aggressor, though he be in society and a fellow subject. Thus a thief, whom I cannot harm but by appeal to the law, for having stolen all that I am worth, I may kill, when he sets on me to rob me, but of my horse or coat: because the law, which was made for my preservation, where it cannot interpose to secure my life from present force, which if lost, is capable of no reparation, permits me my own defence, and the right of war, a liberty to kill the aggressor, because the aggressor allows not time to appeal to our common judge, nor the decision of the law, for remedy in a case, where the mischief may be irreparable. Want of a common judge with authority, puts all men in a state of nature: force without right, upon a man's person, makes a state of war, both where there is, and is not, a common judge.

20. But when the actual force is over, the state of war ceases between those that are in society, and are equally on both sides subjected to the fair determination of the law; because then there lies open the remedy of appeal for the past injury, and to prevent future harm: but where no such appeal is, as in the state of nature, for want of positive laws, and judges with authority to appeal to, the state of war once begun, continues, with a right to the innocent party, to destroy the other whenever he can, until the aggressor offers peace, and desires reconciliation on such terms, as may repair any wrongs he has already done, and secure the innocent for the future: nay where an appeal to the law, and constituted judges lies open, but the remedy is denied by a manifest perverting of justice, and a barefaced wresting of the laws, to protect or indemnify the violence or injuries of some men, or party of men, there it is hard to imagine anything but a state of war. For

wherever violence is used, and injury done, though by hands appointed to administer justice, it is still violence and injury, however coloured with the name, pretences, or forms of law, the end whereof being to protect and redress the innocent, by an unbiased application of it, to all who are under it; wherever that is not *bona fide* done, war is made upon the sufferers, who having no appeal on earth to right them, they are left to the only remedy in such cases, an appeal to heaven.

21. To avoid this state of war (wherein there is no appeal but to heaven, and wherein every the least difference is apt to end, where there is no authority to decide between the contenders) is one great reason of men's putting themselves into society, and quitting the state of nature. For where there is an authority, a power on earth, from which relief can be had by appeal, there the continuance of the state of war is excluded, and the controversy is decided by that power. Had there been any such court, any superior jurisdiction on earth, to determine the right between Jephtha and the Ammonites, they had never come to a state of war, but we see he was forced to appeal to heaven. 'The Lord the judge' (says he) 'be judge this day between the children of Israel, and the children of Ammon' (*Judges* 11:27) and then prosecuting, and relying on his appeal, he leads out his army to battle: and therefore in such controversies, where the question is put, who shall be judge? it cannot be meant, who shall decide the controversy; everyone knows what Jephtha here tells us, that 'the Lord the judge', shall judge. Where there is no judge on earth, the appeal lies to God in heaven. That question then cannot mean, who shall judge? whether another hath put himself in a state of war with me, and whether I may as Jephtha did, appeal to heaven in it? Of that I myself can only be judge in my own conscience, as I will answer it at the great day, to the supreme judge of all men.

Chapter 4
OF SLAVERY

22. The natural liberty of man is to be free from any superior power on earth, and not to be under the will or legislative authority of man, but to have only the law of nature for his rule.

The liberty of man, in society, is to be under no other legislative power, but that established, by consent, in the commonwealth, nor under the dominion of any will, or restraint of any law, but what the legislative shall enact, according to the trust put in it. Freedom then is not what Sir Robert Filmer tells us [275], 'a liberty for everyone to do what he lists, to live as he pleases, and not to be tied by any laws': but freedom of men under government, is, to have a standing rule to live by, common to everyone of that society, and made by the legislative power erected in it; a liberty to follow my own will in all things, where the rule prescribes not; and not to be subject to the inconstant, uncertain, unknown, arbitrary will of another man. As freedom of nature is to be under no other restraint but the law of nature.

23. This freedom from absolute, arbitrary power, is so necessary to, and closely joined with a man's preservation, that he cannot part with it, but by what forfeits his preservation and life together. For a man, not having the power of his own life, cannot, by compact, or his own consent, enslave himself to anyone, nor put himself under the absolute, arbitrary power of another, to take away his life, when he pleases. Nobody can give more power than he has himself; and he that cannot take away his own life, cannot give another power over it. Indeed having, by his fault, forfeited his own life, by some act that deserves death; he, to whom he has forfeited it, may (when he has him in his power) delay to take it, and make use of him to his own service, and he does him no injury by it. For, whenever he finds the hardship of his slavery outweigh the value of his life, 'tis in his power, by resisting the will of his master, to draw on himself the death he desires.

24. This is the perfect condition of slavery, which is nothing else, but the state of war continued, between a lawful conqueror, and a captive. For, if once compact enter between them, and make an agreement for a limited power on the one side, and obedience on the other, the state of war and slavery ceases, as long as the compact endures. For, as has been said, no man can, by agreement, pass over to another that which he hath not in himself, a power over his own life.

I confess, we find among the Jews, as well as other nations, that men did sell themselves; but, 'tis plain, this was only to drudgery, not to slavery. For, it is evident, the person sold was not under an absolute, arbitrary, despotical power. For the master could not have power to kill him, at any time, whom, at a certain time, he was obliged to let go free out of his service: and the master of such a servant was so far from having an arbitrary power over his life, that he could not, at pleasure, so much as maim him, but the loss of an eye, or tooth, set him free (*Exodus* 21).

Chapter 5
OF PROPERTY

25. Whether we consider natural reason, which tells us, that men, being once born, have a right to their preservation, and consequently to meat and drink, and such other things, as nature affords for their subsistence: or revelation, which gives us an account of those grants God made of the world to Adam, and to Noah, and his sons, 'tis very clear, that God, as King David says (*Psalms* 115:16) 'has given the earth to the children of men', given it to mankind in common. But this being supposed, it seems to some a very great difficulty, how anyone should ever come to have a property in anything: I will not content myself to answer, that if it be difficult to make out property, upon a supposition, that God gave the world to Adam and his posterity in common; it is impossible that any man, but one universal monarch, should have any property, upon a supposition, that God gave the world to Adam, and his heirs in succession, exclusive of all the rest of his posterity. But I shall endeavour to show, how men might come to have a property in several parts of that which God gave to mankind in common, and that without any express compact of all the commoners.

26. God, who hath given the world to men in common, hath also given them reason to make use of it to the best advantage of life, and convenience. The earth, and all that is therein, is given to men for the support and comfort of their being. And though all the fruits it naturally produces, and beasts it feeds, belong to mankind in common, as they are produced by the spontaneous hand of nature; and nobody has originally a private dominion, exclusive of the rest of mankind, in any of them, as they are thus

in their natural state: yet being given for the use of men, there must of necessity be a means to appropriate them some way or other before they can be of any use, or at all beneficial to any particular man. The fruit, or venison, which nourishes the wild Indian, who knows no enclosure, and is still a tenant in common, must be his, and so his, i.e. a part of him, that another can no longer have any right to it, before it can do him any good for the support of his life.

27. Though the earth, and all inferior creatures be common to all men, yet every man has a property in his own person. This nobody has any right to but himself. The labour of his body, and the work of his hands, we may say, are properly his. Whatsoever then he removes out of the state that nature hath provided, and left it in, he hath mixed his labour with, and joined to it something that is his own, and thereby makes it his property. It being by him removed from the common state nature placed it in, it hath by this labour something annexed to it, that excludes the common right of other men. For this labour being the unquestionable property of the labourer, no man but he can have a right to what that is once joined to, at least where there is enough, and as good left in common for others.

28. He that is nourished by the acorns he picked up under an oak, or the apples he gathered from the trees in the wood, has certainly appropriated them to himself. Nobody can deny but the nourishment is his. I ask then, when did they begin to be his? When he digested? Or when he eat? Or when he boiled? Or when he brought them home? Or when he picked them up? And 'tis plain, if the first gathering made them not his, nothing else could. That labour put a distinction between them and common. That added something to them more than nature, the common mother of all, had done; and so they became his private right. And will anyone say he had no right to those acorns or apples he thus appropriated, because he had not the consent of all mankind to make them his? Was it a robbery thus to assume to himself what belonged to all in common? If such a consent as that was necessary, man had starved, notwithstanding the plenty God had given him. We see in commons, which remain so by compact, that 'tis the taking any part of what is common, and removing it out of the state nature leaves it in, which begins the property; without

which the common is of no use. And the taking of this or that part, does not depend on the express consent of all the commoners. Thus the grass my horse has bit; the turfs my servant has cut; and the ore I have digged in any place where I have a right to them in common with others, become my property, without the assignation or consent of anybody. The labour that was mine, removing them out of that common state they were in, hath fixed my property in them.

29. By making an explicit consent of every commoner, necessary to anyone's appropriating to himself any part of what is given in common, children or servants could not cut the meat which their father or master had provided for them in common, without assigning to everyone his peculiar part. Though the water running in the fountain be everyone's, yet who can doubt, but that in the pitcher is his only who drew it out? His labour hath taken it out of the hands of nature, where it was common, and belonged equally to all her children, and hath thereby appropriated it to himself.

30. Thus this law of reason makes the deer, that Indian's who hath killed it; 'tis allowed to be his goods who hath bestowed his labour upon it, though before, it was the common right of everyone. And amongst those who are counted the civilized part of mankind, who have made and multiplied positive laws to determine property, this original law of nature for the beginning of property, in what was before common, still takes place; and by virtue thereof, what fish anyone catches in the ocean, that great and still remaining common of mankind; or what ambergris anyone takes up here, is by the labour that removes it out of that common state nature left it in, made his property who takes that pains about it. And even amongst us the hare that anyone is hunting, is thought his who pursues her during the chase. For being a beast that is still looked upon as common, and no man's private possession; whoever has employed so much labour about any of that kind, as to find and pursue her, has thereby removed her from the state of nature, wherein she was common, and hath begun a property.

31. It will perhaps be objected to this, that if gathering the acorns, or other fruits of the earth, etc. makes a right to them, then anyone may engross as much as he will. To which I answer,

not so. The same law of nature, that does by this means give us property, does also bound that property too. 'God has given us all things richly' (1 *Timothy* 6:17) is the voice of reason confirmed by inspiration. But how far has he given it us? 'To enjoy.' As much as anyone can make use of to any advantage of life before it spoils; so much he may by his labour fix a property in. Whatever is beyond this, is more than his share, and belongs to others. Nothing was made by God for man to spoil or destroy. And thus considering the plenty of natural provisions there was a long time in the world, and the few spenders, and to how small a part of that provision the industry of one man could extend itself, and engross it to the prejudice of others; especially keeping within the bounds, set by reason of what might serve for his use; there could be then little room for quarrels or contentions about property so established.

32. But the chief matter of property being now not the fruits of the earth, and the beasts that subsist on it, but the earth itself; as that which takes in and carries with it all the rest: I think it is plain, that property in that too is acquired as the former. As much land as a man tills, plants, improves, cultivates, and can use the product of, so much is his property. He by his labour does, as it were, enclose it from the common. Nor will it invalidate his right to say, everybody else has an equal title to it; and therefore he cannot appropriate, he cannot enclose, without the consent of all his fellow commoners, all mankind. God, when he gave the world in common to all mankind, commanded man also to labour, and the penury of his condition required it of him. God and his reason commanded him to subdue the earth, i.e. improve it for the benefit of life, and therein lay out something upon it that was his own, his labour. He that in obedience to this command of God, subdued, tilled and sowed any part of it, thereby annexed to it something that was his property, which another had no title to, nor could without injury take from him.

33. Nor was this appropriation of any parcel of land, by improving it, any prejudice to any other man, since there was still enough, and as good left; and more than the yet unprovided could use. So that in effect, there was never the less left for others because of his enclosure for himself. For he that leaves as much as another can make use of, does as good as take nothing at all.

Nobody could think himself injured by the drinking of another man, though he took a good draught, who had a whole river of the same water left him to quench his thirst. And the case of land and water, where there is enough of both, is perfectly the same.

34. God gave the world to men in common; but since he gave it them for their benefit, and the greatest conveniences of life they were capable to draw from it, it cannot be supposed he meant it should always remain common and uncultivated. He gave it to the use of the industrious and rational, (and labour was to be his title to it;) not to the fancy or covetousness of the quarrelsome and contentious. He that had as good left for his improvement, as was already taken up, needed not complain, ought not to meddle with what was already improved by another's labour: if he did, 'tis plain he desired the benefit of another's pains, which he had no right to, and not the ground which God had given him in common with others to labour on, and whereof there was as good left, as that already possessed, and more than he knew what to do with, or his industry could reach to.

35. 'Tis true, in land that is common in England, or any other country, where there is plenty of people under government, who have money and commerce, no one can enclose or appropriate any part, without the consent of all his fellow commoners: because this is left common by compact, i.e. by the law of the land, which is not to be violated. And though it be common, in respect of some men, it is not so to all mankind; but is the joint property of this country, or this parish. Besides, the remainder, after such enclosure, would not be as good to the rest of the commoners as the whole was, when they could all make use of the whole: whereas in the beginning and first peopling of the great common of the world, it was quite otherwise. The law man was under, was rather for appropriating. God commanded, and his wants forced him to labour. That was his property which could not be taken from him wherever he had fixed it. And hence subduing or cultivating the earth, and having dominion, we see are joined together. The one gave title to the other. So that God, by commanding to subdue, gave authority so far to appropriate. And the condition of human life, which requires labour and materials to work on, necessarily introduces private possessions.

36. The measure of property, nature has well set, by the extent of men's labour, and the conveniency of life: no man's labour could subdue, or appropriate all: nor could his enjoyment consume more than a small part; so that it was impossible for any man, this way, to entrench upon the right of another, or acquire, to himself, a property, to the prejudice of his neighbour, who would still have room, for as good, and as large a possession (after the other had taken out his) as before it was appropriated. This measure did confine every man's possession, to a very moderate proportion, and such as he might appropriate to himself, without injury to anybody in the first ages of the world, when men were more in danger to be lost, by wandering from their company, in the then vast wilderness of the earth, than to be straitened for want of room to plant in. And the same measure may be allowed still, without prejudice to anybody, as full as the world seems. For supposing a man, or family, in the state they were, at [the] first peopling of the world by the children of Adam, or Noah; let him plant in some inland, vacant places of America, we shall find that the possessions he could make himself upon the measures we have given, would not be very large, nor, even to this day, prejudice the rest of mankind, or give them reason to complain, or think themselves injured by this man's encroachment, though the race of men have now spread themselves to all the corners of the world, and do infinitely exceed the small number [which] was at the beginning. Nay, the extent of ground is of so little value, without labour, that I have heard it affirmed, that in Spain itself, a man may be permitted to plough, sow, and reap, without being disturbed, upon land he has no other title to, but only his making use of it. But, on the contrary, the inhabitants think themselves beholden to him, who, by his industry on neglected, and consequently waste land, has increased the stock of corn, which they wanted. But be this as it will, which I lay no stress on; this I dare boldly affirm, that the same rule of propriety, (*viz.*) that every man should have as much as he could make use of, would hold still in the world, without straitening anybody, since there is land enough in the world to suffice double the inhabitants had not the invention of money, and the tacit agreement of men to put a value on it, introduced (by consent) larger possessions, and a right to them; which, how it has done, I shall, by and by, show more at large.

37. This is certain, that in the beginning, before the desire of having more than men needed, had altered the intrinsic value of things, which depends only on their usefulness to the life of man; or [men] had agreed, that a little piece of yellow metal, which would keep without wasting or decay, should be worth a great piece of flesh, or a whole heap of corn; though men had a right to appropriate, by their labour, each one to himself, as much of the things of nature, as he could use: yet this could not be much, nor to the prejudice of others, where the same plenty was still left, to those who would use the same industry. To which let me add, that he who appropriates land to himself by his labour, does not lessen but increase the common stock of mankind. For the provisions serving to the support of human life, produced by one acre of enclosed and cultivated land, are (to speak much within compass) ten times more, than those, which are yielded by an acre of land, of an equal richness, lying waste in common. And therefore he, that encloses land and has a greater plenty of the conveniences of life from ten acres, than he could have from a hundred left to nature, may truly be said, to give ninety acres to mankind. For his labour now supplies him with provisions out of ten acres, which were but the product of a hundred lying in common. I have here rated the improved land very low in making its product but as ten to one, when it is much nearer a hundred to one. For I ask whether in the wild woods and uncultivated waste of America left to nature, without any improvement, tillage or husbandry, a thousand acres [will] yield the needy and wretched inhabitants as many conveniences of life as ten acres of equally fertile land do in Devonshire where they are well cultivated?

Before the appropriation of land, he who gathered as much of the wild fruit, killed, caught, or tamed, as many of the beasts as he could; he that so employed his pains about any of the spontaneous products of nature, as any way to alter them, from the state which nature put them in, by placing any of his labour on them, did thereby acquire a propriety in them: but if they perished, in his possession, without their due use; if the fruits rotted, or the venison putrefied, before he could spend it, he offended against the common law of nature, and was liable to be punished; he invaded his neighbour's share, for he had no right, further than his use called for any of them, and they might serve to afford him conveniences of life.

38. The same measures governed the possession of land too: whatsoever he tilled and reaped, laid up and made use of, before it spoiled, that was his peculiar right; whatsoever he enclosed, and could feed, and make use of, the cattle and product was also his. But if either the grass of his enclosure rotted on the ground, or the fruit of his planting perished without gathering, and laying up, this part of the earth, notwithstanding his enclosure, was still to be looked on as waste, and might be the possession of any other. Thus, at the beginning, Cain might take as much ground as he could till, and make it his own land, and yet leave enough to Abel's sheep to feed on; a few acres would serve for both their possessions. But as families increased, and industry enlarged their stocks, their possessions enlarged with the need of them; but yet it was commonly without any fixed property in the ground they made use of, till they incorporated, settled themselves together, and built cities, and then, by consent, they came in time, to set out the bounds of their distinct territories, and agree on limits between them and their neighbours, and by laws within themselves, settled the properties of those of the same society. For we see, that in that part of the world which was first inhabited, and therefore like to be best peopled, even as low down as Abraham's time, they wandered with their flocks, and their herds, which was their substance, freely up and down; and this Abraham did, in a country where he was a stranger. Whence it is plain, that at least, a great part of the land lay in common; that the inhabitants valued it not, nor claimed property in any more than they made use of. But when there was not room enough in the same place, for their herds to feed together, they, by consent, as Abraham and Lot did (*Genesis* 13:5[-9]) separated and enlarged their pasture, where it best liked them. And for the same reason Esau went from his father, and his brother, and planted in Mount Seir (*Genesis* 36:6[-8]).

39. And thus, without supposing any private dominion, and property in Adam, over all the world, exclusive of all other men, which can no way be proved, nor anyone's property be made out from it; but supposing the world given as it was to the children of men in common, we see how labour could make men distinct titles

to several parcels of it, for their private uses; wherein there could be no doubt of right, no room for quarrel.

40. Nor is it so strange, as perhaps before consideration it may appear, that the property of labour should be able to overbalance the community of land. For 'tis labour indeed that puts the difference of value on everything; and let anyone consider, what the difference is between an acre of land planted with tobacco, or sugar, sown with wheat or barley; and an acre of the same land lying in common, without any husbandry upon it, and he will find, that the improvement of labour makes the far greater part of the value. I think it will be but a very modest computation to say, that of the products of the earth useful to the life of man nine tenths are the effects of labour: nay, if we will rightly estimate things as they come to our use, and cast up the several expenses about them, what in them is purely owing to nature, and what to labour, we shall find, that in most of them ninety-nine hundredths are wholly to be put on the account of labour.

41. There cannot be a clearer demonstration of anything, than several nations of the Americans are of this, who are rich in land, and poor in all the comforts of life; whom nature having furnished as liberally as any other people, with the materials of plenty, i.e. a fruitful soil, apt to produce in abundance, what might serve for food, raiment, and delight; yet for want of improving it by labour, have not one hundredth part of the conveniences we enjoy: and a king of a large and fruitful territory there feeds, lodges, and is clad worse than a day labourer in England.

42. To make this a little clearer, let us but trace some of the ordinary provisions of life, through their several progresses, before they come to our use, and see how much they receive of their value from human industry. Bread, wine and cloth, are things of daily use, and great plenty, yet notwithstanding, acorns, water, and leaves, or skins, must be our bread, drink and clothing, did not labour furnish us with these more useful commodities. For whatever bread is more worth than acorns, wine than water, and cloth or silk than leaves, skins, or moss, that is wholly owing to labour and industry. The one of these being the food and raiment which unassisted nature furnishes us with; the other provisions which our industry and pains prepare for us, which how much they exceed the other in value, when anyone hath computed, he

will then see, how much labour makes the far greatest part of the
value of things, we enjoy in this world: and the ground which
produces the materials, is scarce to be reckoned in, as any, or at
most, but a very small, part of it; so little, that even amongst us,
land that is left wholly to nature, that hath no improvement of
pasturage, tillage, or planting, is called, as indeed it is, waste; and
we shall find the benefit of it amount to little more than nothing.
This shows, how much numbers of men are to be preferred to
largeness of dominions, and that the increase of lands [hands?]
and the right employing of them is the great art of government.
And that prince who shall be so wise and godlike as by established
laws of liberty to secure protection and encouragement to the
honest industry of mankind against the oppression of power and
narrowness of party will quickly be too hard for his neighbours.
But this by the by. To return to the argument in hand.

43. An acre of land that bears here twenty bushels of wheat,
and another in America, which, with the same husbandry, would
do the like, are, without doubt, of the same natural, intrinsic
value. But yet the benefit mankind receives from the one, in a year,
is worth five pounds and from the other possibly not worth a
penny, if all the profit an Indian received from it were to be valued,
and sold here; at least, I may truly say, not one thousandth. 'Tis
labour then which puts the greatest part of value upon land,
without which it would scarcely be worth anything: 'tis to that
we owe the greatest part of all its useful products: for all that the
straw, bran, bread, of that acre of wheat, is more worth than the
product of an acre of as good land, which lies waste, is all the
effect of labour. For 'tis not barely the ploughman's pains, the
reaper's and thresher's toil, and the baker's sweat, [that] is to be
counted into the bread we eat; the labour of those who broke the
oxen, who digged and wrought the iron and stones, who felled
and framed the timber employed about the plough, mill, oven, or
any other utensils, which are a vast number, requisite to this corn,
from its being seed to be sown to its being made bread, must all
be charged on the account of labour, and received as an effect of
that: nature and the earth furnished only the almost worthless
materials, as in themselves. 'Twould be a strange catalogue of
things, that industry provided and made use of, about every loaf
of bread, before it came to our use, if we could trace them; iron,

wood, leather, bark, timber, stone, bricks, coals, lime, cloth, dyeing-drugs, pitch, tar, masts, ropes, and all the materials made use of in the ship, that brought any of the commodities made use of by any of the workmen, to any part of the work, all which, 'twould be almost impossible, at least too long, to reckon up.

44. From all which it is evident, that though the things of nature are given in common, yet man (by being master of himself, and proprietor of his own person, and the actions or labour of it) had still in himself the great foundation of property; and that which made up the great part of what he applied to the support or comfort of his being, when invention and arts had improved the conveniences of life, was perfectly his own, and did not belong in common to others.

45. Thus labour, in the beginning, gave a right of property, wherever anyone was pleased to employ it, upon what was common, which remained, a long while, the far greater part, and is yet more than mankind makes use of. Men, at first, for the most part, contented themselves with what unassisted nature offered to their necessities: and though afterwards, in some parts of the world, (where the increase of people and stock, with the use of money) had made land scarce, and so of some value, the several communities settled the bounds of their distinct territories, and by laws within themselves, regulated the properties of the private men of their society, and so, by compact and agreement, settled the property which labour and industry began; and the leagues that have been made between several states and kingdoms, either expressly or tacitly disowning all claim and right to the land in the others' possession, have, by common consent, given up their pretences to their natural common right, which originally they had to those countries, and so have, by positive agreement, settled a property amongst themselves, in distinct parts and parcels of the earth: yet there are still great tracts of ground to be found, which (the inhabitants thereof not having joined with the rest of mankind, in the consent of the use of their common money) lie waste, and are more than the people, who dwell on it, do, or can make use of, and so still lie in common. Though this can scarce happen amongst that part of mankind, that have consented to the use of money.

46. The greatest part of things really useful to the life of man,

and such as the necessity of subsisting made the first commoners of the world look after, as it doth the Americans now, are generally things of short duration; such as, if they are not consumed by use, will decay and perish of themselves: gold, silver, and diamonds, are things, that fancy or agreement hath put the value on, more than real use, and the necessary support of life. Now of those good things which nature hath provided in common, everyone had a right (as hath been said) to as much as he could use, and had a property in all that he could effect with his labour: all that his industry could extend to, to alter from the state nature had put it in, was his. He that gathered a hundred bushels of acorns or apples, had thereby a property in them; they were his goods as soon as gathered. He was only to look that he used them before they spoiled; else he took more than his share, and robbed others. And indeed it was a foolish thing, as well as dishonest, to hoard up more than he could make use of. If he gave away a part to anybody else, so that it perished not uselessly in his possession, these he also made use of. And if he also bartered away plums that would have rotted in a week, for nuts that would last good for his eating a whole year, he did no injury; he wasted not the common stock; destroyed no part of the portion of goods that belonged to others, so long as nothing perished uselessly in his hands. Again, if he would give his nuts for a piece of metal, pleased with its colour; or exchange his sheep for shells, or wool for a sparkling pebble or a diamond, and keep those by him all his life, he invaded not the right of others, he might heap up as much of these durable things as he pleased; the exceeding of the bounds of his just property not lying in the largeness of his possession, but the perishing of anything uselessly in it.

47. And thus came in the use of money, some lasting thing that men might keep without spoiling, and that by mutual consent men would take in exchange for the truly useful, but perishable supports of life.

48. And as different degrees of industry were apt to give men possessions in different proportions, so this invention of money gave them the opportunity to continue and enlarge them. For supposing an island, separate from all possible commerce with the rest of the world, wherein there were but a hundred families, but there were sheep, horses and cows, with other useful animals,

wholesome fruits, and land enough for corn for a hundred thousand times as many, but nothing in the island, either because of its commonness, or perishableness, fit to supply the place of money: what reason could anyone have there to enlarge his possessions beyond the use of his family, and a plentiful supply to its consumption, either in what their own industry produced, or they could barter for like perishable, useful commodities, with others? Where there is not something both lasting and scarce, and so valuable to be hoarded up, there men will not be apt to enlarge their possessions of land, were it never so rich, never so free for them to take. For I ask, what would a man value ten thousand, or a hundred thousand acres of excellent land, ready cultivated, and well stocked too with cattle, in the middle of the inland parts of America, where he had no hopes of commerce with other parts of the world, to draw money to him by the sale of the product? It would not be worth the enclosing, and we should see him give up again to the wild common of nature, whatever was more than would supply the conveniences of life to be had there for him and his family.

49. Thus in the beginning all the world was America, and more so than that is now; for no such thing as money was anywhere known. Find out something that hath the use and value of money amongst his neighbours, you shall see the same man will begin presently to enlarge his possessions.

50. But since gold and silver, being little useful to the life of man in proportion to food, raiment, and carriage, has its value only from the consent of men, whereof labour yet makes, in great part, the measure, it is plain, that men have agreed to disproportionate and unequal possession of the earth, they having by a tacit and voluntary consent found out a way, how a man may fairly possess more land than he himself can use the product of, by receiving in exchange for the overplus, gold and silver, which may be hoarded up without injury to anyone, these metals not spoiling or decaying in the hands of the possessor. This partage [division] of things, in an inequality of private possessions, men have made practicable out of the bounds of society, and without compact, only by putting a value on gold and silver and tacitly agreeing in the use of money. For in governments the laws regulate the right of property, and the possession of land is determined by positive constitutions.

51. And thus, I think, it is very easy to conceive without any difficulty, how labour could at first begin a title of property in the common things of nature, and how the spending it upon our uses bounded it. So that there could then be no reason of quarrelling about title, nor any doubt about the largeness of possession it gave. Right and conveniency went together; for as a man had a right to all he could employ his labour upon, so he had no temptation to labour for more than he could make use of. This left no room for controversy about the title, nor for encroachment on the right of others; what portion a man carved to himself, was easily seen; and it was useless as well as dishonest to carve himself too much, or take more than he needed.

Chapter 6
OF PATERNAL POWER

52. It may perhaps be censured as an impertinent criticism in a discourse of this nature, to find fault with words and names that have obtained in the world: and yet possibly it may not be amiss to offer new ones when the old are apt to lead men into mistakes, as this of paternal power probably has done, which seems so to place the power of parents over their children wholly in the father, as if the mother had no share in it, whereas if we consult reason or revelation, we shall find she hath an equal title. This may give one reason to ask, whether this might not be more properly called parental power. For whatever obligation nature and the right of generation lays on children, it must certainly bind them equal to both the concurrent causes of it. And accordingly we see the positive law of God everywhere joins them together, without distinction, when it commands the obedience of children, 'Honour thy father and thy mother' (*Exodus* 20:12), 'Whosoever curseth his father or his mother' (*Leviticus* 20:9), 'Ye shall fear every man his mother and his father' (*Leviticus* 19:3), 'Children obey your parents', etc. (*Ephesians* 6:1), is the style of the Old and New Testament.

53. Had but this one thing been well considered without looking any deeper into the matter, it might perhaps have kept men from running into those gross mistakes, they have made,

about this power of parents: which however it might, without any great harshness, bear the name of absolute dominion, and regal authority, when under the title of paternal power it seemed appropriated to the father, would yet have sounded but oddly, and in the very name shown the absurdity, if this supposed absolute power over children had been called parental, and thereby have discovered, that it belonged to the mother too; for it will but very ill serve the turn of those men who contend so much for the absolute power and authority of the fatherhood, as they call it, that the mother should have any share in it. And it would have but ill supported the monarchy they contend for, when by the very name it appeared that that fundamental authority from whence they would derive their government of a single person only, was not placed in one, but two persons jointly. But to let this of names pass.

54. Though I have said above, chapter 2, that all men by nature are equal, I cannot be supposed to understand all sorts of equality: age or virtue may give men a just precedency: excellency of parts and merit may place others above the common level: birth may subject some, and alliance or benefits others, to pay an observance to those to whom nature, gratitude or other respects may have made it due; and yet all this consists with the equality, which all men are in, in respect of jurisdiction or dominion one over another, which was the equality I there spoke of, as proper to the business in hand, being that equal right that every man hath, to his natural freedom, without being subjected to the will or authority of any other man.

55. Children, I confess are not born in this full state of equality, though they are born to it. Their parents have a sort of rule and jurisdiction over them when they come into the world, and for some time after, but 'tis but a temporary one. The bonds of this subjection are like the swaddling clothes they are wrapped up in, and supported by, in the weakness of their infancy. Age and reason as they grow up, loosen them till at length they drop quite off, and leave a man at his own free disposal.

56. Adam was created a perfect man, his body and mind in full possession of their strength and reason, and so was capable from the first instant of his being to provide for his own support and preservation, and govern his actions according to the dictates

of the law of reason which God had implanted in him. From him
the world is peopled with his descendants, who are all born
infants, weak and helpless, without knowledge or understanding.
But to supply the defects of this imperfect state, till the improvement of growth and age hath removed them, Adam and Eve, and
after them all parents were, by the law of nature, under an
obligation to preserve, nourish, and educate the children, they had
begotten, not as their own workmanship, but the workmanship
of their own Maker, the Almighty, to whom they were to be
accountable for them.

57. The law that was to govern Adam, was the same that was
to govern all his posterity, the law of reason. But his offspring
having another way of entrance into the world, different from
him, by a natural birth, that produced them ignorant and without
the use of reason, they were not presently under that law: for
nobody can be under a law, which is not promulgated to him; and
this law being promulgated or made known by reason only, he
that is not come to the use of his reason, cannot be said to be
under this law; and Adam's children being not presently as soon
as born, under this law of reason were not presently free. For law,
in its true notion, is not so much the limitation as the direction of
a free and intelligent agent to his proper interest, and prescribes
no further than is for the general good of those under that law.
Could they be happier without it, the law, as a useless thing would
of itself vanish; and that ill deserves the name of confinement
which hedges us in only from bogs and precipices. So that,
however it may be mistaken, the end of law is not to abolish or
restrain, but to preserve and enlarge freedom: for in all the states
of created beings capable of laws, where there is no law, there is
no freedom. For liberty is to be free from restraint and violence
from others which cannot be, where there is no law: but freedom
is not, as we are told, 'a liberty for every man to do what he lists':
(for who could be free, when every other man's humour might
domineer over him?) but a liberty to dispose, and order, as he lists,
his person, actions, possessions, and his whole property, within
the allowance of those laws under which he is; and therein not to
be subject to the arbitrary will of another, but freely follow his
own.

58. The power, then, that parents have over their children,

arises from that duty which is incumbent on them, to take care of their offspring, during the imperfect state of childhood. To inform the mind, and govern the actions of their yet ignorant nonage, till reason shall take its place, and ease them of that trouble, is what the children want, and the parents are bound to. For God having given man an understanding to direct his actions, has allowed him a freedom of will, and liberty of acting, as properly belonging thereunto, within the bounds of that law he is under. But whilst he is in an estate, wherein he has not understanding of his own to direct his will, he is not to have any will of his own to follow: he that understands for him, must will for him too; he must prescribe to his will, and regulate his actions; but when he comes to the estate that made his father a free man, the son is a free man too.

59. This holds in all the laws a man is under, whether natural or civil. Is a man under the law of nature? What made him free of that law? What gave him a free disposing of his property according to his own will, within the compass of that law? I answer; [a] state of maturity wherein he might be supposed capable to know that law, that so he might keep his actions within the bounds of it. When he has acquired that state, he is presumed to know how far that law is to be his guide, and how far he may make use of his freedom, and so comes to have it; till then, somebody else must guide him, who is presumed to know how far the law allows a liberty. If such a state of reason, such an age of discretion made him free, the same shall make his son free too. Is a man under the law of England? What made him free of that law? That is, to have the liberty to dispose of his actions and possessions according to his own will, within the permission of that law? A capacity of knowing that law. Which is supposed by that law, at the age of one and twenty years, and in some cases sooner. If this made the father free, it shall make the son free too. Till then we see the law allows the son to have no will, but he is to be guided by the will of his father or guardian, who is to understand for him. And if the father die, and fail to substitute a deputy in this trust, if he hath not provided a tutor to govern his son during his minority, during his want of understanding, the law takes care to do it; some other must govern him, and be a will to him, till he hath attained to a state of freedom and his understanding be fit to take the government of his will. But after

that, the father and son are equally free as much as tutor and pupil after nonage; equally subjects of the same law together, without any dominion left in the father over the life, liberty, or estate of his son, whether they be only in the state and under the law of nature, or under the positive laws of an established government.

60. But if through defects that may happen out of the ordinary course of nature, anyone comes not to such a degree of reason, wherein he might be supposed capable of knowing the law, and so living within the rules of it, he is never capable of being a free man, he is never let loose to the disposure of his own will (because he knows no bounds to it, has not understanding, its proper guide) but is continued under the tuition and government of others, all the time his own understanding is incapable of that charge. And so lunatics and idiots are never set free from the government of their parents; 'children, who are not as yet come unto those years whereat they may have; and innocents which are excluded by a natural defect from ever having'; thirdly, 'madmen, which for the present cannot possibly have the use of right reason to guide themselves, have for their guide, the reason that guideth other men which are tutors over them, to seek and procure their good for them', says Hooker (*Ecclesiastical Polity*, Bk I, Ch. 7 [p. 72]). All which seems no more than that duty, which God and nature has laid on man as well as other creatures, to preserve their offspring, till they can be able to shift for themselves, and will scarce amount to an instance or proof of parents' regal authority.

61. Thus we are born free, as we are born rational; not that we have actually the exercise of either: age that brings one, brings with it the other too. And thus we see how natural freedom and subjection to parents may consist together, and are both founded on the same principle. A child is free by his father's title, by his father's understanding, which is to govern him, till he hath it of his own. The freedom of a man at years of discretion, and the subjection of a child to his parents, whilst yet short of that age, are so consistent, and so distinguishable, that the most blinded contenders for monarchy, by right of fatherhood, cannot miss this difference, the most obstinate cannot but allow their consistency. For were their doctrine all true, were the right heir of Adam now known, and by that title settled a monarch in his throne, invested with all the absolute, unlimited power Sir Robert Filmer talks of;

if he should die as soon as his heir was born, must not the child, notwithstanding he were never so free,never so much sovereign, be in subjection to his mother and nurse, to tutors and governors, till age and education brought him reason and ability to govern himself, and others? The necessities of his life, the health of his body, and the information of his mind would require him to be directed by the will of others and not his own: and yet will anyone think, that this restraint and subjection were inconsistent with, or spoiled him of that liberty or sovereignty he had a right to, or gave away his empire to those who had the government of his nonage? This government over him only prepared him the better and sooner for it. If anybody should ask me, when my son is of age to be free? I shall answer, just when his monarch is of age to govern. 'But at what time', says the judicious Hooker (*Ecclesiastical Polity*, Bk I, Ch. 6 [p. 70]), 'a man may be said to have attained so far forth the use of reason, as sufficeth to make him capable of those laws whereby he is then bound to guide his actions; this is a great deal more easy for sense to discern, than for anyone by skill and learning to determine'.

62. Commonwealths themselves take notice of, and allow that there is a time when men are to begin to act like free men, and therefore till that time require not oaths of fealty, or allegiance, or other public owning of, or submission to the government of their countries.

63. The freedom then of man and liberty of acting according to his own will, is grounded on his having reason, which is able to instruct him in that law he is to govern himself by, and make him know how far he is left to the freedom of his own will. To turn him loose to an unrestrained liberty, before he has reason to guide him, is not the allowing him the privilege of his nature, to be free; but to thrust him out amongst brutes, and abandon him to a state as wretched, and as much beneath that of a man, as theirs. This is that which puts the authority into the parents' hands to govern the minority of their children. God hath made it their business to employ this care on their offspring, and hath placed in them suitable inclinations of tenderness and concern to temper this power, to apply it as his wisdom designed it, to the children's good, as long as they should need to be under it.

64. But what reason can hence advance this care of the parents

due to their offspring into an absolute arbitrary dominion of the father, whose power reaches no further, than by such a discipline as he finds most effectual to give such strength and health to their bodies, such vigour and rectitude to their minds, as may best fit his children to be most useful to themselves and others; and, if it be necessary to his condition, to make them work when they are able for their own subsistence. But in this power the mother too has her share with the father.

65. Nay, this power so little belongs to the father by any peculiar right of nature, but only as he is guardian of his children, that when he quits his care of them, he loses his power over them, which goes along with their nourishment and education, to which it is inseparably annexed, and it belongs as much to the foster-father of an exposed child, as to the natural father of another: so little power does the bare act of begetting give a man over his issue, if all his care ends there, and this be all the title he hath to the name and authority of a father. And what will become of this paternal power in that part of the world where one woman hath more than one husband at a time? Or in those parts of America where when the husband and wife part, which happens frequently, the children are all left to the mother, follow her, and are wholly under her care and provision? If the father die whilst the children are young, do they not naturally everywhere owe the same obedience to their mother, during their minority, as to their father were he alive? And will anyone say, that the mother hath a legislative power over her children? that she can make standing rules, which shall be of perpetual obligation, by which they ought to regulate all the concerns of their property, and bound their liberty all the course of their lives? Or can she enforce the observation of them with capital punishments? For this is the proper power of the magistrate, of which the father hath not so much as the shadow. His command over his children is but temporary, and reaches not their life or property. It is but a help to the weakness and imperfection of their nonage, a discipline necessary to their education: and though a father may dispose of his own possessions as he pleases, when his children are out of danger of perishing for want, yet his power extends not to the lives or goods, which either their own industry, or another's bounty has made theirs; nor to their liberty neither, when they are

once arrived to the enfranchisement of the years of discretion. The father's empire then ceases, and he can from thenceforward no more dispose of the liberty of his son, than that of any other man: and it must be far from an absolute or perpetual jurisdiction, from which a man may withdraw himself, having licence from divine authority to 'leave father and mother and cleave to his wife' [*Genesis* 2:24, *Matthew* 19:5].

66. But though there be a time when a child comes to be as free from subjection to the will and command of his father, as the father himself is free from subjection to the will of anybody else, and they are each under no other restraint but that which is common to them both, whether it be the law of nature, or municipal law of their country: yet this freedom exempts not a son from that honour which he ought, by the law of God and nature, to pay his parents. God having made the parents instruments in his great design of continuing the race of mankind, and the occasions of life to their children, as he hath laid on them an obligation to nourish, preserve, and bring up their offspring; so he has laid on the children a perpetual obligation of honouring their parents, which containing in it an inward esteem and reverence to be shown by all outward expressions, ties up the child from anything that may ever injure or affront, disturb, or endanger the happiness or life of those, from whom he received his; and engages him in all actions of defence, relief, assistance and comfort of those, by whose means he entered into being, and has been made capable of any enjoyments of life. From this obligation no state, no freedom, can absolve children. But this is very far from giving parents a power of command over their children, or an authority to make laws and dispose as they please, of their lives or liberties. 'Tis one thing to owe honour, respect, gratitude and assistance; another to require an absolute obedience and submission. The honour due to parents, a monarch in his throne owes his mother, and yet this lessens not his authority, nor subjects him to her government.

67. The subjection of a minor places in the father a temporary government, which terminates with the minority of the child: and the honour due from a child, places in the parents a perpetual right to respect, reverence, support and compliance too, more or less, as the father's care, cost and kindness in his education, has been more or less. This ends not with minority, but holds in all

parts and conditions of a man's life. The want of distinguishing these two powers; *viz.* that which the father hath in the right of tuition, during minority, and the right of honour all his life, may perhaps have caused a great part of the mistakes about this matter. For to speak properly of them, the first of these is rather the privilege of children, and duty of parents, than any prerogative of paternal power. The nourishment and education of their children, is a charge so incumbent on parents for their children's good, that nothing can absolve them from taking care of it. And though the power of commanding and chastising them go along with it, yet God hath woven into the principles of human nature such a tenderness for their offspring, that there is little fear that parents should use their power with too much rigour; the excess is seldom on the severe side, the strong bias of nature drawing the other way. And therefore God Almighty when he would express his gentle dealing with the Israelites, he tells them, that though he chastened them, 'he chastened them as a man chastens his son', (*Deuteronomy* 8:5), i.e. with tenderness and affection, and kept them under no severer discipline than what was absolutely best for them, and had been less kindness to have slackened. This is that power to which children are commanded obedience, that the pains and care of their parents may not be increased, or ill rewarded.

68. On the other side, honour and support, all that which gratitude requires to return for the benefits received by and from them is the indispensable duty of the child, and the proper privilege of the parents. This is intended for the parent's advantage, as the other is for the child's; though education, the parent's duty, seems to have most power, because the ignorance and infirmities of childhood stand in need of restraint and correction; which is a visible exercise of rule, and a kind of dominion. And that duty which is comprehended in the word honour, requires less obedience, though the obligation be stronger on grown than younger children. For who can think the command, 'children obey your parents', requires in a man that has children of his own the same submission to his father, as it does in his yet young children to him; and that by this precept he were bound to obey all his father's commands, if out of a conceit of authority he should have the indiscretion to treat him still as a boy?

69. The first part then of paternal power, or rather duty, which is education, belongs so to the father that it terminates at a certain season; when the business of education is over it ceases of itself, and is also alienable before. For a man may put the tuition of his son in other hands; and he that has made his son an apprentice to another, has discharged him, during that time, of a great part of his obedience both to himself and to his mother. But all the duty of honour, the other part, remains nevertheless entire to them; nothing can cancel that. It is so inseparable from them both, that the father's authority cannot dispossess the mother of this right, nor can any man discharge his son from honouring her that bore him. But both these are very far from a power to make laws, and enforcing them with penalties that may reach estate, liberty, limbs and life. The power of commanding ends with nonage; and though after that, honour and respect, support and defence, and whatsoever gratitude can oblige a man to for the highest benefits he is naturally capable of, be always due from a son to his parents; yet all this puts no sceptre into the father's hand, no sovereign power of commanding. He has no dominion over his son's property or actions, nor any right, that his will should prescribe to his son's in all things; however it may become his son in many things, not very inconvenient to him and his family, to pay a deference to it.

70. A man may owe honour and respect to an ancient, or wise man; defence to his child or friend; relief and support to the distressed; and gratitude to a benefactor, to such a degree, that all he has, all he can do, cannot sufficiently pay it: but all these give no authority, no right to anyone of making laws over him from whom they are owing. And 'tis plain, all this is due not to bare title of father; not only because, as has been said, it is owing to the mother too; but because these obligations to parents, and the degrees of what is required of children, may be varied, by the different care and kindness, trouble and expense, which is often employed upon one child, more than another.

71. This shows the reason how it comes to pass, that parents in societies, where they themselves are subjects, retain a power over their children, and have as much right to their subjection, as those who are in the state of nature, which could not possibly be, if all political power were only paternal, and that in truth they

were one and the same thing: for then, all paternal power being in the prince, the subject could naturally have none of it. But these two powers, political and paternal, are so perfectly distinct and separate; are built upon so different foundations, and given to so different ends, that every subject that is a father, has as much a paternal power over his children, as the prince has over his; and every prince that has parents owes them as much filial duty and obedience as the meanest of his subjects do to theirs; and can therefore contain not any part or degree of that kind of dominion, which a prince, or magistrate has over his subject.

72. Though the obligation on the parents to bring up their children, and the obligation on children to honour their parents, contain all the power on the one hand, and submission on the other, which are proper to this relation; yet there is another power ordinarily in the father, whereby he has a tie on the obedience of his children: which though it be common to him with other men, yet the occasions of showing it, almost constantly happening to fathers in their private families, and the instances of it elsewhere being rare, and less taken notice of, it passes in the world for a part of paternal jurisdiction. And this is the power men generally have to bestow their estates on those, who please them best. The possession of the father being the expectation and inheritance of the children ordinarily in certain proportions, according to the law and custom of each country; yet it is commonly in the father's power to bestow it with a more sparing or liberal hand, according as the behaviour of this or that child hath comported with his will and humour.

73. This is no small tie on the obedience of children: and there being always annexed to the enjoyment of land, a submission to the government of the country, of which that land is a part; it has been commonly supposed, that a father could oblige his posterity to that government, of which he himself was a subject, and that his compact held them; whereas, it being only a necessary condition annexed to the land, and the inheritance of an estate which is under that government, reaches only those who will take it on that condition, and so is no natural tie or engagement, but a voluntary submission. For every man's children being by nature as free as himself, or any of his ancestors ever were, may, whilst they are in that freedom, choose what society they will join

themselves to, what commonwealth they will put themselves under. But if they will enjoy the inheritance of their ancestors, they must take it on the same terms their ancestors had it, and submit to all the conditions annexed to such a possession. By this power indeed fathers oblige their children to obedience to themselves, even when they are past minority, and most commonly too subject them to this or that political power. But neither of these by any peculiar right of fatherhood, but by the reward they have in their hands to enforce and recompense such a compliance; and is no more power than what a Frenchman has over an Englishman, who by the hopes of an estate he will leave him, will certainly have a strong tie on his obedience: and if when it is left him, he will enjoy it, he must certainly take it upon the conditions annexed to the possession of land in that country where it lies, whether it be France or England.

74. To conclude then, though the father's power of commanding extends no further than the minority of his children, and to a degree only fit for the discipline and government of that age: and though that honour and respect, and all that which the Latins call piety, which they indispensably owe to their parents all their lifetimes, and in all estates, with all that support and defence [which] is due to them, gives the father no power of governing, i.e. making laws and enacting penalties on his children; though by all this he has no dominion over the property or actions of his son: yet 'tis obvious to conceive how easy it was in the first ages of the world, and in places still, where the thinness of people gives families leave to separate into unpossessed quarters, and they have room to remove and plant themselves in yet vacant habitations, for the father of the family to become the prince* of it;

*'It is no improbable opinion, therefore, which the arch-philosopher [Aristotle] was of, that the chief person in every household was always, as it were, a king: so when numbers of households joined themselves in civil societies together, kings were the first kind of governors amongst them, which is also, as it seemeth, the reason why the name of fathers continued still in them, who of fathers, were made rulers; as also the ancient custom of governors to do as Melchizedek, and being kings, to exercise the office of priests, which fathers did, at the first, grew perhaps by the same occasion. Howbeit, this is not the only kind of regiment [i.e. polity] that has been received in the world. The inconveniences of one kind have caused sundry other to be devised; so that in a word, all public regiment of what kind soever, seemeth evidently to have risen from the deliberate advice, consultation and composition between men, judging it convenient, and behoveful; there being no impossibility in nature, considered by itself, but that man might have lived without any public regiment' (Hooker, *Ecclesiastical Polity*, Bk I, Ch. 10 [p. 90]).

he had been a ruler from the beginning of the infancy of his children: and since without some government it would be hard for them to live together, it was likeliest it should, by the express or tacit consent of the children, when they were grown up, be in the father, where it seemed without any change barely to continue; when indeed nothing more was required to it, than the permitting the father to exercise alone in his family that executive power of the law of nature, which every free man naturally hath, and by that permission resigning up to him a monarchical power, whilst they remained in it. But that this was not by any paternal right, but only by the consent of his children, is evident from hence, that nobody doubts but if a stranger, whom chance or business had brought to his family, had there killed any of his children, or committed any other fact, he might condemn and put him to death, or otherwise have punished him as well as any of his children: which it was impossible he should do by virtue of any paternal authority over one, who was not his child, but by virtue of that executive power of the law of nature, which, as a man he had a right to: and he alone could punish him in his family, where the respect of his children had laid by the exercise of such a power, to give way to the dignity and authority, they were willing should remain in him, above the rest of his family.

75. Thus 'twas easy, and almost natural for children by a tacit, and scarce avoidable consent to make way for the father's authority and government. They had been accustomed in their childhood to follow his direction, and to refer their little differences to him, and when they were men, who fitter to rule them? Their little properties, and less covetousness seldom afforded greater controversies; and when any should arise, where could they have a fitter umpire than he, by whose care they had every one been sustained, and brought up, and who had a tenderness for them all? 'Tis no wonder, that they made no distinction betwixt minority, and full age; nor looked after one and twenty, or any other age, that might make them the free disposers of themselves and fortunes, when they could have no desire to be out of their pupillage. The government they had been under, during it, continued still to be more their protection than restraint: and they could nowhere find a greater security to their peace, liberties, and fortunes, than in the rule of a father.

76. Thus the natural fathers of families, by an insensible change, became the politic monarchs of them too: and as they chanced to live long, and leave able, and worthy heirs, for several successions, or otherwise; so they laid the foundations of hereditary, or elective kingdoms, under several constitutions, and manners, according as chance, contrivance, or occasions happened to mould them. But if princes have their titles in the father's right, and it be a sufficient proof of the natural right of fathers to political authority, because they commonly were those, in whose hands we find, *de facto*, the exercise of government: I say, if this argument be good, it will as strongly prove that all princes, nay princes only, ought to be priests, since 'tis as certain, that in the beginning, the father of the family was priest, as that he was ruler in his own household.

Chapter 7
OF POLITICAL OR CIVIL SOCIETY

77. God having made man such a creature, that, in his own judgment, it was not good for him to be alone, put him under strong obligations of necessity, convenience, and inclination to drive him into society, as well as fitted him with understanding and language to continue and enjoy it. The first society was between man and wife, which gave beginning to that between parents and children; to which, in time, that between master and servant came to be added: and though all these might, and commonly did meet together, and make up but one family, wherein the master or mistress of it had some sort of rule proper to a family; each of these, or all together came short of political society, as we shall see, if we consider the different ends, ties, and bounds of each of these.

78. Conjugal society is made by a voluntary compact between man and woman: and though it consist chiefly in such a communion of right in one another's bodies, as is necessary to its chief end, procreation; yet it draws with it mutual support, and assistance, and a communion of interest too, as necessary not only to unite their care, and affection, but also necessary to their common offspring, who have a right to be nourished and

maintained by them, till they are able to provide for themselves.

79. For the end of conjunction between male and female, being not barely procreation, but the continuation of the species, this conjunction betwixt male and female ought to last, even after procreation, so long as is necessary to the nourishment and support of the young ones, who are to be sustained by those that got them, till they are able to shift and provide for themselves. This rule, which the infinite wise Maker hath set to the works of his hands, we find the inferior creatures steadily obey. In those viviparous animals which feed on grass, the conjunction between male and female lasts no longer than the very act of copulation: because the teat of the dam being sufficient to nourish the young, till it be able to feed on grass, the male only begets, but concerns not himself for the female or young, to whose sustenance he can contribute nothing. But in beasts of prey the conjunction lasts longer: because the dam not being able well to subsist herself, and nourish her numerous offspring by her own prey alone, a more laborious, as well as more dangerous way of living, than by feeding on grass, the assistance of the male is necessary to the maintenance of their common family, which cannot subsist till they are able to prey for themselves, but by the joint care of male and female. The same is to be observed in all birds (except some domestic ones, where plenty of food excuses the cock from feeding, and taking care of the young brood) whose young needing food in the nest, the cock and hen continue mates, till the young are able to use their wing, and provide for themselves.

80. And herein I think lies the chief, if not the only reason, why the male and female in mankind are tied to a longer conjunction than other creatures, viz. because the female is capable of conceiving, and de facto is commonly with child again, and brings forth too a new birth long before the former is out of a dependency for support on his parents' help, and able to shift for himself, and has all the assistance [which] is due to him from his parents: whereby the father, who is bound to take care for those he hath begot, is under an obligation to continue in conjugal society with the same woman longer than other creatures, whose young being able to subsist of themselves, before the time of procreation returns again, the conjugal bond dissolves of itself, and they are

at liberty, till Hymen, at his usual anniversary season, summons them again to choose new mates. Wherein one cannot but admire the wisdom of the great Creator, who having given to man foresight and an ability to lay up for the future, as well as to supply the present necessity, hath made it necessary, that society of man and wife should be more lasting, than of male and female amongst other creatures; that so their industry might be encouraged, and their interest better united, to make provision, and lay up goods for their common issue, which uncertain mixture, or easy and frequent solutions of conjugal society would mightily disturb.

81. But though these are ties upon mankind, which make the conjugal bonds more firm and lasting in man, than the other species of animals; yet it would give one reason to enquire, why this compact, where procreation and education are secured, and inheritance taken care for, may not be made determinable, either by consent, or at a certain time, or upon certain conditions, as well as any other voluntary compacts, there being no necessity in the nature of the thing, nor to the ends of it, that it should always be for life; I mean, to such as are under no restraint of any positive law, which ordains all such contracts to be perpetual.

82. But the husband and wife, though they have but one common concern, yet having different understandings, will unavoidably sometimes have different wills too; it therefore being necessary, that the last determination, i.e. the rule, should be placed somewhere, it naturally falls to the man's share, as the abler and the stronger. But this reaching but to the things of their common interest and property, leaves the wife in the full and free possession of what by contract is her peculiar right, and gives the husband no more power over her life, than she has over his. The power of the husband being so far from that of an absolute monarch, that the wife has, in many cases, a liberty to separate from him; where natural right, or their contract allows it, whether that contract be made by themselves in the state of nature, or by the customs or laws of the country they live in; and the children upon such separation fall to the father or mother's lot, as such contract does determine.

83. For all the ends of marriage being to be obtained under politic government, as well as in the state of nature, the civil

magistrate doth not abridge the right, or power of either
naturally necessary to those ends, *viz.* procreation and mutual
support and assistance whilst they are together; but only decides any controversy that may arise between man and wife
about them. If it were otherwise, and that absolute sovereignty
and power of life and death naturally belonged to the husband,
and were necessary to the society between man and wife, there
could be no matrimony in any of those countries where the
husband is allowed no such absolute authority. But the ends of
matrimony requiring no such power in the husband, the condition of conjugal society put it not in him, it being not at all
necessary to that state. Conjugal society could subsist and
obtain its ends without it; nay, community of goods, and the
power over them, mutual assistance, and maintenance, and
other things belonging to conjugal society, might be varied and
regulated by that contract, which unites man and wife in that
society, as far as may consist with procreation and the bringing
up of children till they could shift for themselves; nothing being
necessary to any society, that is not necessary to the ends for
which it is made.

84. The society betwixt parents and children, and the distinct
rights and powers belonging respectively to them, I have treated
of so largely, in the foregoing chapter, that I shall not here need
to say anything of it. And I think it is plain, that it is far different
from a politic society.

85. Master and servant are names as old as history, but given
to those of far different condition; for a free man makes himself
a servant to another, by selling him for a certain time, the service
he undertakes to do, in exchange for wages he is to receive: and
though this commonly puts him into the family of his master, and
under the ordinary discipline thereof; yet it gives the master but
a temporary power over him, and no greater, than what is
contained in the contract between them. But there is another sort
of servants, which by a peculiar name we call slaves, who being
captives taken in a just war, are by the right of nature subjected
to the absolute dominion and arbitrary power of their masters.
These men having, as I say, forfeited their lives, and with it their
liberties, and lost their estates; and being in the state of slavery,
not capable of any property, cannot in that state be considered as

any part of civil society; the chief end whereof is the preservation of property.

86. Let us therefore consider a master of a family with all these subordinate relations of wife, children, servants and slaves united under the domestic rule of a family; which what resemblance soever it may have in its order, offices, and number too, with a little commonwealth, yet is very far from it, both in its constitution, power and end: or if it must be thought a monarchy, and the paterfamilias the absolute monarch in it, absolute monarchy will have but a very shattered and short power, when 'tis plain, by what has been said before, that the master of the family has a very distinct and differently limited power, both as to time and extent, over those several persons that are in it; for excepting the slave (and the family is as much a family, and his power as paterfamilias as great, whether there be any slaves in his family or no) he has no legislative power of life and death over any of them, and none too but what a mistress of a family may have as well as he. And he certainly can have no absolute power over the whole family, who has but a very limited one over every individual in it. But how a family, or any other society of men, differ from that, which is properly political society, we shall best see, by considering wherein political society itself consists.

87. Man being born, as has been proved, with a title to perfect freedom, and an uncontrolled enjoyment of all the rights and privileges of the law of nature, equally with any other man, or number of men in the world, hath by nature a power, not only to preserve his property, that is, his life, liberty and estate, against the injuries and attempts of other men; but to judge of, and punish the breaches of that law in others, as he is persuaded the offence deserves, even with death itself, in crimes where the heinousness of the fact, in his opinion, requires it. But because no political society can be, nor subsist without having in itself the power to preserve the property, and in order thereunto punish the offences of all those of that society; there, and there only is political society, where every one of the members hath quitted this natural power, resigned it up into the hands of the community in all cases that exclude him not from appealing for protection to the law established by it. And thus all private judgment of every particular member being excluded, the community comes to be umpire, by

settled standing rules, indifferent, and the same to all parties; and by men having authority from the community, for the execution of those rules, decides all the differences that may happen between any members of that society, concerning any matter of right; and punishes those offences, which any member hath committed against the society, with such penalties as the law has established: whereby it is easy to discern who are, and who are not, in political society together. Those who are united into one body, and have a common established law and judicature to appeal to, with authority to decide controversies between them, and punish offenders, are in civil society one with another: but those who have no such common appeal, I mean on earth, are still in the state of nature, each being, where there is no other, judge for himself, and executioner; which is, as I have before showed it, the perfect state of nature.

88. And thus the commonwealth comes by a power to set down, what punishment shall belong to the several transgressions which they think worthy of it, committed amongst the members of that society, (which is the power of making laws) as well as it has the power to punish any injury done unto any of its members, by anyone that is not of it, (which is the power of war and peace;) and all this for the preservation of the property of all the members of that society, as far as is possible. But though every man who has entered into civil society, and is become a member of any commonwealth, has thereby quitted his power to punish offences against the law of nature, in prosecution of his own private judgment; yet with the judgment of offences which he has given up to the legislative in all cases, where he can appeal to the magistrate, he has given a right to the commonwealth to employ his force, for the execution of the judgments of the commonwealth, whenever he shall be called to it; which indeed are his own judgments, they being made by himself, or his representative. And herein we have the original of the legislative and executive power of civil society, which is to judge by standing laws how far offences are to be punished, when committed within the commonwealth; and also to determine, by occasional judgments founded on the present circumstances of the fact, how far injuries from without are to be vindicated, and in both these to employ all the force of all the members when there shall be need.

89. Wherever therefore any number of men are so united into one society, as to quit every one his executive power of the law of nature, and to resign it to the public, there and there only is a political, or civil society. And this is done wherever any number of men, in the state of nature, enter into society to make one people, one body politic under one supreme government, or else when anyone joins himself to, and incorporates with any government already made. For hereby he authorizes the society, or which is all one, the legislative thereof to make laws for him as the public good of the society shall require; to the execution whereof, his own assistance (as to his own decrees) is due. And this puts men out of a state of nature into that of a commonwealth, by setting up a judge on earth, with authority to determine all the controversies, and redress the injuries, that may happen to any member of the commonwealth; which judge is the legislative, or magistrates appointed by it. And wherever there are any number of men, however associated, that have no such decisive power to appeal to, there they are still in the state of nature.

90. Hence it is evident, that absolute monarchy, which by some men is counted the only government in the world, is indeed inconsistent with civil society, and so can be no form of civil government at all. For the end of civil society, being to avoid, and remedy those inconveniences of the state of nature, which necessarily follow from every man's being judge in his own case, by setting up a known authority, to which everyone of that society may appeal upon any injury received, or controversy that may arise, and which everyone of the society ought to obey;* wherever any persons are, who have not such an authority to appeal to, for the decision of any difference between them, there those persons are still in the state of nature. And so is every absolute prince in respect of those who are under his dominion.

91. For he being supposed to have all, both legislative and executive power in himself alone, there is no judge to be found, no appeal lies open to anyone, who may fairly, and indifferently,

*'The public power of all society is above every soul contained in the same society; and the principal use of that power is to give laws unto all that are under it, which laws in such cases we must obey, unless there be reason showed which may necessarily enforce, that the law of reason, or of God, doth enjoin the contrary' (Hooker, *Ecclesiastical Polity*, Bk I, Ch. 16 [p. 125]).

and with authority decide, and from whose decision relief and redress may be expected of any injury or inconveniency, that may be suffered from the prince or by his order: so that such a man, however entitled, Czar, or Grand Signior, or how you please, is as much in the state of nature, with all under his dominion, as he is with the rest of mankind. For wherever any two men are, who have no standing rule, and common judge to appeal to on earth for the determination of controversies of right betwixt them, there they are still in the state of nature, and under all the inconveniences of it,* with only this woeful difference to the subject, or rather slave of an absolute prince: that whereas, in the ordinary state of nature, he has a liberty to judge of his right, and according to the best of his power, to maintain it; now whenever his property is invaded by the will and order of his monarch, he has not only no appeal, as those in society ought to have, but as if he were degraded from the common state of rational creatures, is denied a liberty to judge of, or to defend his right, and so is exposed to all the misery and inconveniences that a man can fear from one, who being in the unrestrained state of nature, is yet corrupted with flattery, and armed with power.

92. For he that thinks absolute power purifies men's bloods, and corrects the baseness of human nature, need read but the history of this, or any other age to be convinced of the contrary. He that would have been insolent and injurious in the woods of America, would not probably be much better in a throne; where perhaps learning and religion shall be found out to justify all, that he shall do to his subjects, and the sword presently silence all those that dare question it. For what the protection of absolute monar-

---

*'To take away all such mutual grievances, injuries and wrongs', i.e. such as attend men in the state of nature, 'there was no way but only by growing into composition and agreement amongst themselves, by ordaining some kind of government public, and by yielding themselves subject thereunto, that unto whom they granted authority to rule and govern, by them the peace, tranquility, and happy estate of the rest might be procured. Men always knew that where force and injury was offered, they might be defenders of themselves; they knew that however men may seek their own commodity; yet if this were done with injury unto others, it was not to be suffered, but by all men, and all good means to be withstood. Finally, they knew that no man might in reason take upon him to determine his own right, and according to his own determination proceed in maintenance thereof, in as much as every man is towards himself, and them whom he greatly affects, partial; and therefore that strifes and troubles would be endless, except they gave their common consent, all to be ordered by some, whom they should agree upon, without which consent there would be no reason that one man should take upon him to be lord or judge over another' (Hooker, *Ecclesiastical Polity*, Bk I, Ch. 10 [pp. 89–90]).

chy is, what kind of fathers of their countries it makes princes to be, and to what a degree of happiness and security it carries civil society, where this sort of government is grown to perfection, he that will look into the late relation of Ceylon [by Robert Knox], may easily see.

93. In absolute monarchies indeed, as well as other governments of the world, the subjects have an appeal to the law, and judges to decide any controversies, and restrain any violence that may happen betwixt the subjects themselves, one amongst another. This everyone thinks necessary, and believes he deserves to be thought a declared enemy to society and mankind, who should go about to take it away. But whether this be from a true love of mankind and society, and such a charity as we owe all one to another, there is reason to doubt. For this is no more, than what every man who loves his own power, profit, or greatness, may, and naturally must do, [to] keep those animals from hurting or destroying one another who labour and drudge only for his pleasure and advantage, and so are taken care of, not out of any love the master has for them, but love of himself, and the profit they bring him. For if it be asked, what security, what fence is there in such a state, against the violence and oppression of this absolute ruler? The very question can scarce be borne. They are ready to tell you, that it deserves death only to ask after safety. Betwixt subject and subject, they will grant, there must be measures, laws, and judges, for their mutual peace and security: but as for the ruler, he ought to be absolute, and is above all such circumstances: because he has power to do more hurt and wrong, 'tis right when he does it. To ask how you may be guarded from harm, or injury on that side where the strongest hand is to do it, is presently the voice of faction and rebellion. As if when men quitting the state of nature entered into society, they agreed that all of them but one, should be under the restraint of laws, but that he should still retain all the liberty of the state of nature, increased with power, and made licentious by impunity. This is to think that men are so foolish that they take care to avoid what mischiefs may be done them by polecats, or foxes, but are content, nay think it safety, to be devoured by lions.

94. But whatever flatterers may talk to amuse people's understandings, it hinders not men, from feeling: and when they

perceive, that any man, in what station soever, is out of the bounds of the civil society which they are of; and that they have no appeal on earth against any harm they may receive from him, they are apt to think themselves in the state of nature, in respect of him, whom they find to be so; and to take care as soon as they can, to have that safety and security in civil society, for which it was first instituted, and for which only they entered into it. And therefore, though perhaps at first, (as shall be showed more at large hereafter in the following part of this discourse) some one good and excellent man, having got a pre-eminency amongst the rest, had this deference paid to his goodness and virtue, as to a kind of natural authority, that the chief rule, with arbitration of their differences, by a tacit consent devolved into his hands, without any other caution, but the assurance they had of his uprightness and wisdom: yet when time, giving authority, and (as some men would persuade us) sacredness to customs, which the negligent, and unforeseeing innocence of the first ages began, had brought in successors of another stamp, the people finding their properties not secure under the government, as then it was, (whereas government has no other end but the preservation of property) could never be safe nor at rest, nor think themselves in civil society, till the legislature was placed in collective bodies of men, call them senate, parliament, or what you please.* By which means every single person became subject, equally with other the meanest men, to those laws, which he himself, as part of the legislative had established: nor could anyone, by his own authority, avoid the force of the law, when once made, nor by any pretence of superiority, plead exemption, thereby to license his own, or the miscarriages of any of his dependants. No man in civil society can be exempted from the laws of it.** For if any man may do, what he thinks fit, and there be no appeal on earth, for redress or

* 'At the first, when some certain kind of regiment [i.e. polity] was once appointed, it may be that nothing was then further thought upon for the manner of governing, but all permitted unto their wisdom and discretion, which were to rule, till by experience they found this for all parts very inconvenient, so as the thing which they had devised for a remedy, did indeed but increase the sore, which it should have cured. They saw, that to live by one man's will, became the cause of all men's misery. This constrained them to come unto laws wherein all men might see their duty beforehand, and know the penalties of transgressing them' (Hooker, *Ecclesiastical Polity*, Bk I, Ch. 10 [p. 91]).

** 'Civil law being the act of the whole body politic, doth therefore overrule each several part of the same body' (Hooker, *ibid.* [p. 98]).

security against any harm he shall do; I ask, whether he be not perfectly still in the state of nature, and so can be no part or member of that civil society: unless anyone will say, the state of nature and civil society are one and the same thing, which I have never yet found anyone so great a patron of anarchy as to affirm.

Chapter 8
OF THE BEGINNING OF
POLITICAL SOCIETIES

95. Men being, as has been said, by nature, all free, equal and independent, no one can be put out of this estate, and subjected to the political power of another, without his own consent. The only way whereby anyone divests himself of his natural liberty, and puts on the bonds of civil society is by agreeing with other men to join and unite into a community, for their comfortable, safe, and peaceable living one amongst another, in a secure enjoyment of their properties, and a greater security against any that are not of it. This any number of men may do, because it injures not the freedom of the rest; they are left as they were in the liberty of the state of nature. When any number of men have so consented to make one community or government, they are thereby presently incorporated, and make one body politic, wherein the majority have a right to act and conclude the rest.

96. For when any number of men have, by the consent of every individual, made a community, they have thereby made that community one body, with a power to act as one body, which is only by the will and determination of the majority. For that which acts any community, being only the consent of the individuals of it, and it being necessary to that which is one body to move one way; it is necessary the body should move that way whither the greater force carries it, which is the consent of the majority: or else it is impossible it should act or continue one body, one community, which the consent of every individual that united into it, agreed that it should; and so everyone is bound by that consent to be concluded by the majority. And therefore we see that in assemblies empowered to act by positive laws where no

number is set by that positive law which empowers them, the act
of the majority passes for the act of the whole, and of course
determines, as having by the law of nature and reason, the power
of the whole.

97. And thus every man, by consenting with others to make
one body politic under one government, puts himself under an
obligation to everyone of that society, to submit to the determination of the majority, and to be concluded by it; or else this
original compact, whereby he with others incorporates into one
society, would signify nothing, and be no compact, if he be left
free, and under no other ties, than he was in before in the state of
nature. For what appearance would there be of any compact?
What new engagement if he were no further tied by any decrees
of the society, than he himself thought fit, and did actually consent
to? This would be still as great a liberty, as he himself had before
his compact, or anyone else in the state of nature hath, who may
submit himself and consent to any acts of it if he thinks fit.

98. For if the consent of the majority shall not in reason, be
received, as the act of the whole, and conclude every individual;
nothing but the consent of every individual can make anything to
be the act of the whole: but such a consent is next impossible ever
to be had, if we consider the infirmities of health, and avocations
of business, which in a number, though much less than that of a
commonwealth, will necessarily keep many away from the public
assembly. To which if we add the variety of opinions, and
contrariety of interests, which unavoidably happen in all collec-
tions of men, the coming into society upon such terms, would be
only like Cato's coming into the theatre, only to go out again.
Such a constitution as this would make the mighty Leviathan of
a shorter duration, than the feeblest creatures; and not let it outlast
the day it was born in: which cannot be supposed, till we can
think, that rational creatures should desire and constitute societies
only to be dissolved. For where the majority cannot conclude the
rest, there they cannot act as one body, and consequently will be
immediately dissolved again.

99. Whosoever therefore out of a state of nature unite into a
community, must be understood to give up all the power, necessary to the ends for which they unite into society, to the majority
of the community, unless they expressly agreed in any number

greater than the majority. And this is done by barely agreeing to unite into one political society, which is all the compact that is, or needs be, between the individuals, that enter into, or make up a commonwealth. And thus that, which begins and actually constitutes any political society, is nothing but the consent of any number of free men capable of a majority to unite and incorporate into such a society. And this is that, and that only, which did, or could give beginning to any lawful government in the world.

100. To this I find two objections made.

First, that there are no instances to be found in [hi]story of a company of men independent and equal one amongst another, that met together, and in this way began and set up a government.

Secondly, 'tis impossible of right that men should do so, because all men being born under government, they are to submit to that, and are not at liberty to begin a new one.

101. To the first there is this to answer. That it is not at all to be wondered, that history gives us but a very little account of men, that lived together in the state of nature. The inconveniences of that condition, and the love, and want of society no sooner brought any number of them together, but they presently united and incorporated, if they designed to continue together. And if we may not suppose men ever to have been in the state of nature, because we hear not much of them in such a state, we may as well suppose the armies of Salmanasser, or Xerxes were never children, because we hear little of them, till they were men, and embodied in armies. Government is everywhere antecedent to records, and letters seldom come in amongst a people, till a long continuation of civil society has, by other more necessary arts provided for their safety, ease, and plenty. And then they begin to look after the history of their founders, and search into their original, when they have outlived the memory of it. For 'tis with commonwealths as with particular persons, they are commonly ignorant of their own births and infancies: and if they know anything of their original, they are beholding, for it, to the accidental records, that others have kept of it. And those that we have, of the beginning of any polities in the world, excepting that of the Jews, where God himself immediately interposed, and which favours not at all paternal dominion, are all either plain instances of such a

beginning, as I have mentioned, or at least have manifest footsteps of it.

102. He must show a strange inclination to deny evident matter of fact, when it agrees not with his hypothesis, who will not allow that the beginning of Rome and Venice were by the uniting together of several men free and independent one of another, amongst whom there was no natural superiority or subjection. And if Josephus Acosta's word may be taken, he tells us, that in many parts of America there was no government at all. 'There are great and apparent conjectures', says he, 'that these men', speaking of those of Peru, 'for a long time had neither kings not commonwealths, but lived in troops, as they do this day in Florida, the Cheriquanas, those of Brazil, and many other nations, which have no certain kings, but as occasion is offered in peace and war, they choose their captains as they please' (Bk. I, Ch. 25). If it be said, that every man there was born subject to his father, or the head of his family. That the subjection due from a child to a father, took not away his freedom of uniting into what political society he thought fit, has been already proved. But be that as it will, these men, 'tis evident, were actually free; and whatever superiority some politicians now would place in any of them, they themselves claimed it not; but by consent were all equal, till by the same consent they set rulers over themselves. So that their politic societies all began from a voluntary union, and the mutual agreement of men freely acting in the choice of their governors, and forms of government.

103. And I hope those who went away from Sparta with Palantus, mentioned by Justin, Bk. 3, Ch. 4, will be allowed to have been free men independent one of another, and to have set up a government over themselves, by their own consent. Thus I have given several examples out of history, of people free and in the state of nature, that being met together incorporated and began a commonwealth. And if the want of such instances be an argument to prove that government were not, nor could not be so begun, I suppose the contenders for paternal empire were better [to] let it alone, than urge it against natural liberty. For if they can give so many instances out of history, of governments begun upon paternal right, I think (though at best an argument from what has been, to what should of right be, has no great force) one might,

without any great danger, yield them the cause. But if I might advise them in the case, they would do well not to search too much into the original of governments, as they have begun *de facto*, lest they should find at the foundation of most of them, something very little favourable to the design they promote, and such a power as they contend for.

104. But to conclude, reason being plain on our side, that men are naturally free, and the examples of history showing, that the governments of the world, that were begun in peace, had their beginning laid on that foundation, and were made by the consent of the people; there can be little room for doubt, either where the right is, or what has been the opinion, or practice of mankind, about the first erecting of governments.

105. I will not deny, that if we look back as far as history will direct us, towards the original of commonwealths, we shall generally find them under the government and administration of one man. And I am also apt to believe, that where a family was numerous enough to subsist by itself, and continued entire together, without mixing with others, as it often happens, where there is much land and few people, the government commonly began in the father. For the father having, by the law of nature, the same power with every man else to punish, as he thought fit, any offences against that law, might thereby punish his transgressing children even when they were men, and out of their pupillage; and they were very likely to submit to his punishment, and all join with him against the offender, in their turns, giving him thereby power to execute his sentence against any transgression, and so in effect make him the law-maker, and governor over all, that remained in conjunction with his family. He was fittest to be trusted; paternal affection secured their property, and interest under his care, and the custom of obeying him, in their childhood, made it easier to submit to him, rather than to any other. If therefore they must have one to rule them, as government is hardly to be avoided amongst men that live together; who [was] so likely to be the man, as he that was their common father; unless negligence, cruelty, or any other defect of mind, or body made him unfit for it? But when either the father died, and left his next heir for want of age, wisdom, courage, or any other qualities, less fit for rule: or where several families met, and consented to

continue together: there, 'tis not to be doubted, but they used their natural freedom, to set up him, whom they judged the ablest, and most likely, to rule well over them. Conformable hereunto we find the people of America, who (living out of the reach of the conquering swords, and spreading domination of the two great empires of Peru and Mexico) enjoyed their own natural freedom, though, *ceteris paribus* [other things being equal], they commonly prefer the heir of their deceased king; yet if they find him [in] any way weak, or incapable, they pass him by and set up the stoutest and bravest man for their ruler.

106. Thus, though looking back as far as records give us any account of peopling the world, and the history of nations, we commonly find the government to be in one hand, yet it destroys not that, which I affirm, (*viz.*) that the beginning of politic society depends upon the consent of the individuals, to join into and make one society; who, when they are thus incorporated, might set up what form of government they thought fit. But this having given occasion to men to mistake, and think, that by nature government was monarchical, and belonged to the father, it may not be amiss here to consider, why people in the beginning generally pitched upon this form, which though perhaps the father's pre-eminency might in the first institution of some commonwealths, give a rise to, and place, in the beginning, the power in one hand; yet it is plain, that the reason, that continued the form of government in a single person, was not any regard, or respect to paternal authority; since all petty monarchies, that is, almost all monarchies, near their original, have been commonly, at least upon occasion, elective.

107. First then, in the beginning of things, the father's government of the childhood of those sprung from him, having accustomed them to the rule of one man, and taught them that where it was exercised with care and skill, with affection and love to those under it, it was sufficient to procure and preserve to men all the political happiness they sought for, in society. It was no wonder, that they should pitch upon, and naturally run into that form of government, which from their infancy they had been all accustomed to; and which, by experience they had found both easy and safe. To which, if we add, that monarchy being simple, and most obvious to men, whom neither experience had in-

structed in forms of government, nor the ambition or insolence of empire had taught to beware of the encroachments of prerogative, or the inconveniences of absolute power, which monarchy, in succession, was apt to lay claim to, and bring upon them, it was not at all strange, that they should not much trouble themselves to think of methods of restraining any exorbitances of those, to whom they had given the authority over them, and of balancing the power of government, by placing several parts of it in different hands. They had neither felt the oppression of tyrannical dominion, nor did the fashion of the age, nor their possessions, or way of living (which afforded little matter for covetousness or ambition) give them any reason to apprehend or provide against it: and therefore 'tis no wonder they put themselves into such a frame of government, as was not only as I said, most obvious and simple, but also best suited to their present state and condition; which stood more in need of defence against foreign invasions and injuries, than of multiplicity of laws. The equality of a simple poor way of living confining their desires within the narrow bounds of each man's small property made few controversies and so no need of many laws to decide them: and there wanted not of justice where there were but few trespasses, and few offenders. Since then those, who liked one another so well as to join into society, cannot but be supposed to have some acquaintance and friendship together, and some trust one in another; they could not but have greater apprehensions of others, than of one another: and therefore their first care and thought cannot but be supposed to be, how to secure themselves against foreign force. 'Twas natural for them to put themselves under a frame of government, which might best serve to that end; and choose the wisest and bravest man to conduct them in their wars, and lead them out against their enemies, and in this chiefly be their ruler.

108. Thus we see, that the kings of the Indians in America, which is still a pattern of the first ages in Asia and Europe, whilst the inhabitants were too few for the country, and want of people and money gave men no temptation to enlarge their possessions of land, or contest for wider extent of ground, are little more than generals of their armies; and though they command absolutely in war, yet at home and in time of peace they exercise very little

dominion, and have but a very moderate sovereignty, the resolutions of peace and war, being ordinarily either in the people, or in a council. Though the war itself, which admits not of plurality of governors, naturally devolves the command into the king's sole authority.

109. And thus in Israel itself, the chief business of their judges, and first kings seems to have been to be captains in war, and leaders of their armies; which, (besides what is signified by 'going out and in before the people' [*Numbers* 27:17], which was, to march forth to war, and home again in [i.e. at] the heads of their forces) appears plainly in the story of Jephtha. The Ammonites making war upon Israel, the Gileadites, in fear send to Jephtha, a bastard of their family, whom they had cast off, and article with him, if he will assist them against the Ammonites, to make him their ruler; which they do in these words, 'and the people made him head and captain over them' (*Judges* 11:11), which was, as it seems, all one as to be judge. 'And he judged Israel' (*Judges* 12:7) that is, was their captain-general, 'six years'. So when Jotham upbraids the Shechemites with the obligation they had to Gideon, who had been their judge and ruler, he tells them, 'he fought for you, and adventured his life far, and delivered you out of the hands of Midian' (*Judges* 9:17). Nothing mentioned of him, but what he did as a general, and indeed that is all is found in his history, or in any of the rest of the judges. And Abimelech particularly is called king, though at most he was but their general. And when, being weary of the ill conduct of Samuel's sons, the children of Israel desired a king, 'like all the nations to judge them, and to go out before them, and to fight their battles' (1 Samuel 8:20), God granting their desire, says to Samuel, 'I will send thee a man, and thou shalt anoint him to be captain over my people Israel, that he may save my people out of the hands of the Philistines' (9:16). As if the only business of a king had been to lead out their armies, and fight in their defence; and accordingly at his inauguration, pouring a vial of oil upon him, declares to Saul, that 'the Lord had anointed him to be captain over his inheritance' (10:1). And therefore those, who after Saul's being solemnly chosen and saluted king by the tribes at Mizpah, were unwilling to have him their king, make no other objection but this, 'how shall this man save us?' (verse 27) as if they should have

said, 'this man is unfit to be our king, not having skill and conduct enough in war, to be able to defend us'. And when God resolved to transfer the government to David, it is in these words, 'but now thy kingdom shall not continue: the Lord hath sought him a man after his own heart, and the Lord hath commanded him to be captain over his people' (13:14). As if the whole kingly authority were nothing else but to be their general: and therefore the tribes who had stuck to Saul's family, and opposed David's reign, when they came to Hebron with terms of submission to him, they tell him, amongst other arguments they had to submit to him as to their king, that he was in effect their king in Saul's time, and therefore they had no reason but to receive him as their king now. 'Also' (say they) 'in time past, when Saul was king over us, thou wast he that leddest out and broughtest in Israel, and the Lord said unto thee, thou shalt feed my people Israel, and thou shalt be a captain over Israel' [2 Samuel 5:2].

110. Thus, whether a family by degrees grew up into a commonwealth, and the fatherly authority being continued on to the elder son, everyone in his turn growing up under it, tacitly submitted to it, and the easiness and equality of it not offending anyone, everyone acquiesced, till time seemed to have confirmed it, and settled a right of succession by prescription: or whether several families, or the descendants of several families, whom chance, neighbourhood, or business brought together, uniting into society, the need of a general, whose conduct might defend them against their enemies in war, and the great confidence the innocence and sincerity of that poor but virtuous age (such as are almost all those which begin governments, that ever come to last in the world) gave men one of another, made the first beginners of commonwealths generally put the rule into one man's hand, without any other express limitation or restraint, but what the nature of the thing, and the end of government required: whichever of these it was, that at first put the rule into the hands of a single person, certain it is that nobody was ever entrusted with it but for the public good and safety, and to those ends in the infancies of commonwealths those who had it, commonly used it: and unless they had done so, young societies could not have subsisted: without such nursing fathers tender and careful of the public weal, all governments would have sunk under the weakness

and infirmities of their infancy; and the prince and the people had soon perished together.

111. But though the golden age (before vain ambition, and *amor sceleratus habendi* [the accursed love of possessing], evil concupiscence, had corrupted men's minds into a mistake of true power and honour) had more virtue, and consequently better governors, as well as less vicious subjects; and there was then no stretching prerogative on the one side to oppress the people; nor consequently on the other any dispute about privilege, to lessen or restrain the power of the magistrate;* and so no contest betwixt rulers and people about governors or government: yet, when ambition and luxury, in future ages would retain and increase the power, without doing the business, for which it was given, and aided by flattery, taught princes to have distinct and separate interests from their people, men found it necessary to examine more carefully the original and rights of government; and to find out ways to restrain the exorbitances; and prevent the abuses of that power which they having entrusted in another's hands only for their own good, they found was made use of to hurt them.

112. Thus we may see how probable it is, that people that were naturally free, and by their own consent either submitted to the government of their father, or united together, out of different families to make a government, should generally put the rule into one man's hands, and choose to be under the conduct of a single person, without so much as by express conditions limiting or regulating his power, which they thought safe enough in his honesty and prudence. Though they never dreamed of monarchy being *jure divino* [by divine right], which we never heard of among mankind, till it was revealed to us by the divinity of this last age; nor ever allowed paternal power to have a right to dominion, or to be the foundation of all government. And thus much may suffice to show, that as far as we have any light from history, we

---

*'At first, when some certain kind of regiment [i.e. polity] was once approved, it may be nothing was then further thought upon for the manner of governing, but all permitted unto their wisdom and discretion which were to rule, till by experience they found this for all parts very inconvenient, so as the thing which they had devised for a remedy, did indeed but increase the sore which it should have cured. They saw, that to live by one man's will, became the cause of all men's misery. This constrained them to come unto laws wherein all men might see their duty beforehand, and know the penalties of transgressing them' (Hooker, *Ecclesiastical Polity*, Bk I, Ch. 10 [p. 91]).

have reason to conclude, that all peaceful beginnings of government have been laid in the consent of the people. I say peaceful, because I shall have occasion in another place to speak of conquest, which some esteem a way of beginning of governments.

The other objection I find urged against the beginning of polities, in the way I have mentioned, is this, *viz.*

113. That all men being born under government, some or other, it is impossible any of them should ever be free, and at liberty to unite together, and begin a new one, or ever be able to erect a lawful government.

If this argument be good; I ask, how came so many lawful monarchies into the world? For if anybody, upon this supposition, can show me any one man in any age of the world free to begin a lawful monarchy; I will be bound to show him ten other free men at liberty, at the same time to unite and begin a new government under a regal, or any other form. It being demonstration, that if anyone, born under the dominion of another, may be so free as to have a right to command others in a new and distinct empire; everyone that is born under the dominion of another may be so free too, and may become a ruler, or subject, of a distinct separate government. And so by this their own principle, either all men, however born, are free, or else there is but one lawful prince, one lawful government in the world. And then they have nothing to do but barely to show us, which that is. Which when they have done, I doubt not but all mankind will easily agree to pay obedience to him.

114. Though it be a sufficient answer to their objection to show, that it involves them in the same difficulties that it doth those they use it against; yet I shall endeavour to discover the weakness of this argument a little further.

'All men', say they, 'are born under government, and therefore they cannot be at liberty to begin a new one. Everyone is born a subject to his father, or his prince, and is therefore under the perpetual tie of subjection and allegiance'. 'Tis plain mankind never owned nor considered any such natural subjection, that they were born in, to one or to the other, that tied them, without their own consents, to a subjection to them and their heirs.

115. For there are no examples so frequent in history, both sacred and profane, as those of men withdrawing themselves, and

their obedience, from the jurisdiction they were born under, and the family or community they were bred up in, and setting up new governments in other places; from whence sprang all that number of petty commonwealths in the beginning of ages, and which always multiplied, as long as there was room enough, till the stronger, or more fortunate swallowed the weaker; and those great ones again breaking to pieces, dissolved into lesser dominions. All which are so many testimonies against paternal sovereignty, and plainly prove, that it was not the natural right of the father descending to his heirs, that made governments in the beginning, since it was impossible, upon that ground, there should have been so many little kingdoms; all must have been but only one universal monarchy, if men had not been at liberty to separate themselves from their families, and the government, be it what it will, that was set up in it, and go and make distinct commonwealths and other governments, as they thought fit.

116. This has been the practice of the world from its first beginning to this day: nor is it now any more hindrance to the freedom of mankind, that they are born under constituted and ancient polities, that have established laws and set forms of government, than if they were born in the woods, amongst the unconfined inhabitants that ran loose in them. For those who would persuade us, that by being born under any government, we are naturally subjects to it, and have no more any title or pretence to the freedom of the state of nature, have no other reason (bating [i.e. excepting] that of paternal power, which we have already answered) to produce for it, but only because our fathers or progenitors passed away their natural liberty, and thereby bound up themselves and their posterity to a perpetual subjection to the government, which they themselves submitted to. 'Tis true, that whatever engagements or promises anyone has made for himself, he is under the obligation of them, but cannot by any compact whatsoever, bind his children or posterity. For his son, when a man, being altogether as free as the father, any act of the father can no more give away the liberty of the son, than it can of anybody else: he may indeed annex such conditions to the land, he enjoyed as a subject of any commonwealth, as may oblige his son to be of that community, if he will enjoy those possessions which were his father's; because that estate

being his father's property, he may dispose or settle it as he pleases.

117. And this has generally given the occasion to mistake in this matter; because commonwealths not permitting any part of their dominions to be dismembered, nor to be enjoyed by any but those of their community, the son cannot ordinarily enjoy the possessions of his father, but under the same terms his father did; by becoming a member of the society: whereby he puts himself presently under the government, he finds there established, as much as any other subject of that commonwealth. And thus the consent of free men, born under government, which only makes them members of it, being given separately in their turns, as each comes to be of age, and not in a multitude together; people take no notice of it, and thinking it not done at all, or not necessary, conclude they are naturally subjects as they are men.

118. But, 'tis plain, governments themselves understand it otherwise; they claim no power over the son, because of that they had over the father; nor look on children as being their subjects, by their fathers being so. If a subject of England have a child by an Englishwoman in France, whose subject is he? Not the king of England's; for he must have leave to be admitted to the privileges of it. Nor the king of France's; for how then has his father a liberty to bring him away, and breed him as he pleases? And whoever was judged as a traitor or deserter, if he left, or warred against a country, for being barely born in it of parents that were aliens there? 'Tis plain then, by the practice of governments themselves, as well as by the law of right reason, that a child is born a subject of no country or government. He is under his father's tuition and authority, till he come to age of discretion; and then he is a free man, at liberty what government he will put himself under; what body politic he will unite himself to. For if an Englishman's son, born in France, be at liberty, and may do so, 'tis evident there is no tie upon him by his father being a subject of this kingdom; nor is he bound up, by any compact of his ancestors. And why then hath not his son, by the same reason, the same liberty, though he be born anywhere else? Since the power that a father hath naturally over his children, is the same, wherever they be born; and the ties of natural obligations, are not bounded by the positive limits of kingdoms and commonwealths.

119. Every man being, as has been showed, naturally free, and nothing being able to put him into subjection to any earthly power, but only his own consent; it is to be considered, what shall be understood to be a sufficient declaration of a man's consent, to make him subject to the laws of any government. There is a common distinction of an express and a tacit consent, which will concern our present case. Nobody doubts but an express consent, of any man, entering into any society, makes him a perfect member of that society, a subject of that government. The difficulty is, what ought to be looked upon as a tacit consent, and how far it binds, i.e. how far anyone shall be looked on to have consented, and thereby submitted to any government, where he has made no expressions of it at all. And to this I say, that every man, that hath any possession, or enjoyment, of any part of the dominions of any government, doth thereby give his tacit consent, and is as far forth obliged to obedience to the laws of that government, during such enjoyment, as anyone under it; whether this his possession be of land, to him and his heirs for ever, or a lodging only for a week; or whether it be barely travelling freely on the highway; and in effect, it reaches as far as the very being of anyone within the territories of that government.

120. To understand this the better, it is fit to consider, that every man, when he, at first, incorporates himself into any commonwealth, he, by his uniting himself thereunto, annexed also, and submits to the community those possessions, which he has, or shall acquire, that do not already belong to any other government. For it would be a direct contradiction, for anyone, to enter into society with others for the securing and regulating of property: and yet to suppose his land, whose property is to be regulated by the laws of the society, should be exempt from the jurisdiction of that government, to which he himself the proprietor of the land, is a subject. By the same act therefore, whereby anyone unites his person, which was before free, to any commonwealth; by the same he unites his possessions, which were before free, to it also; and they become, both of them, person and possession, subject to the government and dominion of that commonwealth, as long as it hath a being. Whoever therefore, from thenceforth, by inheritance, purchase, permission, or otherways enjoys any part of the

land, so annexed to, and under the government of that common-wealth, must take it with the condition it is under; that is, of submitting to the government of the commonwealth, under whose jurisdiction it is, as far forth, as any subject of it.

121. But since the government has a direct jurisdiction only over the land, and reaches the possessor of it, (before he has actually incorporated himself in the society) only as he dwells upon, and enjoys that: the obligation anyone is under, by virtue of such enjoyment, to submit to the government, begins and ends with the enjoyment; so that whenever the owner, who has given nothing but such a tacit consent to the government, will, by donation, sale, or otherwise, quit the said possession, he is at liberty to go and incorporate himself into any other common-wealth, or to agree with others to begin a new one, *in vacuis locis* [in empty places], in any part of the world, they can find free and unpossessed: whereas he, that has once, by actual agreement, and any express declaration, given his consent to be of any commonweal, is perpetually and indispensably obliged to be and remain unalterably a subject to it, and can never be again in the liberty of the state of nature; unless by any calamity, the government, he was under, comes to be dissolved; or else by some public act cuts him off from being any longer a member of it.

122. But submitting to the laws of any country, living quietly, and enjoying privileges and protection under them, makes not a man a member of that society: this is only a local protection and homage due to, and from all those, who, not being in a state of war, come within the territories belonging to any government, to all parts whereof the force of its law extends. But this no more makes a man a member of that society, a perpetual subject of that commonwealth, than it would make a man a subject to another in whose family he found it convenient to abide for some time; though, whilst he continued in it, he were obliged to comply with the laws, and submit to the government he found there. And thus we see, that foreigners, by living all their lives under another government, and enjoying the privileges and protection of it, though they are bound, even in conscience, to submit to its administration, as far forth as any denizen; yet do not thereby come to be subjects or members of that commonwealth. Nothing

can make any man so, but his actually entering into it by positive engagement, and express promise and compact. This is that, which I think, concerning the beginning of political societies, and that consent which makes anyone a member of any commonwealth.

Chapter 9
OF THE ENDS OF POLITICAL SOCIETY
AND GOVERNMENT

123. If man in the state of nature be so free, as has been said; if he be absolute lord of his own person and possessions, equal to the greatest, and subject to nobody, why will he part with his freedom? Why will he give up this empire, and subject himself to the dominion and control of any other power? To which 'tis obvious to answer, that though in the state of nature he hath such a right, yet the enjoyment of it is very uncertain, and constantly exposed to the invasion of others. For all being kings as much as he, every man his equal, and the greater part no strict observers of equity and justice, the enjoyment of the property he has in this state is very unsafe, very insecure. This makes him willing to quit this condition, which however free, is full of fears and continual dangers: and 'tis not without reason, that he seeks out, and is willing to join in society with others who are already united, or have a mind to unite for the mutual preservation of their lives, liberties and estates, which I call by the general name, property.

124. The great and chief end therefore, of men's uniting into commonwealths, and putting themselves under government, is the preservation of their property. To which in the state of nature there are many things wanting.

First, there wants an established, settled, known law, received and allowed by common consent to be the standard of right and wrong, and the common measure to decide all controversies between them. For though the law of nature be plain and intelligible to all rational creatures; yet men being biased by their interest, as well as ignorant for want of study of it, are not apt to allow of it as a law binding to them in the application of it to their particular cases.

125. Secondly, in the state of nature there wants a known and indifferent judge, with authority to determine all differences according to the established law. For everyone in that state being both judge and executioner of the law of nature, men being partial to themselves, passion and revenge is very apt to carry them too far, and with too much heat, in their own cases; as well as negligence, and unconcernedness, to make them too remiss, in other men's.

126. Thirdly, in the state of nature there often wants power to back and support the sentence when right, and to give it due execution. They who by any injustice offended, will seldom fail, where they are able, by force to make good their injustice: such resistance many times makes the punishment dangerous, and frequently destructive, to those who attempt it.

127. Thus mankind, notwithstanding all the privileges of the state of nature, being but in an ill condition, while they remain in it, are quickly driven into society. Hence it comes to pass, that we seldom find any number of men live any time together in this state. The inconveniences, that they are therein exposed to, by the irregular and uncertain exercise of the power every man has of punishing the transgressions of others, make them take sanctuary under the established laws of government, and therein seek the preservation of their property. 'Tis this make them so willingly give up everyone his single power of punishing to be exercised by such alone as shall be appointed to it amongst them; and by such rules as the community, or those authorized by them to that purpose, shall agree on. And in this we have the original right and rise of both the legislative and executive power, as well as of the governments and societies themselves.

128. For in the state of nature, to omit the liberty he has of innocent delights, a man has two powers.

The first is to do whatsoever he thinks fit for the preservation of himself and others within the permission of the law of nature; by which law common to them all, he and all the rest of mankind are one community, make up one society distinct from all other creatures. And were it not for the corruption, and viciousness of degenerate men, there would be no need of any other; no necessity that men should separate from this great and natural community, and by positive agreements combine into smaller and divided associations.

The other power a man has in the state of nature, is the power to punish the crimes committed against that law. Both these he gives up, when he joins in a private, if I may so call it, or particular political society, and incorporates into any commonwealth, separate from the rest of mankind.

129. The first power, *viz.* of doing whatsoever he thought fit for the preservation of himself, and the rest of mankind, he gives up to be regulated by laws made by the society, so far forth as the preservation of himself, and the rest of that society shall require; which laws of the society in many things confine the liberty he had by the law of nature.

130. Secondly, the power of punishing he wholly gives up, and engages his natural force, (which he might before employ in the execution of the law of nature, by his own single authority, as he thought fit) to assist the executive power of the society, as the law thereof shall require. For being now in a new state, wherein he is to enjoy many conveniences, from the labour, assistance, and society of others in the same community, as well as protection from its whole strength; he is to part also with as much of his natural liberty in providing for himself, as the good, prosperity, and safety of the society shall require: which is not only necessary, but just; since the other members of the society do the like.

131. But though men when they enter into society, give up the equality, liberty, and executive power they had in the state of nature, into the hands of the society, to be so far disposed of by the legislative, as the good of the society shall require; yet it being only with an intention in everyone the better to preserve himself his liberty and property; (for no rational creature can be supposed to change his condition with an intention to be worse) the power of the society, or legislative constituted by them, can never be supposed to extend further than the common good; but is obliged to secure everyone's property by providing against those three defects above mentioned, that made the state of nature so unsafe and uneasy. And so whoever has the legislative or supreme power of any commonwealth, is bound to govern by established standing laws, promulgated and known to the people, and not by extemporary decrees; by indifferent and upright judges, who are to

decide controversies by those laws; and to employ the force of the community at home, only in the execution of such laws, or abroad to prevent or redress foreign injuries, and secure the community from inroads and invasion. And all this to be directed to no other end, but the peace, safety, and public good of the people.

Chapter 10
OF THE FORMS OF A COMMONWEALTH

132. The majority having, as has been showed, upon men's first uniting into society, the whole power of the community, naturally in them, may employ all that power in making laws for the community from time to time, and executing those laws by officers of their own appointing; and then the form of the government is a perfect democracy: or else may put the power of making laws into the hands of a few select men, and their heirs or successors; and then it is an oligarchy: or else into the hands of one man, and then it is a monarchy: if to him and his heirs, it is a hereditary monarchy: if to him only for life, but upon his death the power only of nominating a successor to return to them; an elective monarchy. And so accordingly of these the community may make compounded and mixed forms of government, as they think good. And if the legislative power be at first given by the majority to one or more persons only for their lives, or any limited time, and then the supreme power to revert to them again; when it is so reverted, the community may dispose of it again anew into what hands they please, and so constitute a new form of government. For the form of government depending upon the placing of supreme power, which is the legislative, it being impossible to conceive that an inferior power should prescribe to a superior, or any but the supreme make laws, according as the power of making laws is placed, such is the form of the commonwealth.

133. By 'commonwealth', I must be understood all along to mean, not a democracy, or any form of government, but any independent community which the Latins signified by the word *civitas*, to which the word which best answers in our language, is 'commonwealth', and most properly expresses such a society of men, which 'community' or 'city' in English does not, for there

may be subordinate communities in a government; and 'city' amongst us has a quite different notion from 'commonwealth'; and therefore to avoid ambiguity, I crave leave to use the word 'commonwealth' in that sense, in which I find it used by King James the First, and I take it to be its genuine signification; which if anybody dislike, I consent with him to change it for a better.

Chapter 11
OF THE EXTENT OF THE
LEGISLATIVE POWER

134. The great end of men's entering into society, being the enjoyment of their properties in peace and safety, and the great instrument and means of that being the laws established in that society; the first and fundamental positive law of all commonwealths, is the establishing of the legislative power; as the first and fundamental natural law, which is to govern even the legislative itself, is the preservation of the society, and (as far as will consist with the public good) of every person in it. This legislative is not only the supreme power of the commonwealth, but sacred and unalterable in the hands where the community have once placed it; nor can any edict of anybody else, in which form soever conceived, or by what power soever backed, have the force and obligation of a law, which has not its sanction from that legislative, which the public has chosen and appointed. For without this the law could not have that, which is absolutely necessary to its being a law, the consent of the society, over whom nobody can have a power to make laws, but by their own consent,* and by

*'The lawful power of making laws to command whole politic societies of men belonging so properly unto the same entire societies, that for any prince or potentate of what kind soever upon earth, to exercise the same of himself, and not by express commission immediately and personally received from God, or else by authority derived at the first from their consent, upon whose persons they impose laws, it is no better than mere tyranny. Laws they are not therefore which public approbation hath not made so' (Hooker, *Ecclesiastical Polity*, Bk I, Ch. 10 [p. 93]). 'Of this point therefore we are to note, that since men naturally have no full and perfect power to command whole politic multitudes of men, therefore utterly without our consent, we could in such sort be at no man's commandment living. And to be commanded we do consent when that society, whereof we be a part, hath at any time before consented, without revoking the same after by the like universal agreement. [...] Laws therefore human, of what kind soever, are available by consent' (*Ibid.*)

authority received from them; and therefore all the obedience, which by the most solemn ties anyone can be obliged to pay, ultimately terminates in this supreme power, and is directed by those laws which it enacts: nor can any oaths to any foreign power whatsoever, or any domestic subordinate power, discharge any member of the society from his obedience to the legislative, acting pursuant to their trust, nor oblige him to any obedience contrary to the laws so enacted, or further than they do allow; it being ridiculous to imagine one can be tied ultimately to obey any power in the society, which is not the supreme.

135. Though the legislative, whether placed in one or more, whether it be always in being, or only by intervals, though it be the supreme power in every commonwealth; yet,

First, it is not, nor can possibly be absolutely arbitrary over the lives and fortunes of the people. For it being but the joint power of every member of the society given up to that person, or assembly, which is legislator, it can be no more than those persons had in a state of nature before they entered into society, and gave up to the community. For nobody can transfer to another more power than he has in himself; and nobody has an absolute arbitrary power over himself, or over any other, to destroy his own life, or take away the life or property of another. A man, as has been proved, cannot subject himself to the arbitrary power of another; and having in the state of nature no arbitrary power over the life, liberty, or possession of another, but only so much as the law of nature gave him for the preservation of himself, and the rest of mankind; this is all he doth, or can give up to the commonwealth, and by it to the legislative power, so that the legislative can have no more than this. Their power in the utmost bounds of it, is limited to the public good of the society.* It is a power, that hath

* 'Two foundations there are which bear up public societies, the one a natural inclination, whereby all men desire sociable life and fellowship; the other an order, expressly or secretly agreed upon, touching the manner of their union in living together; the latter is that which we call the law of a commonweal, the very soul of a politic body, the parts whereof are by law animated, held together, and set on work in such actions as the common good requireth. Laws politic, ordained for external order and regiment amongst men, are never framed as they should be, unless presuming the will of man to be inwardly obstinate, rebellious, and averse from all obedience to the sacred laws of his nature; in a word, unless presuming man to be in regard of his depraved mind, little better than a wild beast, they do accordingly provide notwithstanding, so to frame his outward actions, that they be no hindrance unto the common good, for which societies are instituted. Unless they do this they are not perfect' (Hooker, *Ecclesiastical Polity*, Bk I, Ch. 10 [pp. 87–8]).

no other end but preservation, and therefore can never have a right to destroy, enslave, or designedly to impoverish the subjects. The obligations of the law of nature, cease not in society, but only in many cases are drawn closer, and have by human laws known penalties annexed to them, to enforce their observation. Thus the law of nature stands as an eternal rule to all men, legislators as well as others. The rules that they make for other men's actions, must, as well as their own and other men's actions, be conformable to the law of nature, i.e. to the will of God, of which that is a declaration, and the fundamental law of nature being the preservation of mankind, no human sanction can be good, or valid against it.

136. Secondly, the legislative, or supreme authority, cannot assume to itself a power to rule by extemporary arbitrary decrees,* but is bound to dispense justice, and decide the rights of the subject by promulgated standing laws, and known authorized judges. For the law of nature being unwritten, and so nowhere to be found but in the minds of men, they who through passion or interest shall mis-cite, or misapply it, cannot so easily be convinced of their mistake where there is no established judge: and so it serves not, as it ought, to determine the rights, and fence the properties of those that live under it, especially where everyone is judge, interpreter, and executioner of it too, and that in his own case: and he that has right on his side, having ordinarily but his own single strength, hath not force enough to defend himself from injuries, or to punish delinquents. To avoid these inconveniences which disorder men's properties in the state of nature, men unite into societies, that they may have the united strength of the whole society to secure and defend their properties, and may have standing rules to bound it, by which everyone may know what is his. To this end it is that men give up all their natural power to the society which they enter into, and the community put the legislative power into such hands as they think fit, with this trust, that they shall be governed by declared laws, or else their peace,

---

* 'Human laws are measures in respect of men, whose actions they must direct, howbeit such measures they are as have also their higher rules to be measured by, which rules are two, the law of God, and the law of nature; so that laws human must be made according to the general laws of nature, and without contradiction to any positive law of Scripture, otherwise they are ill made' ([Hooker, *Ecclesiastical Polity*], Bk III, Ch. 9). 'To constrain men to anything inconvenient doth seem unreasonable' (*Ibid.*, Bk I, Ch. 10 [p. 92]).

quiet, and property will still be at the same uncertainty, as it was in the state of nature.

137. Absolute arbitrary power, or governing without settled standing laws, can neither of them consist with the ends of society and government, which men would not quit the freedom of the state of nature for, and tie themselves up under, were it not to preserve their lives, liberties and fortunes; and by stated rules of right and property to secure their peace and quiet. It cannot be supposed that they should intend, had they a power so to do, to give to any one, or more, an absolute arbitrary power over their persons and estates, and put a force into the magistrate's hand to execute his unlimited will arbitrarily upon them: this were to put themselves into a worse condition than the state of nature, wherein they had a liberty to defend their right against the injuries of others, and were upon equal terms of force to maintain it, whether invaded by a single man, or many in combination. Whereas by supposing they have given up themselves to the absolute arbitrary power and will of a legislator, they have disarmed themselves, and armed him, to make a prey of them when he pleases. He being in a much worse condition who is exposed to the arbitrary power of one man, who has the command of 100,000 than he that is exposed to the arbitrary power of 100,000 single men: nobody being secure, that his will, who has such a command, is better, than that of other men, though his force be 100,000 times stronger. And therefore whatever form the commonwealth is under, the ruling power ought to govern by declared and received laws, and not by extemporary dictates and undetermined resolutions. For then mankind will be in a far worse condition, than in the state of nature, if they shall have armed one or a few men with the joint power of a multitude, to force them to obey at pleasure the exorbitant and unlimited decrees of their sudden thoughts, or unrestrained, and till that moment unknown wills without having any measures set down which may guide and justify their actions. For all the power the government has, being only for the good of the society, as it ought not to be arbitrary and at pleasure, so it ought to be exercised by established and promulgated laws: that both the people may know their duty, and be safe and secure within the limits of the law, and the rulers too kept within their due bounds, and not to be tempted, by the power

they have in their hands, to employ it to such purposes, and by such measures, as they would not have known, and own not willingly.

138. Thirdly, the supreme power cannot take from any man any part of his property without his own consent. For the preservation of property being the end of government, and that for which men enter into society, it necessarily supposes and requires, that the people should have property, without which they must be supposed to lose that by entering into society, which was the end for which they entered into it, too gross an absurdity for any man to own. Men therefore in society having property, they have such a right to the goods, which by the law of the community are theirs, that nobody hath a right to take their substance, or any part of it from them, without their own consent; without this, they have no property at all. For I have truly no property in that, which another can by right take from me, when he pleases, against my consent. Hence it is a mistake to think, that the supreme or legislative power of any commonwealth, can do what it will, and dispose of the estates of the subject arbitrarily, or take any part of them at pleasure. This is not much to be feared in governments where the legislative consists, wholly or in part, in assemblies which are variable, whose members upon the dissolution of the assembly, are subjects under the common laws of their country, equally with the rest. But in governments, where the legislative is in one lasting assembly always in being, or in one man, as in absolute monarchies, there is danger still, that they will think themselves to have a distinct interest, from the rest of the community; and so will be apt to increase their own riches and power, by taking, what they think fit, from the people. For a man's property is not at all secure, though there be good and equitable laws to set the bounds of it, between him and his fellow subjects, if he who commands those subjects, have power to take from any private man, what part he pleases of his property, and use and dispose of it as he thinks good.

139. But government into whatsoever hands it is put, being as I have before showed, entrusted with this condition, and for this end, that men might have and secure their properties, the prince or senate, however it may have power to make laws for the regulating of property between the subjects one amongst another, yet can never have a power to take to themselves the whole or any

part of the subjects' property, without their own consent. For this would be in effect to leave them no property at all. And to let us see, that even absolute power, where it is necessary, is not arbitrary by being absolute, but is still limited by that reason, and confined to those ends, which required it in some cases to be absolute, we need look no further than the common practice of martial discipline. For the preservation of the army, and in it of the whole commonwealth, requires an absolute obedience to the command of every superior officer, and it is justly death to disobey or dispute the most dangerous or unreasonable of them: but yet we see, that neither the sergeant, that could command a soldier to march up to the mouth of a cannon, or stand in a breach, where he is almost sure to perish, can command that soldier to give him one penny of his money; nor the general, that can condemn him to death for deserting his post, or for not obeying the most desperate orders, can yet with all his absolute power of life and death, dispose of one farthing of that soldier's estate, or seize one jot of his goods; whom yet he can command anything, and hang for the least disobedience. Because such a blind obedience is necessary to that end for which the commander has his power, *viz.* the preservation of the rest; but the disposing of his goods has nothing to do with it.

140. 'Tis true, governments cannot be supported without great charge, and 'tis fit everyone who enjoys his share of the protection, should pay out of his estate his proportion of the maintenance of it. But still it must be with his own consent, i.e. the consent of the majority, giving it either by themselves, or their representatives chosen by them. For if anyone shall claim a power to lay and levy taxes on the people, by his own authority, and without such consent of the people, he thereby invades the fundamental law of property, and subverts the end of government. For what property have I in that which another may by right take, when he pleases to himself?

141. Fourthly, the legislative cannot transfer the power of making laws to any other hands. For it being but a delegated power from the people, they, who have it, cannot pass it over to others. The people alone can appoint the form of the commonwealth, which is by constituting the legislative, and appointing in whose hands that shall be. And when the people have said, 'we

will submit to rules, and be governed by laws made by such men, and in such forms', nobody else can say other men shall make laws for them; nor can the people be bound by any laws but such as are enacted by those, whom they have chosen, and authorized to make laws for them. The power of the legislative being derived from the people by a positive voluntary grant and institution, can be no other, than what that positive grant conveyed, which being only to make laws, and not to make legislators, the legislative can have no power to transfer their authority of making laws, and place it in other hands.

142. These are the bounds which the trust that is put in them by the society, and the law of God and nature, have set to the legislative power of every commonwealth, in all forms of government.

First, they are to govern by promulgated established laws, not to be varied in particular cases, but to have one rule for rich and poor, for the favourite at court, and the countryman at plough.

Secondly, these laws also ought to be designed for no other end ultimately than the good of the people.

Thirdly, they must not raise taxes on the property of the people, without the consent of the people, given by themselves, or their deputies. And this properly concerns only such governments where the legislative is always in being, or at least where the people have not reserved any part of the legislative to deputies, to be from time to time chosen by themselves.

Fourthly, the legislative neither must nor can transfer the power of making laws to anybody else, or place it anywhere but where the people have.

Chapter 12
OF THE LEGISLATIVE, EXECUTIVE,
AND FEDERATIVE POWER OF THE COMMONWEALTH

143. The legislative power is that which has a right to direct how the force of the commonwealth shall be employed for preserving the community and the members of it. But because those laws which are constantly to be executed, and whose force is always to continue, may be made in a little time; therefore there

is no need, that the legislative should be always in being, not having always business to do. And because it may be too great a temptation to human frailty apt to grasp at power, for the same persons who have the power of making laws, to have also in their hands the power to execute them, whereby they may exempt themselves from obedience to the laws they make, and suit the law, both in its making and execution, to their own private advantage, and thereby come to have a distinct interest from the rest of the community, contrary to the end of society and government: therefore in well ordered commonwealths, where the good of the whole is so considered, as it ought, the legislative power is put into the hands of divers persons who duly assembled, have by themselves, or jointly with others, a power to make laws, which when they have done, being separated again, they are themselves subject to the laws, they have made; which is a new and near tie upon them, to take care, that they make them for the public good.

144. But because the laws, that are at once, and in a short time made, have a constant and lasting force, and need a perpetual execution, or an attendance thereunto: therefore 'tis necessary there should be a power always in being, which should see to the execution of the laws that are made, and remain in force. And thus the legislative and executive power come often to be separated.

145. There is another power in every commonwealth, which one may call natural, because it is that which answers to the power every man naturally had before he entered into society. For though in a commonwealth the members of it are distinct persons still in reference to one another, and as such are governed by the laws of the society; yet in reference to the rest of mankind, they make one body, which is, as every member of it before was, still in the state of nature with the rest of mankind. Hence it is, that the controversies that happen between any man of the society with those that are out of it, are managed by the public; and an injury done to a member of their body, engages the whole in the reparation of it. So that under this consideration, the whole community is one body in the state of nature, in respect of all other states or persons out of its community.

146. This therefore contains the power of war and peace, leagues and alliances, and all the transactions, with all persons and communities without the commonwealth, and may be called

federative, if anyone pleases. So the thing be understood, I am indifferent as to the name.

147. These two powers, executive and federative, though they be really distinct in themselves, yet one comprehending the execution of the municipal laws of the society within itself, upon all that are parts of it; the other the management of the security and interest of the public without, with all those that it may receive benefit or damage from, yet they are always almost united. And though this federative power in the well or ill management of it be of great moment to the commonwealth, yet it is much less capable to be directed by antecedent, standing, positive laws, than the executive; and so must necessarily be left to the prudence and wisdom of those whose hands it is in, to be managed for the public good. For the laws that concern subjects one amongst another, being to direct their actions, may well enough precede them. But what is to be done in reference to foreigners, depending much upon their actions, and the variation of designs and interests, must be left in great part to the prudence of those who have this power committed to them, to be managed by the best of their skill, for the advantage of the commonwealth.

148. Though, as I said, the executive and federative power of every community be really distinct in themselves, yet they are hardly to be separated, and placed, at the same time, in the hands of distinct persons. For both of them requiring the force of the society for their exercise, it is almost impracticable to place the force of the commonwealth in distinct, and not subordinate hands; or that the executive and federative power should be placed in persons that might act separately, whereby the force of the public would be under different commands: which would be apt some time or other to cause disorder and ruin.

Chapter 13
OF THE SUBORDINATION OF THE POWERS
OF THE COMMONWEALTH

149. Though in a constituted commonwealth, standing upon its own basis, and acting according to its own nature, that is, acting for the preservation of the community, there can be but

one supreme power, which is the legislative, to which all the rest are and must be subordinate, yet the legislative being only a fiduciary power to act for certain ends, there remains still in the people a supreme power to remove or alter the legislative, when they find the legislative act contrary to the trust reposed in them. For all power given with trust for the attaining an end, being limited by that end, whenever that end is manifestly neglected, or opposed, the trust must necessarily be forfeited, and the power devolve into the hands of those that gave it, who may place it anew where they shall think best for their safety and security. And thus the community perpetually retains a supreme power of saving themselves from the attempts and designs of anybody, even of their legislators, whenever they shall be so foolish, or so wicked, as to lay and carry on designs against the liberties and properties of the subject. For no man, or society of men, having a power to deliver up their preservation, or consequently the means of it, to the absolute will and arbitrary dominion of another; whenever anyone shall go about to bring them into such a slavish condition, they will always have a right to preserve what they have not a power to part with; and to rid themselves of those who invade this fundamental, sacred, and unalterable law of self-preservation, for which they entered into society. And thus the community may be said in this respect to be always the supreme power, but not as considered under any form of government, because this power of the people can never take place till the government be dissolved.

150. In all cases, whilst the government subsists, the legislative is the supreme power. For what can give laws to another, must needs be superior to him: and since the legislative is no otherwise legislative of the society, but by the right it has to make laws for all the parts and for every member of the society, prescribing rules to their actions, and giving power of execution, where they are transgressed, the legislative must needs be the supreme, and all other powers in any members or parts of the society, derived from and subordinate to it.

151. In some commonwealths where the legislative is not always in being, and the executive is vested in a single person, who has also a share in the legislative; there that single person in a very tolerable sense may also be called supreme, not that he has

in himself all the supreme power, which is that of law-making:
but because he has in him the supreme execution, from whom all
inferior magistrates derive all their several subordinate powers,
or at least the greatest part of them: having also no legislative
superior to him, there being no law to be made without his
consent, which cannot be expected should ever subject him to the
other part of the legislative, he is properly enough in this sense
supreme. But yet it is to be observed, that though oaths of
allegiance and fealty are taken to him, 'tis not to him as supreme
legislator, but as supreme executor of the law, made by a joint
power of him with others; allegiance being nothing but an obedience according to law, which when he violates, he has no right to
obedience, nor can claim it otherwise than as the public person
vested with the power of the law, and so is to be considered as
the image, phantom, or representative of the commonwealth,
acted by the will of the society, declared in its laws; and thus he
has no will, no power, but that of the law. But when he quits this
representation, this public will, and acts by his own private will,
he degrades himself, and is but a single private person without
power, and without will, that has any right to obedience; the
members owing no obedience but to the public will of the
society.

152. The executive power placed anywhere but in a person,
that has also a share in the legislative, is visibly subordinate and
accountable to it, and may be at pleasure changed and dis-
placed; so that it is not the supreme executive power that is
exempt from subordination, but the supreme executive power
vested in one, who having a share in the legislative, has no distinct
superior legislative to be subordinate and accountable to, further
than he himself shall join and consent: so that he is no more
subordinate than he himself shall think fit, which one may certainly conclude will be but very little. Of other ministerial and
subordinate powers in a commonwealth, we need not speak, they
being so multiplied with infinite variety, in the different customs
and constitutions of distinct commonwealths, that it is impossible
to give a particular account of them all. Only thus much, which
is necessary to our present purpose, we may take notice of
concerning them, that they have no manner of authority any of
them, beyond what is, by positive grant, and commission,

delegated to them, and are all of them accountable to some other power in the commonwealth.

153. It is not necessary, no nor so much as convenient, that the legislative should be always in being. But absolutely necessary that the executive power should, because there is not always need of new laws to be made, but always need of execution of the laws that are made. When the legislative hath put the execution of the laws, they make, into other hands, they have a power still to resume it out of those hands, when they find cause, and to punish for any maladministration against the laws. The same holds also in regard of the federative power, that and the executive being both ministerial and subordinate to the legislative, which as has been showed in a constituted commonwealth, is the supreme. The legislative also in this case being supposed to consist of several persons (for if it be a single person, it cannot but be always in being, and so will as supreme, naturally have the supreme executive power, together with the legislative) may assemble and exercise their legislature, at the times that either their original constitution, or their own adjournment appoints, or when they please; if neither of these hath appointed any time, or there be no other way prescribed to convoke them. For the supreme power being placed in them by the people, 'tis always in them, and they may exercise it when they please, unless by their original constitution they are limited to certain seasons, or by an act of their supreme power they have adjourned to a certain time, and when that time comes, they have a right to assemble and act again.

154. If the legislative, or any part of it be made up of representatives chosen for that time by the people, which afterwards return into the ordinary state of subjects, and have no share in the legislature but upon a new choice, this power of choosing must also be exercised by the people, either at certain appointed seasons, or else when they are summoned to it: and in this latter case, the power of convoking the legislative, is ordinarily placed in the executive, and has one of these two limitations in respect of time: that either the original constitution requires their assembling and acting at certain intervals, and then the executive power does nothing but ministerially issue directions for their electing and assembling, according to due forms: or else it is left to his

prudence to call them by new elections, when the occasions or exigencies of the public require the amendment of old, or making of new laws, or the redress or prevention of any inconveniences, that lie on, or threaten the people.

155. It may be demanded here, what if the executive power being possessed of the force of the commonwealth, shall make use of that force to hinder the meeting and acting of the legislative, when the original constitution, or the public exigencies require it? I say using force upon the people without authority, and contrary to the trust put in him, that does so, is a state of war with the people, who have a right to reinstate their legislative in the exercise of their power. For having erected a legislative, with an intent they should exercise the power of making laws, either at certain set times, or when there is need of it; when they are hindered by any force from, what is so necessary to the society, and wherein the safety and preservation of the people consists, the people have a right to remove it by force. In all states and conditions the true remedy of force without authority, is to oppose force to it. The use of force without authority, always puts him that uses it into a state of war, as the aggressor, and renders him liable to be treated accordingly.

156. The power of assembling and dismissing the legislative, placed in the executive, gives not the executive a superiority over it, but is a fiduciary trust, placed in him, for the safety of the people, in a case where the uncertainty, and variableness of human affairs could not bear a steady fixed rule. For it not being possible, that the first framers of the government should, by any foresight, be so much masters of future events, as to be able to prefix so just periods of return and duration to the assemblies of the legislative, in all times to come, that might exactly answer all the exigencies of the commonwealth; the best remedy could be found for this defect, was to trust this to the prudence of one, who was always to be present, and whose business it was to watch over the public good. Constant frequent meetings of the legislative, and long continuations of their assemblies, without necessary occasion, could not but be burdensome to the people, and must necessarily in time produce more dangerous inconveniences, and yet the quick turn of affairs might be sometimes such as to need their present help: any delay of their convening might endanger

the public; and sometimes too their business might be so great, that the limited time of their sitting might be too short for their work, and rob the public of that benefit, which could be had only from their mature deliberation. What then could be done, in this case, to prevent the community, from being exposed sometime or other to eminent hazard, on one side, or the other, by fixed intervals and periods, set to the meeting and acting of the legislative, but to entrust it to the prudence of some, who being present, and acquainted with the state of public affairs, might make use of this prerogative for the public good? And where else could this be so well placed as in his hands, who was entrusted with the execution of the laws, for the same end? Thus supposing the regulation of times for the assembling and sitting of the legislative, not settled by the original constitution, it naturally fell into the hands of the executive, not as an arbitrary power depending on his good pleasure, but with this trust always to have it exercised only for the public weal, as the occurrences of times and change of affairs might require. Whether settled periods of their convening, or a liberty left to the prince for convoking the legislative, or perhaps a mixture of both, hath the least inconvenience attending it, 'tis not my business here to enquire, but only to show, that though the executive power may have the prerogative of convoking and dissolving such conventions of the legislative, yet it is not thereby superior to it.

157. Things of this world are in so constant a flux, that nothing remains long in the same state. Thus people, riches, trade, power, change their stations; flourishing mighty cities come to ruin, and prove in time neglected desolate corners, whilst other unfrequented places grow into populous countries, filled with wealth and inhabitants. But things not always changing equally, and private interest often keeping up customs and privileges, when the reasons of them are ceased, it often comes to pass, that in governments, where part of the legislative consists of representatives chosen by the people, that in tract of time this representation becomes very unequal and disproportionate to the reasons it was at first established upon. To what gross absurdities the following of custom, when reason has left it, may lead, we may be satisfied when we see the bare name of a town, of which there remains not so much as the ruins, where scarce so much

housing as a sheepcote; or more inhabitants than a shepherd is to be found, sends as many representatives to the grand assembly of law-makers, as a whole county numerous in people, and powerful in riches. This strangers stand amazed at, and everyone must confess needs a remedy. Though most think it hard to find one, because the constitution of the legislative being the original and supreme act of the society, antecedent to all positive laws in it, and depending wholly on the people, no inferior power can alter it. And therefore the people, when the legislative is once constituted, having in such a government as we have been speaking of, no power to act as long as the government stands; this inconvenience is thought incapable of remedy.

158. *Salus populi suprema lex* [the people's safety is the supreme law], is certainly so just and fundamental a rule, that he, who sincerely follows it, cannot dangerously err. If therefore the executive, who has the power of convoking the legislative, observing rather the true proportion, than fashion of representation, regulates, not by old custom, but true reason, the number of members, in all places, that have a right to be distinctly represented, which no part of the people however incorporated can pretend to, but in proportion to the assistance, which it affords to the public, it cannot be judged, to have set up a new legislative, but to have restored the old and true one, and to have rectified the disorders, which succession of time had insensibly, as well as inevitably introduced. For it being the interest, as well as intention of the people, to have a fair and equal representative; whoever brings it nearest to that, is an undoubted friend, to, and establisher of the government, and cannot miss the consent and approbation of the community. Prerogative being nothing, but a power in the hands of the prince to provide for the public good, in such cases, which depending upon unforeseen and uncertain occurrences, certain and unalterable laws could not safely direct, whatsoever shall be done manifestly for the good of the people, and the establishing the government upon its true foundations, is, and always will be just prerogative. The power of erecting new corporations, and therewith new representatives, carries with it a supposition, that in time the measures of representation might vary, and those places have a just right to be represented which before had none; and by the same reason, those cease to have a

right, and be too inconsiderable for such a privilege, which before had it. 'Tis not change from the present state, which perhaps corruption, or decay has introduced, that makes an inroad upon the government, but the tendency of it to injure or oppress the people, and to set up one part, or party, with a distinction from, and an unequal subjection of the rest. Whatsoever cannot but be acknowledged to be of advantage to the society, and people in general, upon just and lasting measures, will always, when done, justify itself; and whenever the people shall choose their representatives upon just and undeniably equal measures suitable to the original frame of the government, it cannot be doubted to be the will and act of the society, whoever permitted, or caused them so to do.

Chapter 14
OF PREROGATIVE

159. Where the legislative and executive power are in distinct hands, (as they are in all moderated monarchies, and well-framed governments) there the good of the society requires, that several things should be left to the discretion of him, that has the executive power. For the legislators not being able to foresee, and provide, by laws, for all, that may be useful to the community, the executor of the laws, having the power in his hands, has by the common law of nature, a right to make use of it, for the good of the society, in many cases, where the municipal law has given no direction, till the legislative can conveniently be assembled to provide for it. Many things there are, which the law can by no means provide for, and those must necessarily be left to the discretion of him, that has the executive power in his hands, to be ordered by him, as the public good and advantage shall require: nay, 'tis fit that the laws themselves should in some cases give way to the executive power, or rather to this fundamental law of nature and government, viz. that as much as may be, all the members of the society are to be preserved. For since many accidents may happen, wherein a strict and rigid observation of the laws may do harm; (as not to pull down an innocent man's house to stop the fire, when the next to it is burning) and a man may come sometimes

within the reach of the law, which makes no distinction of persons, by an action, that may deserve reward and pardon; 'tis fit, the ruler should have a power, in many cases, to mitigate the severity of the law, and pardon some offenders: for the end of government being the preservation of all, as much as may be, even the guilty are to be spared, where it can prove no prejudice to the innocent.

160. This power to act according to discretion, for the public good, without the prescription of the law, and sometimes even against it, is that which is called prerogative. For since in some governments the law-making power is not always in being, and is usually too numerous, and so too slow, for the dispatch requisite to execution: and because also it is impossible to foresee, and so by laws to provide for, all accidents and necessities, that may concern the public; or to make such laws, as will do no harm, if they are executed with an inflexible rigour, on all occasions, and upon all persons, that may come in their way, therefore here is a latitude left to the executive power, to do many things of choice, which the laws do not prescribe.

161. This power whilst employed for the benefit of the community, and suitably to the trust and ends of the government, is undoubted prerogative, and never is questioned. For the people are very seldom, or never scrupulous, or nice in the point: they are far from examining prerogative, whilst it is in any tolerable degree employed for the use it was meant; that is, for the good of the people, and not manifestly against it. But if there comes to be a question between the executive power and the people, about a thing claimed as a prerogative; the tendency of the exercise of such prerogative to the good or hurt of the people, will easily decide that question.

162. It is easy to conceive, that in the infancy of governments, when commonwealths differed little from families in number of people, they differed from them too but little in number of laws: and the governors, being as the fathers of them, watching over them for their good, the government was almost all prerogative. A few established laws served the turn, and the discretion and care of the ruler supplied the rest. But when mistake, or flattery prevailed with weak princes to make use of this power, for private ends of their own, and not for the public good, the people were

fain by express laws to get prerogative determined, in those points, wherein they found disadvantage from it: and thus declared limitations of prerogative were by the people found necessary in cases, which they and their ancestors had left, in the utmost latitude, to the wisdom of those princes, who made no other but a right use of it, that is, for the good of their people.

163. And therefore they have a very wrong notion of government, who say, that the people have encroached upon the prerogative, when they have got any part of it to be defined by positive laws. For in so doing, they have not pulled from the prince anything, that of right belonged to him, but only declared, that that power which they indefinitely left in his, or his ancestors', hands, to be exercised for their good, was not a thing, which they intended him, when he used it otherwise. For the end of government being the good of the community, whatsoever alterations are made in it, tending to that end, cannot be an encroachment upon anybody: since nobody in government can have a right tending to any other end. And those only are encroachments which prejudice or hinder the public good. Those who say otherwise, speak as if the prince had a distinct and separate interest from the good of the community, and was not made for it, the root and source, from which spring almost all those evils, and disorders, which happen in kingly governments. And indeed if that be so, the people under his government are not a society of rational creatures entered into a community for their mutual good; they are not such as have set rulers over themselves, to guard, and promote that good; but are to be looked on as a herd of inferior creatures, under the dominion of a master, who keeps them, and works them for his own pleasure or profit. If men were so void of reason, and brutish, as to enter into society upon such terms, prerogative might indeed be, what some men would have it, an arbitrary power to do things hurtful to the people.

164. But since a rational creature cannot be supposed when free, to put himself into subjection to another, for his own harm: (though where he finds a good and wise ruler, he may not perhaps think it either necessary, or useful to set precise bounds to his power in all things) prerogative can be nothing, but the people's permitting their rulers, to do several things of their own free choice, where the law was silent, and sometimes too against the

direct letter of the law, for the public good; and their acquiescing in it when so done. For as a good prince, who is mindful of the trust put into his hands, and careful of the good of his people, cannot have too much prerogative, that is, power to do good: so a weak and ill prince, who would claim that power, which his predecessors exercised without the direction of the law, as a prerogative belonging to him by right of his office, which he may exercise at his pleasure, to make or promote an interest distinct from that of the public, gives the people an occasion, to claim their right, and limit that power, which, whilst it was exercised for their good, they were content should be tacitly allowed.

165. And therefore he, that will look into the history of England, will find, that prerogative was always largest in the hands of our wisest and best princes: because the people observing the whole tendency of their actions to be the public good, contested not what was done without law to that end; or if any human frailty or mistake (for princes are but men, made as others) appeared in some small declinations from that end; yet 'twas visible, the main of their conduct tended to nothing but the care of the public. The people therefore finding reason to be satisfied with these princes, whenever they acted without or contrary to the letter of the law, acquiesced in what they did, and, without the least complaint, let them enlarge their prerogative as they pleased, judging rightly, that they did nothing herein to the prejudice of their laws, since they acted conformably to the foundation and end of all laws, the public good.

166. Such godlike princes indeed had some title to arbitrary power, by that argument, that would prove absolute monarchy the best government, as that which God himself governs the universe by: because such kings partake of his wisdom and goodness. Upon this is founded that saying, that 'the reigns of good princes have been always most dangerous to the liberties of their people'. For when their successors, managing the government with different thoughts, would draw the actions of those good rulers into precedent, and make them the standard of their prerogative, as if what had been done only for the good of the people, was a right in them to do, for the harm of the people, if they so pleased; it has often occasioned contest, and sometimes public disorders, before the people could recover their original

right, and get that to be declared not to be prerogative, which truly was never so: since it is impossible, that anybody in the society should ever have a right to do the people harm; though it be very possible, and reasonable, that the people should not go about to set any bounds to the prerogative of those kings or rulers, who themselves transgressed not the bounds of the public good. For prerogative is nothing but the power of doing public good without a rule.

167. The power of calling parliaments in England, as to precise time, place, and duration, is certainly a prerogative of the king, but still with this trust, that it shall be made use of for the good of the nation, as the exigencies of the times, and variety of occasions shall require. For it being impossible to foresee, which should always be the fittest place for them to assemble in, and what the best season; the choice of these was left with the executive power, as might be most subservient to the public good, and best suit the ends of parliaments.

168. The old question will be asked in this matter of prerogative, but who shall be judge when this power is made a right use of? I answer: between an executive power in being, with such a prerogative, and a legislative that depends upon his will for their convening, there can be no judge on earth: as there can be none, between the legislative, and the people, should either the executive, or the legislative, when they have got the power in their hands, design, or go about to enslave, or destroy them. The people have no other remedy in this, as in all other cases where they have no judge on earth, but to appeal to heaven. For the rulers, in such attempts, exercising a power the people never put into their hands (who can never be supposed to consent, that anybody should rule over them for their harm) do that, which they have not a right to do. And where the body of the people, or any single man, is deprived of their right, or is under the exercise of a power without right, and have no appeal on earth, there they have a liberty to appeal to heaven, whenever they judge the cause of sufficient moment. And therefore, though the people cannot be judge, so as to have by the constitution of that society any superior power, to determine and give effective sentence in the case; yet they have, by a law antecedent and paramount to all positive laws of men, reserved that ultimate determination to themselves, which belongs

to all mankind, where there lies no appeal on earth, *viz.* to judge whether they have just cause to make their appeal to heaven. And this judgment they cannot part with, it being out of a man's power so to submit himself to another, as to give him a liberty to destroy him; God and nature never allowing a man so to abandon himself, as to neglect his own preservation: and since he cannot take away his own life, neither can he give another power to take it. Nor let anyone think, this lays a perpetual foundation for disorder: for this operates not, till the inconvenience is so great, that the majority feel it, and are weary of it, and find a necessity to have it amended. But this the executive power, or wise princes, never need come in the danger of: and 'tis the thing of all others, they have most need to avoid, as of all others the most perilous.

Chapter 15
OF PATERNAL, POLITICAL, AND DESPOTICAL POWER, CONSIDERED TOGETHER

169. Though I have had occasion to speak of these separately before, yet the great mistakes of late about government, having, as I suppose, arisen from confounding these distinct powers one with another, it may not, perhaps, be amiss, to consider them here together.

170. First then, paternal or parental power is nothing but that, which parents have over their children, to govern them for the children's good, till they come to the use of reason, or a state of knowledge, wherein they may be supposed capable to understand that rule, whether it be the law of nature, or the municipal law of their country they are to govern themselves by: capable, I say, to know it, as well as several others, who live, as free men, under that law. The affection and tenderness, which God hath planted in the breasts of parents, towards their children, makes it evident, that this is not intended to be a severe arbitrary government, but only for the help, instruction, and preservation of their offspring. But happen it as it will, there is, as I have proved, no reason, why it should be thought, to extend to life and death, at any time, over their children, more than over anybody else, neither can there be any pretence why this parental power should keep the child, when

grown to a man, in subjection to the will of his parents any further, than the having received life and education from his parents, obliges him to respect, honour, gratitude, assistance, and support all his life to both father and mother. And thus, 'tis true, the paternal is a natural government, but not at all extending itself to the ends, and jurisdictions of that which is political. The power of the father doth not reach at all to the property of the child, which is only in his own disposing.

171. Secondly, political power is that power which every man, having in the state of nature, has given up into the hands of the society, and therein to the governors, whom the society hath set over itself, with this express or tacit trust, that it shall be employed for their good, and the preservation of their property: now this power, which every man has in the state of nature, and which he parts with to the society, in all such cases, where the society can secure him, is, to use such means for the preserving of his own property, as he thinks good, and nature allows him; and to punish the breach of the law of nature in others so, as (according to the best of his reason) may most conduce to the preservation of himself, and the rest of mankind. So that the end and measure of this power, when in every man's hands in the state of nature, being the preservation of all of his society, that is, all mankind in general, it can have no other end or measure, when in the hands of the magistrate, but to preserve the members of that society in their lives, liberties, and possessions; and so cannot be an absolute, arbitrary power over their lives and fortunes, which are as much as possible to be preserved; but a power to make laws, and annex such penalties to them, as may tend to the preservation of the whole, by cutting off those parts, and those only, which are so corrupt, that they threaten the sound and healthy, without which no severity is lawful. And this power has its original only from compact and agreement, and the mutual consent of those who make up the community.

172. Thirdly, despotical power is an absolute, arbitrary power one man has over another, to take away his life, whenever he pleases. This is a power, which neither nature gives, for it has made no such distinction between one man and another; nor compact can convey, for man not having such an arbitrary power over his own life, cannot give another man such a power over it;

but it is the effect only of forfeiture, which the aggressor makes of his own life, when he puts himself into the state of war with another. For having quitted reason, which God hath given to be the rule betwixt man and man, and the common bond whereby humankind is united into one fellowship and society; and having renounced the way of peace, which that teaches, and made use of the force of war to compass his unjust ends upon another, where he has no right, and so revolting from his own kind to that of beasts by making force which is theirs, to be his rule of right, he renders himself liable to be destroyed by the injured person and the rest of mankind, that will join with him in the execution of justice, as any other wild beast, or noxious brute with whom mankind can have neither society nor security. And thus captives, taken in a just and lawful war, and such only, are subject to a despotical power, which as it arises not from compact, so neither is it capable of any, but is the state of war continued. For what compact can be made with a man that is not master of his own life? What condition can he perform? And if he be once allowed to be master of his own life, the despotical, arbitrary power of his master ceases. He that is master of himself, and his own life, has a right too to the means of preserving it, so that as soon as compact enters, slavery ceases, and he so far quits his absolute power, and puts an end to the state of war, who enters into conditions with his captive.

173. Nature gives the first of these, *viz.* paternal power to parents for the benefit of their children during their minority, to supply their want of ability, and understanding how to manage their property. (By property I must be understood here, as in other places, to mean that property which men have in their persons as well as goods.) Voluntary agreement gives the second, *viz.* political power to governors for the benefit of their subjects, to secure them in the possession and use of their properties. And forfeiture gives the third, despotical power to lords for their own benefit, over those who are stripped of all property.

174. He, that shall consider the distinct rise and extent, and the different ends of these several powers, will plainly see, that paternal power comes as far short of that of the magistrate, as despotical exceeds it; and that absolute dominion, however placed, is so far from being one kind of civil society, that it is as

inconsistent with it, as slavery is with property. Paternal power is only where minority makes the child incapable to manage his property; political where men have property in their own disposal; and despotical over such as have no property at all.

Chapter 16
OF CONQUEST

175. Though governments can originally have no other rise than that before mentioned, nor polities be founded on anything but the consent of the people; yet such has been the disorders ambition has filled the world with, that in the noise of war, which makes so great a part of the history of mankind, this consent is little taken notice of: and therefore many have mistaken the force of arms, for the consent of the people; and reckon conquest as one of the originals of government. But conquest is as far from setting up any government, as demolishing a house is from building a new one in the place. Indeed it often makes way for a new frame of a commonwealth, by destroying the former; but, without the consent of the people, can never erect a new one.

176. That the aggressor, who puts himself into the state of war with another, and unjustly invades another man's right, can, by such an unjust war, never come to have a right over the conquered, will be easily agreed by all men, who will not think, that robbers and pirates have a right of empire over whomsoever they have force enough to master; or that men are bound by promises, which unlawful force extorts from them. Should a robber break into my house, and with a dagger at my throat, make me seal deeds to convey my estate to him, would this give him any title? Just such a title by his sword, has an unjust conqueror, who forces me into submission. The injury and the crime is equal, whether committed by the wearer of a crown, or some petty villain. The title of the offender, and the number of his followers make no difference in the offence, unless it be to aggravate it. The only difference is, great robbers punish little ones, to keep them in their obedience, but the great ones are rewarded with laurels and triumphs, because they are too big for the weak hands of justice in this world, and have the power in their own possession, which should

punish offenders. What is my remedy against a robber, that so broke into my house? Appeal to the law for justice. But perhaps justice is denied, or I am crippled and cannot stir, robbed and have not the means to do it. If God has taken away all means of seeking remedy, there is nothing left but patience. But my son, when able, may seek the relief of the law, which I am denied: he or his son may renew his appeal, till he recover his right. But the conquered, or their children, have no court, no arbitrator on earth to appeal to. Then they may appeal, as Jephtha did, to heaven, and repeat their appeal, till they have recovered the native right of their ancestors, which was to have such a legislative over them, as the majority should approve, and freely acquiesce in. If it be objected, this would cause endless trouble; I answer, no more than justice does, where she lies open to all that appeal to her. He that troubles his neighbour without a cause, is punished for it by the justice of the court he appeals to. And he that appeals to heaven, must be sure he has right on his side; and a right too that is worth the trouble and cost of the appeal, as he will answer at a tribunal, that cannot be deceived, and will be sure to retribute to everyone according to the mischiefs he hath created to his fellow subjects; that is, any part of mankind. From whence 'tis plain, that he that conquers in an unjust war, can thereby have no title to the subjection and obedience of the conquered.

177. But supposing victory favours the right side, let us consider a conqueror in a lawful war, and see what power he gets, and over whom.

First, 'tis plain he gets no power by his conquest over those that conquered with him. They that fought on his side cannot suffer by the conquest, but must at least be as much free men as they were before. And most commonly they serve upon terms, and on condition to share with their leader, and enjoy a part of the spoil, and other advantages that attend the conquering sword: or at least have a part of the subdued country bestowed upon them. And the conquering people are not, I hope, to be slaves by conquest, and wear their laurels only to show they are sacrifices to their leader's triumph. They that found absolute monarchy upon the title of the sword, make their heroes, who are the founders of such monarchies, arrant Draw-can-Sirs, and forget they had any officers and soldiers that fought on their side in the battles they won, or assisted them in the subduing, or shared in possessing the countries they mastered. We are told by some, that the English monarchy is founded in the Norman Conquest, and that our princes have thereby a title to absolute dominion: which if it were true, (as by the history it appears otherwise) and that William had a right to make war on this island; yet his dominion by conquest could reach no further, than to the Saxons and Britons that were then inhabitants of this country. The Normans that came with him, and helped to conquer, and all descended from them are free men and no subjects by conquest; let that give what dominion it will. And if I, or anybody else, shall claim freedom, as derived from them, it will be very hard to prove the contrary: and 'tis plain, the law that has made no distinction between the one and the other, intends not there should be any difference in their freedom or privileges.

178. But supposing, which seldom happens, that the conquerors and conquered never incorporate into one people, under the same laws and freedom. Let us see next what power a lawful conqueror has over the subdued; and that I say is purely despotical. He has an absolute power over the lives of those, who by an unjust war have forfeited them; but not over the lives or fortunes of those, who engaged not in the war, nor over the possessions even of those, who were actually engaged in it.

179. Secondly, I say then the conqueror gets no power but only over those, who have actually assisted, concurred, or consented to that unjust force, that is used against him. For the people having given to their governors no power to do an unjust thing, such as is to make an unjust war, (for they never had such a power in themselves:) they ought not to be charged, as guilty of the violence and injustice that is committed in an unjust war, any further, than they actually abet it; no more, than they are to be thought guilty of any violence or oppression their governors should use upon the people themselves, or any part of their fellow subjects, they have empowered them no more to the one, than to the other. Conquerors, 'tis true, seldom trouble themselves to make the distinction, but they willingly permit the confusion of war to sweep all together; but yet this alters not the right: for the conqueror's power over the lives of the conquered, being only because they have used force to do, or maintain an injustice, he can have that

power only over those, who have concurred in that force, all the
rest are innocent; and he has no more title over the people of that
country, who have done him no injury, and so have made no
forfeiture of their lives, than he has over any other, who, without
any injuries or provocations, have lived upon fair terms with him.

180. Thirdly, the power a conqueror gets over those he over-
comes in a just war, is perfectly despotical: he has an absolute
power over the lives of those, who by putting themselves in a state
of war, have forfeited them; but he has not thereby a right and
title to their possessions. This I doubt not, but at first sight will
seem a strange doctrine, it being so quite contrary to the practice
of the world; there being nothing more familiar in speaking of the
dominion of countries, than to say, such a one conquered it. As
if conquest, without any more ado, conveyed a right of possession.
But when we consider, that the practice of the strong and powerful, how universal soever it may be, is seldom the rule of right,
however it be one part of the subjection of the conquered, not to
argue against the conditions, cut out to them by the conquering
sword.

181. Though in all war there be usually a complication of force
and damage, and the aggressor seldom fails to harm the estate,
when he uses force against the persons of those he makes war
upon; yet 'tis the use of force only, that puts a man into the state
of war. For whether by force he begins the injury, or else having
quietly, and by fraud, done the injury, he refuses to make reparation, and by force maintains it, (which is the same thing as at first
to have done it by force) 'tis the unjust use of force that makes the
war. For he that breaks open my house, and violently turns me
out of doors; or having peaceably got in, by force keeps me out,
does in effect the same thing; supposing we are in such a state,
that we have no common judge on earth, whom I may appeal to,
and to whom we are both obliged to submit: for of such I am now
speaking. 'Tis the unjust use of force then, that puts a man into
the state of war with another, and thereby he, that is guilty of it,
makes a forfeiture of his life. For quitting reason, which is the rule
given between man and man, and using force the way of beasts,
he becomes liable to be destroyed by him he uses force against, as
any savage ravenous beast, that is dangerous to his being.

182. But because the miscarriages of the father are no faults

of the children, and they may be rational and peaceable, notwithstanding the brutishness and injustice of the father; the father, by his miscarriages and violence, can forfeit but his own life, but involves not his children in his guilt or destruction. His goods, which nature, that willeth the preservation of all mankind as much as is possible, hath made to belong to the children to keep them from perishing, do still continue to belong to his children. For supposing them not to have joined in the war, either through infancy, absence, or choice, they have done nothing to forfeit them: nor has the conqueror any right to take them away, by the bare title of having subdued him, that by force attempted his destruction; though perhaps he may have some right to them, to repair the damages he has sustained by the war, and the defence of his own right, which how far it reaches to the possessions of the conquered, we shall see by and by. So that he that by conquest has a right over a man's person to destroy him if he pleases, has not thereby a right over his estate to possess and enjoy it. For it is the brutal force the aggressor has used, that gives his adversary a right to take away his life, and destroy him if he pleases, as a noxious creature; but 'tis damage sustained that alone gives him title to another man's goods: for though I may kill a thief that sets on me in the highway, yet I may not (which seems less) take away his money and let him go; this would be robbery on my side. His force, and the state of war he put himself in, made him forfeit his life, but gave me no title to his goods. The right then of conquest extends only to the lives of those who joined in the war, not to their estates, but only in order to make reparation for the damages received, and the charges of the war, and that too with reservation of the right of the innocent wife and children.

183. Let the conqueror have as much justice on his side, as could be supposed, he has no right to seize more than the vanquished could forfeit; his life is at the victor's mercy, and his service and goods he may appropriate to make himself reparation; but he cannot take the goods of his wife and children; they too had a title to the goods he enjoyed, and their shares in the estate he possessed. For example, I in the state of nature (and all commonwealths are in the state of nature one with another) have injured another man, and refusing to give satisfaction, it comes to a state of war, wherein my defending by force, what I had gotten

unjustly, makes me the aggressor. I am conquered: my life, 'tis true, as forfeit, is at mercy, but not my wife's and children's. They made not the war, nor assisted in it. I could not forfeit their lives, they were not mine to forfeit. My wife had a share in my estate, that neither could I forfeit. And my children also, being born of me, had a right to be maintained out of my labour or substance. Here then is the case; the conqueror has a title to reparation for damages received, and the children have a title to their father's estate for their subsistence. For as to the wife's share, whether her own labour or compact gave her a title to it, 'tis plain, her husband could not forfeit what was hers. What must be done in the case? I answer; the fundamental law of nature being, that all, as much as may be, should be preserved, it follows, that if there be not enough fully to satisfy both, *viz.* for the conqueror's losses, and children's maintenance, he that hath, and to spare, must remit something of his full satisfaction, and give way to the pressing and preferable title of those, who are in danger to perish without it.

184. But supposing the charge and damages of the war are to be made up to the conqueror, to the utmost farthing, and that the children of the vanquished, spoiled of all their father's goods, are to be left to starve and perish: yet the satisfying of what shall on this score, be due to the conqueror, will scarce give him a title to any country he shall conquer. For the damages of war can scarce amount to the value of any considerable tract of land, in any part of the world, where all the land is possessed, and none lies waste. And if I have not taken away the conqueror's land, which, being vanquished, it is impossible I should; scarce any other spoil I have done him, can amount to the value of mine, supposing it equally cultivated and of an extent any way coming near, what I had overrun of his. The destruction of a year's product or two, (for it seldom reaches four or five) is the utmost spoil, that usually can be done. For as to money, and such riches and treasure taken away, these are none of nature's goods, they have but a fantastical imaginary value: nature has put no such upon them: they are of no more account by her standard, than the wampompeke of the Americans to a European prince, or the silver money of Europe would have been formerly to an American. And five years' product is not worth the perpetual inheritance of land, where all is possessed, and none remains waste to be taken up by him, that

is disseised [dispossessed]: which will be easily granted, if one do but take away the imaginary value of money, the disproportion being more, than between five and five hundred. Though, at the same time, half a year's product is more worth than the inheritance, where there being more land, than the inhabitants possess, and make use of, anyone has liberty to make use of the waste: but there conquerors take little care to possess themselves of the lands of the vanquished. No damage therefore, that men in the state of nature (as all princes and governments are in reference to one another) suffer from one another, can give a conqueror power, to dispossess the posterity of the vanquished, and turn them out of their inheritance, which ought to be the possession of them and their descendants to all generations. The conqueror indeed will be apt to think himself master: and 'tis the very condition of the subdued not to be able to dispute their right. But if that be all, it gives no other title than what bare force gives to the stronger over the weaker. And, by this reason, he that is strongest will have a right to whatever he pleases to seize on.

185. Over those then, that joined with him in the war, and over those of the subdued country that opposed him not, and the posterity even of those that did, the conqueror, even in a just war, hath, by his conquest, no right of dominion: they are free from any subjection to him, and if their former government be dissolved, they are at liberty to begin and erect another to themselves.

186. The conqueror, 'tis true, usually, by the force he has over them, compels them, with a sword at their breasts, to stoop to his conditions, and submit to such a government as he pleases to afford them; but the enquiry is, what right he has to do so? If it be said, they submit by their own consent; then this allows their own consent to be necessary to give the conqueror a title to rule over them. It remains only to be considered, whether promises, extorted by force, without right, can be thought consent, and how far they bind. To which I shall say, they bind not at all; because whatsoever another gets from me by force, I still retain the right of, and he is obliged presently to restore. He that forces my horse from me, ought presently to restore him, and I have still a right to retake him. By the same reason, he that forced a promise from me, ought presently to restore it, i.e. quit me of the obligation of it; or I may resume it myself, i.e. choose whether I will perform

it. For the law of nature laying an obligation on me, only by the rules she prescribes, cannot oblige me by the violation of her rules: such is the extorting anything from me by force. Nor does it at all alter the case, to say I gave my promise, no more than it excuses the force, and passes the right, when I put my hand in my pocket, and deliver my purse myself to a thief, who demands it with a pistol at my breast.

187. From all which it follows, that the government of a conqueror, imposed, by force, on the subdued, against whom he had no right of war, or who joined not in the war against him, where he had right, has no obligation upon them.

188. But let us suppose that all the men of that community being all members of the same body politic, may be taken to have joined in that unjust war, wherein they are subdued, and so their lives are at the mercy of the conqueror.

189. I say, this concerns not their children, who are in their minority. For since a father hath not, in himself, a power over the life or liberty of his child; no act of his can possibly forfeit it: so that the children, whatever may have happened to the fathers, are free men, and the absolute power of the conqueror reaches no further than the persons of the men, that were subdued by him, and dies with them; and should he govern them as slaves, subjected to his absolute, arbitrary power, he has no such right of dominion over their children. He can have no power over them, but by their own consent, whatever he may drive them to say, or do; and he has no lawful authority, whilst force, and not choice, compels them to submission.

190. Every man is born with a double right: first, a right of freedom to his person, which no other man has a power over, but the free disposal of it lies in himself. Secondly, a right, before any other man, to inherit, with his brethren, his father's goods.

191. By the first of these, a man is naturally free from subjection to any government, though he be born in a place under its jurisdiction. But if he disclaim the lawful government of the country he was born in, he must also quit the right that belonged to him by the laws of it, and the possessions there descending to him from his ancestors, if it were a government made by their consent.

192. By the second, the inhabitants of any country, who are

descended, and derive a title to their estates from those, who are subdued, and had a government forced upon them against their free consents, retain a right to the possession of their ancestors, though they consent not freely to the government, whose hard conditions were by force imposed on the possessors of that country. For the first conqueror never having had a title to the land of that country, the people who are the descendants of, or claim under those, who are forced to submit to the yoke of a government by constraint, have always a right to shake it off, and free themselves from the usurpation, or tyranny, which the sword hath brought in upon them, till their rulers put them under such a frame of government, as they willingly, and of choice consent to. Who doubts but the Grecian Christians descendants of the ancient possessors of that country may justly cast off the Turkish yoke which they have so long groaned under whenever they have a power to do it? For no government can have a right to obedience from a people who have not freely consented to it; which they can never be supposed to do, till either they are put in a full state of liberty to choose their government and governors, or at least till they have such standing laws, to which they have by themselves or their representatives, given their free consent, and also till they are allowed their due property, which is so to be proprietors of what they have, that nobody can take away any part of it without their own consent, without which, men under any government are not in the state of free men, but are direct slaves under the force of war.

193. But granting that the conqueror in a just war has a right to the estates, as well as power over the persons of the conquered; which, 'tis plain, he hath not: nothing of absolute power will follow from hence, in the continuance of the government. Because the descendants of these being all free men, if he grants them estates and possessions to inhabit his country (without which it would be worth nothing) whatsoever he grants them, they have, so far as it is granted, property in. The nature whereof is, that without a man's own consent it cannot be taken from him.

194. Their persons are free by a native right, and their properties, be they more or less, are their own, and at their own dispose, and not at his; or else it is no property. Supposing the conqueror gives to one man a thousand acres, to him and his heirs

forever; to another he lets a thousand acres for his life, under the rent of £50 or £500 *per annum*. Has not the one of these a right to his thousand acres forever, and the other, during his life, paying the said rent? And hath not the tenant for life a property in all that he gets over and above his rent, by his labour and industry during the said term, supposing it be double the rent? Can anyone say, the king, or conqueror, after his grant, may by his power of conqueror, take away all, or part of the land from the heirs of one, or from the other, during his life, he paying the rent? Or can he take away from either, the goods or money they have got upon the said land, at his pleasure? If he can, then all free and voluntary contracts cease, and are void, in the world; there needs nothing to dissolve them at any time but power enough: and all the grants and promises of men in power, are but mockery and collusion. For can there be anything more ridiculous than to say, I give you and yours this forever; and that in the surest and most solemn way of conveyance [which] can be devised: and yet it is to be understood, that I have right, if I please, to take it away from you again tomorrow?

195. I will not dispute now whether princes are exempt from the laws of their country; but this I am sure, they owe subjection to the laws of God and nature. No body, no power can exempt them from the obligation of that eternal law. Those are so great, and so strong, in the case of promises, that Omnipotency itself can be tied by them. Grants, promises and oaths are bonds that hold the Almighty: whatever some flatterers say to princes of the world who all together, with all their people joined to them, are in comparison of the great God, but as a drop of the bucket, or a dust on the balance, inconsiderable nothing!

196. The short of the case in conquest is this. The conqueror, if he have a just cause, has a despotical right over the persons of all, that actually aided, and concurred in the war against him, and a right to make up his damage and cost out of their labour and estates, so he injure not the right of any other. Over the rest of the people, if there were any that consented not to the war, and over the children of the captives themselves, or the possessions of either he has no power; and so can have, by virtue of conquest, no lawful title himself to dominion over them, or derive it to his posterity; but is an aggressor, if he attempts upon their properties, and

thereby puts himself in a state of war against them; and has no better a right of principality, he, nor any of his successors, than Hingar, or Hubba the Danes had here in England; or Spartacus, had he conquered Italy would have had; which is to have their yoke cast off, as soon as God shall give those under their subjection courage and opportunity to do it. Thus, notwithstanding whatever title the kings of Assyria had over Judah, by the sword, God assisted Hezekiah to throw off the dominion of that conquering empire. 'And the Lord was with Hezekiah, and he prospered; wherefore he went forth, and he rebelled against the king of Assyria, and served him not' (2 Kings 18:7). Whence it is plain, that shaking off a power, which force, and not right hath set over anyone, though it hath the name of rebellion, yet is no offence before God, but is that, which he allows and countenances, though even promises and covenants, when obtained by force, have intervened. For 'tis very probable to anyone that reads the story of Ahaz, and Hezekiah attentively, that the Assyrians subdued Ahaz, and deposed him, and made Hezekiah king in his father's lifetime; and that Hezekiah by agreement had done him homage, and paid him tribute all this time.

Chapter 17
OF USURPATION

197. As conquest may be called a foreign usurpation, so usurpation is a kind of domestic conquest, with this difference, that a usurper can never have right on his side, it being no usurpation but where one is got into the possession of what another has right to. This, so far as it is usurpation, is a change only of persons, but not of the forms and rules of the government: for if the usurper extend his power beyond, what of right belonged to the lawful princes, or governors of the commonwealth, 'tis tyranny added to usurpation.

198. In all lawful governments the designation of the persons, who are to bear rule, is as natural and necessary a part, as the form of the government itself, and is that which had its establishment originally from the people. Hence all commonwealths with the form of government established, have rules also of appointing

those, who are to have any share in the public authority; and settled methods of conveying the right to them. For the anarchy is much alike to have no form of government at all; or to agree that it shall be monarchical, but to appoint no way to know or design the person that shall have the power and be the monarch. Whoever gets into the exercise of any part of the power, by other ways, than what the laws of the community have prescribed, hath no right to be obeyed, though the form of the commonwealth be still preserved; since he is not the person the laws have appointed, and consequently not the person the people have consented to. Nor can such a usurper, or any deriving from him, ever have a title, till the people are both at liberty to consent, and have actually consented to allow, and confirm in him, the power he hath till then usurped.

Chapter 18
OF TYRANNY

199. As usurpation is the exercise of power, which another hath a right to; so tyranny is the exercise of power beyond right, which nobody can have a right to. And this is making use of the power anyone has in his hands; not for the good of those, who are under it, but for his own private separate advantage. When the governor, however entitled, makes not the law, but his will, the rule; and his commands and actions are not directed to the preservation of the properties of his people, but the satisfaction of his own ambition, revenge, covetousness, or any other irregular passion.

200. If one can doubt this to be truth, or reason, because it comes from the obscure hand of a subject, I hope the authority of a king will make it pass with him. King James the First in his speech to the Parliament, 1603, tells them thus; 'I will ever prefer the weal of the public, and of the whole commonwealth, in making of good laws and constitutions to any particular and private ends of mine. Thinking ever the wealth and weal of the commonwealth, to be my greatest weal, and worldly felicity; a point wherein a lawful king doth directly differ from a tyrant. For I do acknowledge, that the special and greatest point of difference

that is between a rightful king, and a usurping tyrant, is this, that whereas the proud and ambitious tyrant doth think, his kingdom and people are only ordained for satisfaction of his desires and unreasonable appetites; the righteous and just king doth by the contrary acknowledge himself to be ordained for the procuring of the wealth and property of his people.' And again in his speech to the Parliament, 1609, he hath these words: 'The king binds himself by a double oath, to the observation of the fundamental laws of his kingdom. Tacitly, as by being a king, and so bound to protect as well the people as the laws of his kingdom, and expressly by his oath at his coronation; so as every just king, in a settled kingdom is bound to observe that paction made to his people by his laws in framing his government agreeable thereunto, according to that paction which God made with Noah, after the deluge. "Hereafter, seed-time and harvest, and cold and heat, and summer and winter, and day and night shall not cease while the earth remaineth" [*Genesis* 8:22]. And therefore a king governing in a settled kingdom, leaves to be a king, and degenerates into a tyrant as soon as he leaves off to rule according to his laws.' And a little after: 'Therefore all kings that are not tyrants, or perjured, will be glad to bound themselves within the limits of their laws. And they that persuade them the contrary, are vipers, and pests both against them and the commonwealth'. Thus that learned king who well understood the notions of things, makes the difference betwixt a king and a tyrant to consist only in this, that one makes the laws the bounds of his power, and the good of the public, the end of his government; the other makes all give way to his own will and appetite.

201. 'Tis a mistake to think this fault is proper only to monarchies; other forms of government are liable to it, as well as that. For wherever the power that is put in any hands for the government of the people, and the preservation of their properties, is applied to other ends, and made use of to impoverish, harass, or subdue them to the arbitrary and irregular commands of those that have it: there it presently becomes tyranny, whether those that thus use it are one or many. Thus we read of the Thirty Tyrants at Athens, as well as one at Syracuse; and the intolerable dominion of the Decemviri at Rome was nothing better.

202. Wherever law ends, tyranny begins, if the law be

transgressed to another's harm. And whosoever in authority exceeds the power given him by the law, and makes use of the force he has under his command, to compass that upon the subject, which the law allows not, ceases in that to be a magistrate, and acting without authority, may be opposed, as any other man, who by force invades the right of another. This is acknowledged in subordinate magistrates. He that hath authority to seize my person in the street, may be opposed as a thief and a robber, if he endeavours to break into my house to execute a writ, notwithstanding that I know he has such a warrant, and such a legal authority as will empower him to arrest me abroad. And why this should not hold in the highest, as well as in the most inferior magistrate, I would gladly be informed. Is it reasonable that the eldest brother, because he has the greatest part of his father's estate, should thereby have a right to take away any of his younger brothers' portions? Or that a rich man, who possessed a whole country, should from thence have a right to seize, when he pleased, the cottage and garden of his poor neighbour? The being rightfully possessed of great power and riches exceedingly beyond the greatest part of the sons of Adam, is so far from being an excuse, much less a reason, for rapine, and oppression, which the endamaging another without authority is, that it is a great aggravation of it. For the exceeding the bounds of authority is no more a right in a great, than a petty officer; no more justifiable in a king, than a constable. But is so much the worse in him, in that he has more trust put in him, has already a much greater share than the rest of his brethren, and is supposed from the advantage[s] of education, employment and counsellors to be more knowing in the measures of right or wrong.

203. May the commands then of a prince be opposed? May he be resisted as often as anyone shall find himself aggrieved, and but imagine he has not right done him? This will unhinge and overturn all polities, and instead of government and order, leave nothing but anarchy and confusion.

204. To this I answer: that force is to be opposed to nothing, but to unjust and unlawful force; whoever makes any opposition in any other case, draws on himself a just condemnation both from God and man; and so no such danger or confusion will follow, as is often suggested. For,

205. First, as in some countries, the person of the prince by the law is sacred; and so whatever he commands, or does, his person is still free from all question or violence, not liable to force, or any judicial censure or condemnation. But yet opposition may be made to the illegal acts of any inferior officer, or other commissioned by him; unless he will by actually putting himself into a state of war with his people, dissolve the government, and leave them to that defence, which belongs to everyone in the state of nature. For of such things who can tell what the end will be? And a neighbour kingdom has showed the world an odd example. In all other cases the sacredness of the person exempts him from all inconveniences whereby he is secure, whilst the government stands, from all violence and harm whatsoever; than which there cannot be a wiser constitution. For the harm he can do in his own person, not being likely to happen often, nor to extend itself far; nor being able by his single strength to subvert the laws, nor oppress the body of the people, should any prince have so much weakness and ill nature as to be willing to do it, the inconveniency of some particular mischiefs, that may happen sometimes, when a heady prince comes to the throne, are well recompensed, by the peace of the public, and security of the government, in the person of the chief magistrate, thus set out of the reach of danger: it being safer for the body, that some few private men should be sometimes in danger to suffer, than that the head of the republic should be easily, and upon slight occasions exposed.

206. Secondly, but this privilege, belonging only to the king's person, hinders not, but they may be questioned, opposed, and resisted, who use unjust force, though they pretend a commission from him, which the law authorizes not. As is plain in the case of him, that has the king's writ to arrest a man, which is a full commission from the king; and yet he that has it cannot break open a man's house to do it, nor execute this command of the king upon certain days, nor in certain places, though this commission have no such exception in it, but they are the limitations of the law, which if anyone transgress, the king's commission excuses him not. For the king's authority being given him only by the law, he cannot empower anyone to act against the law, or justify him, by his commission in so doing. The commission, or command of any magistrate, where he has no authority, being as

void and insignificant, as that of any private man. The difference between the one and the other, being that the magistrate has some authority so far, and to such ends, and the private man has none at all. For 'tis not the commission, but the authority, that gives the right of acting: and against the laws there can be no authority. But, notwithstanding such resistance, the king's person and authority are still both secured, and so no danger to governor or government.

207. Thirdly, supposing a government wherein the person of the chief magistrate is not thus sacred; yet this doctrine of the lawfulness of resisting all unlawful exercises of his power, will not upon every slight occasion endanger him, or embroil the government. For where the injured party may be relieved, and his damages repaired by appeal to the law, there can be no pretence for force, which is only to be used, where a man is intercepted from appealing to the law. For nothing is to be accounted hostile force, but where it leaves not the remedy of such an appeal. And 'tis such force alone, that puts him that uses it into a state of war, and makes it lawful to resist him. A man with a sword in his hand demands my purse in the highway, when perhaps I have not 12d in my pocket; this man I may lawfully kill. To another I deliver £100 to hold only whilst I alight, which he refuses to restore me, when I am got up again, but draws his sword to defend the possession of it by force, if I endeavour to retake it. The mischief this man does me, is a hundred, or possibly a thousand times more, than the other perhaps intended me, (whom I killed before he really did me any) and yet I might lawfully kill the one, and cannot so much as hurt the other lawfully. The reason whereof is plain; because the one using force, which threatened my life, I could not have time to appeal to the law to secure it: and when it was gone, 'twas too late to appeal. The law could not restore life to my dead carcass: the loss was irreparable; which to prevent, the law of nature gave me a right to destroy him, who had put himself into a state of war with me, and threatened my destruction. But in the other case, my life not being in danger, I may have the benefit of appealing to the law, and have reparation for my £100 that way.

208. Fourthly, but if the unlawful acts done by the magistrate, be maintained (by the power he has got) and the remedy which is due by law, be by the same power obstructed; yet the right of

resisting, even in such manifest acts of tyranny, will not suddenly, or on slight occasions, disturb the government. For if it reach no further than some private men's cases, though they have a right to defend themselves, and to recover by force, what by unlawful force is taken from them; yet the right to do so, will not easily engage them in a contest, wherein they are sure to perish; it being as impossible for one or a few oppressed men to disturb the government, where the body of the people do not think themselves concerned in it, as for a raving madman, or heady malcontent to overturn a well-settled state; the people being as little apt to follow the one, as the other.

209. But if either these illegal acts have extended to the majority of the people; or if the mischief and oppression has light[ed] only on some few, but in such cases, as the precedent, and consequences seem to threaten all, and they are persuaded in their consciences, that their laws, and with them their estates, liberties, and lives are in danger, and perhaps their religion too, how they will be hindered from resisting illegal force, used against them, I cannot tell. This is an inconvenience, I confess, that attends all governments whatsoever, when the governors have brought it to this pass, to be generally suspected of their people; the most dangerous state which they can possibly put themselves in: wherein they are the less to be pitied, because it is so easy to be avoided; it being as impossible for a governor, if he really means the good of his people, and the preservation of them and their laws together, not to make them see and feel it; as it is for the father of a family, not to let his children see he loves, and takes care of them.

210. But if all the world shall observe pretences of one kind, and actions of another; arts used to elude the law, and the trust of prerogative (which is an arbitrary power in some things left in the prince's hand to do good, not harm to the people) employed contrary to the end, for which it was given: if the people shall find the ministers, and subordinate magistrates chosen suitable to such ends, and favoured, or laid by proportionably, as they promote, or oppose them: if they see several experiments made of arbitrary power, and that religion underhand favoured (though publicly proclaimed against) which is readiest to introduce it, and the operators in it supported, as much as may be; and when that

cannot be done, yet approved still, and liked the better: if a long train of actings show the counsels all tending that way, how can a man any more hinder himself from being persuaded in his own mind, which way things are going; or from casting about how to save himself, than he could from believing the captain of a ship he was in, was carrying him, and the rest of the company to Algiers, when he found him always steering that course, though cross winds, leaks in his ship, and want of men and provisions did often force him to turn his course another way for some time, which he steadily returned to again, as soon as the wind, weather, and other circumstances would let him?

Chapter 19
OF THE DISSOLUTION OF GOVERNMENT

211. He that will with any clearness speak of the dissolution of government, ought, in the first place to distinguish between the dissolution of the society, and the dissolution of the government. That which makes the community, and brings men out of the loose state of nature, into one politic society, is the agreement which everyone has with the rest to incorporate, and act as one body, and so be one distinct commonwealth. The usual, and almost only way whereby this union is dissolved, is the inroad of foreign force making a conquest upon them. For in that case, (not being able to maintain and support themselves, as one entire and independent body) the union belonging to that body which consisted therein, must necessarily cease, and so everyone return to the state he was in before, with a liberty to shift for himself, and provide for his own safety as he thinks fit in some other society. Whenever the society is dissolved, 'tis certain the government of that society cannot remain. Thus conquerors' swords often cut up governments by the roots, and mangle societies to pieces, separating the subdued or scattered multitude from the protection of, and dependence on that society which ought to have preserved them from violence. The world is too well instructed in, and too forward to allow of this way of dissolving of governments to need any more to be said of it: and there wants not much argument to prove, that where the society is dissolved, the

government cannot remain; that being as impossible, as for the frame of a house to subsist when the materials of it are scattered, and dissipated by a whirlwind, or jumbled into a confused heap by an earthquake.

212. Besides this overturning from without, governments are dissolved from within,

First, when the legislative is altered. Civil society being a state of peace, amongst those who are of it, from whom the state of war is excluded by the umpirage, which they have provided in their legislative, for the ending all differences, that may arise amongst any of them, 'tis in their legislative, that the members of a commonwealth are united, and combined together into one coherent living body. This is the soul that gives form, life, and unity to the commonwealth: from hence the several members have their mutual influence, sympathy, and connection: and therefore when the legislative is broken, or dissolved, dissolution and death follows. For the essence and union of the society consisting in having one will, the legislative, when once established by the majority, has the declaring, and as it were keeping of that will. The constitution of the legislative is the first and fundamental act of society, whereby provision is made for the continuation of their union, under the direction of persons, and bonds of laws made by persons authorized thereunto, by the consent and appointment of the people, without which no one man, or number of men, amongst them, can have authority of making laws, that shall be binding to the rest. When any one, or more, shall take upon them to make laws, whom the people have not appointed so to do, they make laws without authority, which the people are not therefore bound to obey; by which means they come again to be out of subjection, and may constitute to themselves a new legislative, as they think best, being in full liberty to resist the force of those, who without authority would impose anything upon them. Everyone is at the disposure of his own will, when those who had by the delegation of the society, the declaring of the public will, are excluded from it, and others usurp the place who have no such authority or delegation.

213. This being usually brought about by such in the commonwealth who misuse the power they have: it is hard to consider it aright, and know at whose door to lay it, without

knowing the form of government in which it happens. Let us suppose then the legislative placed in the concurrence of three distinct persons.

(1) A single hereditary person having the constant, supreme, executive power, and with it the power of convoking and dissolving the other two within certain periods of time.

(2) An assembly of hereditary nobility.

(3) An assembly of representatives chosen *pro tempore* [for a period], by the people: such a form of government supposed, it is evident.

214. First, that when such a single person or prince sets up his own arbitrary will in place of the laws, which are the will of the society, declared by the legislative, then the legislative is changed. For that being in effect the legislative whose rules and laws are put in execution, and required to be obeyed; when other laws are set up, and other rules pretended, and enforced, than what the legislative, constituted by the society, have enacted, 'tis plain, that the legislative is changed. Whoever introduces new laws, not being thereunto authorized by the fundamental appointment of the society, or subverts the old, disowns and overturns the power by which they were made, and so sets up a new legislative.

215. Secondly, when the prince hinders the legislative from assembling in its due time, or from acting freely, pursuant to those ends, for which it was constituted, the legislative is altered. For 'tis not a certain number of men, no, nor their meeting, unless they have also freedom of debating, and leisure of perfecting, what is for the good of the society wherein the legislative consists: when these are taken away or altered, so as to deprive the society of the due exercise of their power, the legislative is truly altered. For it is not names, that constitute governments, but the use and exercise of those powers that were intended to accompany them; so that he who takes away the freedom, or hinders the acting of the legislative in its due seasons, in effect takes away the legislative, and puts an end to the government.

216. Thirdly, when by the arbitrary power of the prince, the electors, or ways of election are altered, without the consent, and contrary to the common interest of the people, there also the legislative is altered. For if others, than those whom the society

has authorized thereunto, do choose, or in another way, than what the society hath prescribed, those chosen are not the legislative appointed by the people.

217. Fourthly, the delivery also of the people into the subjection of a foreign power, either by the prince, or by the legislative, is certainly a change of the legislative, and so a dissolution of the government. For the end why people entered into society, being to be preserved one entire, free, independent society, to be governed by its own laws; this is lost, whenever they are given up into the power of another.

218. Why in such a constitution as this, the dissolution of the government in these cases is to be imputed to the prince, is evident: because he having the force, treasure, and offices of the state to employ, and often persuading himself, or being flattered by others, that as supreme magistrate he is incapable of control; he alone is in a condition to make great advances toward such changes, under pretence of lawful authority, and has it in his hands to terrify and suppress opposers, as factious, seditious, and enemies to the government: whereas no other part of the legislative, or people is capable by themselves to attempt any alteration of the legislative, without open and visible rebellion, apt enough to be taken notice of; which when it prevails, produces effects very little different from foreign conquest. Besides the prince in such a form of government, having the power of dissolving the other parts of the legislative, and thereby rendering them private persons, they can never in opposition to him, or without his concurrence, alter the legislative by a law, his consent being necessary to give any of their decrees that sanction. But yet so far as the other parts of the legislative any way contribute to any attempt upon the government, and do either promote, or not, what lies in them, hinder such designs, they are guilty, and partake in this, which is certainly the greatest crime men can be guilty of one towards another.

219. There is one way more whereby such a government may be dissolved, and that is, when he who has the supreme executive power, neglects and abandons that charge, so that the laws already made can no longer be put in execution. This is demonstratively to reduce all to anarchy, and so effectually to dissolve the government. For laws not being made for themselves, but to

be by their execution the bonds of the society, to keep every part of the body politic in its due place and function, when that totally ceases, the government visibly ceases, and the people become a confused multitude, without order or connection. Where there is no longer the administration of justice, for the securing of men's rights, nor any remaining power within the community to direct the force, or provide for the necessities of the public, there certainly is no government left. Where the laws cannot be executed, it is all one as if there were no laws, and a government without laws, is, I suppose, a mystery in politics, inconceivable to human capacity, and inconsistent with human society.

220. In these and the like cases, when the government is dissolved, the people are at liberty to provide for themselves, by erecting a new legislative, differing from the other, by the change of persons, or form, or both as they shall find it most for their safety and good. For the society can never, by the fault of another, lose the native and original right it has to preserve itself, which can only be done by a settled legislative, and a fair and impartial execution of the laws made by it. But the state of mankind is not so miserable that they are not capable of using this remedy, till it be too late to look for any. To tell people they may provide for themselves, by erecting a new legislative, when by oppression, artifice, or being delivered over to a foreign power, their old one is gone, is only to tell them they may expect relief, when it is too late, and the evil is past cure. This is in effect no more than to bid them first be slaves, and then to take care of their liberty; and when their chains are on, tell them, they may act like free men. This, if barely so, is rather mockery than relief; and men can never be secure from tyranny, if there be no means to escape it, till they are perfectly under it: and therefore it is, that they have not only a right to get out of it but to prevent it.

221. There is therefore, secondly, another way whereby governments are dissolved, and that is; when the legislative, or the prince, either of them act contrary to their trust.

First, the legislative acts against the trust reposed in them, when they endeavour to invade the property of the subject, and to make themselves, or any part of the community, masters, or arbitrary disposers of the lives, liberties, or fortunes of the people.

222. The reason why men enter into society, is the preservation

of their property; and the end why they choose and authorize a legislative, is, that there may be laws made, and rules set as guards and fences to the properties of all the members of the society, to limit the power, and moderate the dominion of every part and member of the society. For since it can never be supposed to be the will of the society, that the legislative should have a power to destroy that, which everyone designs to secure, by entering into society, and for which the people submitted themselves to the legislators of their own making; whenever the legislators endeavour to take away, and destroy the property of the people, or to reduce them to slavery under arbitrary power, they put themselves into a state of war with the people, who are thereupon absolved from any further obedience, and are left to the common refuge, which God hath provided for all men, against force and violence. Whensoever therefore the legislative shall transgress this fundamental rule of society; and either by ambition, fear, folly or corruption, endeavour to grasp themselves, or put into the hands of any other an absolute power over the lives, liberties, and estates of the people; by this breach of trust they forfeit the power, the people had put into their hands, for quite contrary ends, and it devolves to the people, who have a right to resume their original liberty, and, by the establishment of a new legislative (such as they shall think fit) provide for their own safety and security, which is the end for which they are in society. What I have said here, concerning the legislative, in general, holds true also concerning the supreme executor, who having a double trust put in him, both to have a part in the legislative, and the supreme execution of the law, acts against both, when he goes about to set up his own arbitrary will, as the law of the society. He acts also contrary to his trust, when he either employs the force, treasure, and offices of the society, to corrupt the representatives, and gain them to his purposes: or openly pre-engages the electors, and prescribes to their choice, such, whom he has by solicitations, threats, promises, or otherwise won to his designs; and employs them to bring in such, who have promised beforehand, what to vote, and what to enact. Thus to regulate candidates and electors, and new model the ways of election, what is it but to cut up the government by the roots, and poison the very fountain of public security? For the people having reserved to themselves the choice of their representatives, as the fence to their properties, could do it for no other end, but that they might always be freely chosen, and so chosen, freely act and advise, as the necessity of the commonwealth, and the public good should, upon examination, and mature debate, be judged to require. This, those who give their votes before they hear the debate, and have weighed the reasons on all sides, are not capable of doing. To prepare such an assembly as this, and endeavour to set up the declared abettors of his own will, for the true representatives of the people, and the law-makers of the society, is certainly as great a breach of trust, and as perfect a declaration of a design to subvert the government, as is possible to be met with. To which, if one shall add rewards and punishments visibly employed to the same end, and all the arts of perverted law made use of, to take off and destroy all that stand in the way of such a design, and will not comply and consent to betray the liberties of their country, 'twill be past doubt what is doing. What power they ought to have in the society, who thus employ it contrary to the trust that went along with it in its first institution, is easy to determine; and one cannot but see, that he, who has once attempted any such thing as this, cannot any longer be trusted.

223. To this perhaps it will be said, that the people being ignorant, and always discontented, to lay the foundation of government in the unsteady opinion, and uncertain humour of the people, is to expose it to certain ruin; and no government will be able long to subsist, if the people may set up a new legislative, whenever they take offence at the old one. To this, I answer: quite the contrary. People are not so easily got out of their old forms, as some are apt to suggest. They are hardly to be prevailed with to amend the acknowledged faults, in the frame they have been accustomed to. And if there be any original defects, or adventitious ones introduced by time, or corruption; 'tis not an easy thing to get them changed, even when all the world sees there is an opportunity for it. This slowness and aversion in the people to quit their old constitutions, has, in the many revolutions which have been seen in this kingdom, in this and former ages, still kept us to, or, after some interval of fruitless attempts, still brought us back again to our old legislative of king, lords and commons: and whatever provocations have made the crown be taken from some

of our princes' heads, they never carried the people so far, as to place it in another line.

224. But 'twill be said, this hypothesis lays a ferment for frequent rebellion. To which I answer,

First, no more than any other hypothesis. For when the people are made miserable, and find themselves exposed to the ill usage of arbitrary power, cry up their governors, as much as you will for sons of Jupiter, let them be sacred and divine, descended or authorized from heaven; give them out for whom or what you please, the same will happen. The people generally ill treated, and contrary to right, will be ready upon any occasion to ease themselves of a burden that sits heavy upon them. They will wish and seek for the opportunity, which, in the change, weakness, and accidents of human affairs, seldom delays long to offer itself. He must have lived but a little while in the world, who has not seen examples of this in his time; and he must have read very little, who cannot produce examples of it in all sorts of governments in the world.

225. Secondly, I answer, such revolutions happen not upon every little mismanagement in public affairs. Great mistakes in the ruling part, many wrong and inconvenient laws, and all the slips of human frailty will be borne by the people, without mutiny or murmur. But if a long train of abuses, prevarications, and artifices, all tending the same way, make the design visible to the people, and they cannot but feel, what they lie under, and see, whither they are going; 'tis not to be wondered, that they should then rouse themselves, and endeavour to put the rule into such hands, which may secure to them the ends for which government was at first erected; and without which, ancient names, and specious forms, are so far from being better, that they are much worse, than the state of nature, or pure anarchy; the inconveniences being all as great and as near, but the remedy further off and more difficult.

226. Thirdly, I answer, that this doctrine of a power in the people of providing for their safety anew by a new legislative, when their legislators have acted contrary to their trust, by invading their property, is the best fence against rebellion, and the probablest means to hinder it. For rebellion being an opposition, not to persons, but authority, which is founded only in the constitutions and laws of the government; those, whoever they

be, who by force break through, and by force justify their violation of them, are truly and properly rebels. For when men by
entering into society and civil government, have excluded force,
and introduced laws for the preservation of property, peace, and
unity amongst themselves; those who set up force again in opposition to the laws, do *rebellare*, that is, bring back again the state
of war, and are properly rebels: which they who are in power (by
the pretence they have to authority, the temptation of force they
have in their hands, and the flattery of those about them) being
likeliest to do; the properest way to prevent the evil, is to show
them the danger and injustice of it, who are under the greatest
temptation to run into it.

227. In both the forementioned cases, when either the legislative is changed, or the legislators act contrary to the end for which
they were constituted; those who are guilty are guilty of rebellion.
For if anyone by force takes away the established legislative of
any society, and the laws by them made pursuant to their trust,
he thereby takes away the umpirage, which everyone had consented to, for a peaceable decision of all their controversies, and
a bar to the state of war amongst them. They, who remove, or
change the legislative, take away this decisive power, which
nobody can have, but by the appointment and consent of the
people; and so destroying the authority, which the people did, and
nobody else can set up, and introducing a power, which the people
hath not authorized, they actually introduce a state of war, which
is that of force without authority: and thus by removing the
legislative established by the society (in whose decisions the
people acquiesced and united, as to that of their own will) they
untie the knot, and expose the people anew to the state of war.
And if those, who by force take away the legislative, are rebels,
the legislators themselves, as has been shown, can be no less
esteemed so; when they, who were set up for the protection, and
preservation of the people, their liberties and properties, shall by
force invade, and endeavour to take them away; and so they
putting themselves into a state of war with those, who made them
the protectors and guardians of their peace, are properly, and with
the greatest aggravation, *rebellantes* rebels.

228. But if they, who say it lays a foundation for rebellion,
mean that it may occasion civil wars, or intestine broils, to tell the

people they are absolved from obedience, when illegal attempts are made upon their liberties or properties, and may oppose the unlawful violence of those, who were their magistrates, when they invade their properties contrary to the trust put in them; and that therefore this doctrine is not to be allowed, being so destructive to the peace of the world. They may as well say upon the same ground, that honest men may not oppose robbers or pirates, because this may occasion disorder or bloodshed. If any mischief come in such cases, it is not to be charged upon him, who defends his own right, but on him, that invades his neighbour's. If the innocent honest man must quietly quit all he has for peace sake, to him who will lay violent hands upon it, I desire it may be considered, what a kind of peace there will be in the world, which consists only in violence and rapine; and which is to be maintained only for the benefit of robbers and oppressors. Who would not think it an admirable peace betwixt the mighty and the mean, when the lamb, without resistance, yielded his throat to be torn by the imperious wolf? Polyphemus's den gives us a perfect pattern of such a peace, and such a government, wherein Ulysses and his companions had nothing to do, but quietly to suffer themselves to be devoured. And no doubt Ulysses, who was a prudent man, preached up passive obedience, and exhorted them to a quiet submission, by representing to them of what concernment peace was to mankind; and by showing the inconveniences [that] might happen, if they should offer to resist Polyphemus, who had now the power over them.

229. The end of government is the good of mankind, and which is best for mankind, that the people should be always exposed to the boundless will of tyranny, or that the rulers should be sometimes liable to be opposed, when they grow exorbitant in the use of their power, and employ it for the destruction, and not the preservation of the properties of their people?

230. Nor let anyone say, that mischief can arise from hence, as often as it shall please a busy head, or turbulent spirit, to desire the alteration of the government. 'Tis true, such men may stir, whenever they please, but it will be only to their own just ruin and perdition. For till the mischief be grown general, and the ill designs of the rulers become visible, or their attempts sensible to the greater part, the people, who are more disposed to suffer,

than right themselves by resistance, are not apt to stir. The examples of particular injustice, or oppression of here and there an unfortunate man, moves them not. But if they universally have a persuasion, grounded upon manifest evidence, that designs are carrying on against their liberties, and the general course and tendency of things cannot but give them strong suspicions of the evil intention of their governors, who is to be blamed for it? Who can help it, if they, who might avoid it, bring themselves into this suspicion? Are the people to be blamed, if they have the sense of rational creatures, and can think of things no otherwise than as they find and feel them? And is it not rather their fault, who puts things in such a posture that they would not have them thought, to be as they are? I grant, that the pride, ambition, and turbulency of private men have sometimes caused great disorders in common-wealths, and factions have been fatal to states and kingdoms. But whether the mischief hath oftener begun in the people's wantonness, and a desire to cast off the lawful authority of their rulers; or in the ruler's insolence, and endeavours to get, and exercise an arbitrary power over their people; whether oppression, or disobedience gave the first rise to the disorder, I leave it to impartial history to determine. This I am sure, whoever, either ruler or subject, by force goes about to invade the rights of either prince or people, and lays the foundation for overturning the constitution and frame of any just government, is guilty of the greatest crime, I think, a man is capable of, being to answer for all those mischiefs of blood, rapine, and desolation, which the breaking to pieces of governments bring on a country. And he who does it, is justly to be esteemed the common enemy and pest of mankind; and is to be treated accordingly.

231. That subjects, or foreigners attempting by force on the properties of any people, may be resisted with force, is agreed on all hands. But that magistrates doing the same thing, may be resisted, hath of late been denied: as if those who had the greatest privileges and advantages by the law, had thereby a power to break those laws, by which alone they were set in a better place than their brethren: whereas their offence is thereby the greater, both as being ungrateful for the greater share they have by the law, and breaking also that trust, which is put into their hands by their brethren.

232. Whosoever uses force without right, as everyone does in

society, who does it without law, puts himself into a state of war with those, against whom he so uses it, and in that state all former ties are cancelled, all other rights cease, and everyone has a right to defend himself, and to resist the aggressor. This is so evident, that Barclay himself, that great assertor of the power and sacredness of kings, is forced to confess, that it is lawful for the people, in some cases, to resist their king; and that too in a chapter, wherein he pretends to show that the divine law shuts up the people from all manner of rebellion. Whereby it is evident, even by his own doctrine, that, since they may in some cases resist, all resisting of princes is not rebellion. His words are these. 'Quod siquis dicat, ergone populus tyrannicae crudelitati & furori jugulum semper praebebit? Ergone multitudo civitates suas famae ferro, & flammâ vastari, seque, conjuges, & liberos fortunae ludibrio & tyranni libidini exponi, inque omnia vitae pericula omnesque miserias & molestias a 'rege deduci patientur? Num illis quod omni animantium generi est à naturâ tributum, denegari debet, ut sc. vim vi repellant, seseq.; ab injuriâ tueantur? Huic brevitur responsum sit, populo universo non negari defensionem, quae juris naturalis est, neque ultionem quae praeter naturam est adversus regem concedi debere. Quapropter si rex non in singulares tantum personas aliquot privatum odium exerceat, sed corpus etiam reipublicae, cujus ipse caput est, i.e. totum populum, vel insignem aliquam ejus partem immani & intolerandâ saevitiâ seu tyrannide divexet; populo, quidem hoc casu resistendi ac tuendi se ab injuriâ potestas competit, sed tuendi se tantum, non enim in principem invadendi: & restituendae injuriae illatae, non recedendi à debitâ reverentiâ propter acceptam injuriam. Praesentem denique impetum propulsandi non vim praeteritam ulciscendi jus habet. Horum enim alterum à naturâ est, ut vitam scilicet corpusque tueamur. Alterum vero contra naturam, ut inferior de superiori supplicium sumat. Quod itaque populus malum, antequam factum sit, impedire potest, ne fiat, id postquam factum est, in regem authorem sceleris vindicare non potest: populus igitur hoc ampliùs quam privatus quisquam habet: quod huic, vel ipsis adversariis judicibus, excepto Buchanano, nullum nisi in patientia remedium superest. Cùm ille si intolerabilis tyrannis est (modicum enim ferre omnino debet) resistere cum reverentiâ possit' (Barclay, *De Regno* ... *Monarchomachos*, Bk III, Ch. 8).

In English thus.

233. 'But if anyone should ask, must the people then always lay themselves open to the cruelty and rage of tyranny? Must they see their cities pillaged, and laid in ashes, their wives and children exposed to the tyrant's lust and fury, and themselves and families reduced by their king, to ruin and all the miseries of want and oppression, and yet sit still? Must men alone be debarred the common privilege of opposing force with force, which nature allows so freely to all other creatures for their preservation from injury? I answer: self-defence is a part of the law of nature; nor can it be denied the community, even against the king himself: but to revenge themselves upon him, must by no means be allowed them; it being not agreeable to that law. Wherefore if the king shall show a hatred, not only to some particular persons, but sets himself against the body of the commonwealth, whereof he is the head, and shall, with intolerable ill usage, cruelly tyrannize over the whole, or a considerable part of the people; in this case the people have a right to resist and defend themselves from injury: but it must be with this caution, that they only defend themselves, but do not attack their prince: they may repair the damages received, but must not for any provocation exceed the bounds of due reverence and respect. They may repulse the present attempt, but must not revenge past violences. For it is natural for us to defend life and limb, but that an inferior should punish a superior, is against nature. The mischief which is designed them, the people may prevent before it be done, but when it is done, they must not revenge it on the king, though author of the villainy. This therefore is the privilege of the people in general, above what any private person hath; that particular men are allowed by our adversaries themselves, (Buchanan only excepted) to have no other remedy but patience; but the body of the people may with respect resist intolerable tyranny; for when it is but moderate, they ought to endure it.'

234. Thus far that great advocate of monarchical power allows of resistance.

235. 'Tis true he has annexed two limitations to it, to no purpose: First, he says, it must be with reverence.

Secondly, it must be without retribution, or punishment; and the reason he gives, is, 'because an inferior cannot punish a superior'.

First, how to resist force without striking again, or how to strike with reverence, will need some skill to make intelligible. He that shall oppose an assault only with a shield to receive the blows, or in any more respectful posture, without a sword in his hand, to abate the confidence and force of the assailant, will quickly be at an end of his resistance, and will find such a defence serve only to draw on himself the worse usage. This is as ridiculous a way of resisting, as Juvenal thought it of fighting; 'ubi tu pulsas, ego vapulo tantum' [when you strike, I'm just a punchbag]. And the success of the combat will be unavoidably the same he there describes it:

'Libertas pauperis haec est:
Pulsatus rogat, et pugnis concisus, adorat,
Ut liceat paucis cum dentibus inde reverti.'

[Such is the poor man's freedom: after being beaten to a pulp, he may beg, as a special favour, to be left with his few remaining teeth.]

This will always be the event of such an imaginary resistance, where men may not strike again. He therefore who may resist, must be allowed to strike. And then let our author, or anybody else join a knock on the head, or a cut on the face, with as much reverence and respect as he thinks fit. He that can reconcile blows and reverence, may, for aught I know, deserve for his pains, a civil respectful cudgelling wherever he can meet with it.

Secondly, as to his second, 'an inferior cannot punish a superior'; that's true, generally speaking, whilst he is his superior. But to resist force with force, being the state of war that levels the parties, cancels all former relation of reverence, respect, and superiority: and then the odds that remains, is, that he, who opposes the unjust aggressor, has this superiority over him, that he has a right, when he prevails, to punish the offender, both for the breach of the peace, and all the evils that followed upon it. Barclay therefore, in another place, more coherently to himself, denies it to be lawful to resist a king in any case. But he there assigns two cases, whereby a king may unking himself. His words are,

'Quid ergo nulline casus incidere possunt quibus populo sese erigere atque in regem impotentius dominantem arma capere &

invadere jure suo suâque authoritate liceat? Nulli certe quamdiu rex manet. Semper enim ex divinis id obstat, "regem honorificato"; & "qui potestati resistit, Dei ordinationi resistit": non aliàs igitur in eum populo potestas est quam si id committat propter quod ipso jure rex esse desinat. Tunc enim se ipse principatu exuit atque in privatis constituit liber: hoc modo populus & superior efficitur, reverso ad eum sc. jure illo quod ante regem inauguratum in interregno habuit. At sunt paucorum generum commissa ejusmodi quae hunc effectum pariunt. At ego cum plurima animo perlustrem, duo tantum invenio, duos, inquam, casus quibus rex ipso facto ex rege non regem se facit & omni honore & dignitate regali atque in subditos potestate destituit; quorum etiam meminit Winzerus. Horum unus est, si regnum [& rempublicam evertere conetur, hoc est, si id ei propositum, eaque intentio fuerit ut] disperdat, quemadmodum de Nerone fertur, quod is nempe senatum populumque Romanum, atque adeo urbem ipsam ferro flammaque vastare, ac novas sibi sedes quaerere decrevisset. Et de Caligula, quod palam denunciarit se neque civem neque principem senatui ampliùs fore, inque animo habuerit, interempto utrisque ordinis electissimo quoque Alexandriam commigrare, ac ut populum uno ictu interimeret, unam ei cervicem optavit. Talia cum rex aliquis meditatur & molitur serio, omnem regnandi curam & animum illico abjicit, ac proinde imperium in subditos amittit, ut dominus servi pro derelicto habiti, dominium.

236. 'Alter casus est, si rex in alicujus clientelam se contulit, ac regnum quod liberum à majoribus & populo traditum accepit, alienae ditioni mancipavit. Nam tunc quamvis forte non eâ mente id agit populo plane ut incommodet: tamen quia quod praecipuum est regiae dignitatis amisit, ut summus scilicet in regno secundum Deum sit, & solo Deo inferior, atque populum etiam totum ignorantem vel invitum, cujus libertatem sartam & tectam conservare debuit, in alterius gentis ditionem & potestatem dedidit; hâc velut quadam regni ab alienatione effecit, ut nec quod ipse in regno imperium habuit retineat, nec in eum cui collatum voluit, juris quicquam transferat; atque ita eo facto liberum jam & suae potestatis populum relinquit, cujus rei exemplum unum annales Scotici suppeditant' (Barclay, *De Regno . . . Monarchomachos*, Bk 3, Ch. 16).

Which in English runs thus.

237. 'What then, can there no case happen wherein the people may of right, and by their own authority help themselves, take arms, and set upon their king, imperiously domineering over them? None at all, whilst he remains a king. "Honour the king" [*Exodus* 20:12], and "he that resists the power, resists the ordinance of God" [*Romans* 13:2]; are divine oracles that will never permit it. The people therefore can never come by a power over him, unless he does something that makes him cease to be a king. For then he divests himself of his crown and dignity, and returns to the state of a private man, and the people become free and superior; the power which they had in the interregnum, before they crowned him king, devolving to them again. But there are but few miscarriages which bring the matter to this state. After considering it well on all sides, I can find but two. Two cases there are, I say, whereby a king, *ipso facto*, becomes no king; and loses all power and regal authority over his people; which are also taken notice of by Winzerus.

'The first is, if he endeavour to overturn the government, that is, if he have a purpose and design to ruin the kingdom and commonwealth, as it is recorded of Nero, that he resolved to cut off the senate and people of Rome, lay the city waste with fire and sword, and then remove to some other place. And of Caligula, that he openly declared, that he would be no longer a head to the people or senate, and that he had it in his thoughts to cut off the worthiest men of both ranks, and then retire to Alexandria: and he wished that the people had but one neck, that he might dispatch them all at a blow. Such designs as these, when any king harbours in his thoughts and seriously promotes, he immediately gives up all care and thought of the commonwealth; and consequently forfeits the power of governing his subjects, as a master does the dominion over his slaves whom he hath abandoned.

238. 'The other case is, when a king makes himself the dependant of another, and subjects his kingdom which his ancestors left him, and the people put free into his hands, to the dominion of another. For however perhaps it may not be in his intention to prejudice the people; yet because he has hereby lost the principal part of regal dignity, *viz.* to be next and immediately under God, supreme in his kingdom; and also because he betrayed or forced his people, whose liberty he ought to have carefully preserved,

into the power and dominion of a foreign nation. By this as it were alienation of his kingdom, he himself loses the power he had in it before, without transferring any the least right to those on whom he would have bestowed it; and so by this act sets the people free, and leaves them at their [own] disposal. One example of this is to be found in the Scotch annals'.

239. In these cases Barclay the great champion of absolute monarchy, is forced to allow, that a king may be resisted, and ceases to be a king. That is in short, not to multiply cases: in whatsoever he has no authority, there he is no king, and may be resisted: for wheresoever the authority ceases, the king ceases too, and becomes like other men who have no authority. And these two cases he instances in, differ little from those above mentioned, to be destructive to governments, only that he has omitted the principle from which his doctrine flows; and that is, the breach of trust, in not preserving the form of government agreed on, and in not intending the end of government itself, which is the public good and preservation of property. When a king has dethroned himself, and put himself in a state of war with his people, what shall hinder them from prosecuting him who is no king, as they would any other man, who has put himself into a state of war with them; Barclay, and those of his opinion, would do well to tell us. This further I desire may be taken notice of out of Barclay, that he says, 'the mischief that is designed them, the people may prevent before it be done', whereby he allows resistance when tyranny is but in design. 'Such designs as these' (says he) 'when any king harbours in his thoughts and seriously promotes, he immediately gives up all care and thought of the commonwealth'; so that according to him the neglect of the public good is to be taken as an evidence of such a design, or at least for a sufficient cause of resistance. And the reason of all he gives in these words, 'because he betrayed or forced his people whose liberty he ought carefully to have preserved'. What he adds 'into the power and dominion of a foreign nation', signifies nothing, the fault and forfeiture lying in the loss of their liberty which he ought to have preserved, and not in any distinction of the persons to whose dominion they were subjected. The people's right is equally invaded, and their liberty lost, whether they are made slaves to any of their own, or a foreign nation; and in this lies the injury, and against

this only have they the right of defence. And there are instances to be found in all countries, which show that 'tis not the change of nations in the persons of their governors, but the change of government, that gives the offence. Bilson, a bishop of our church, and a great stickler for the power and prerogative of princes, does, if I mistake not, in his treatise of *Christian Subjection*, acknowledge, that princes may forfeit their power, and their title to the obedience of their subjects; and if there needed authority in a case where reason is so plain, I could send my reader to Bracton, Fortescue, and the author of the *Mirror*, and others; writers, who cannot be suspected to be ignorant of our government, or enemies to it. But I thought Hooker alone might be enough to satisfy those men, who relying on him for their ecclesiastical polity, are by strange fate carried to deny those principles upon which he builds it. Whether they are herein made the tools of cunninger workmen, to pull down their own fabric, they were best look. This I am sure, their civil policy is so new, so dangerous, and so destructive to both rulers and people, that as former ages never could bear the broaching of it; so it may be hoped those to come, redeemed from the impositions of those Egyptian under-taskmasters, will abhor the memory of such servile flatterers, who whilst it seemed to serve their turn, resolved all government into absolute tyranny, and would have all men born to, what their mean souls fitted them for, slavery.

240. Here, 'tis like, the common question will be made, who shall be judge whether the prince or legislative act contrary to their trust? This, perhaps, ill affected and factious men may spread amongst the people, when the prince only makes use of his due prerogative. To this I reply, the people shall be judge; for who shall be judge whether his trustee or deputy acts well, and according to the trust reposed in him, but he who deputes him, and must, by having deputed him have still a power to discard him, when he fails in his trust? If this be reasonable in particular cases of private men, why should it be otherwise in that of the greatest moment; where the welfare of millions is concerned, and also where the evil, if not prevented, is greater, and the redress very difficult, dear, and dangerous?

241. But further, this question, (who shall be judge?) cannot mean, that there is no judge at all. For where there is no judicature on earth, to decide controversies amongst men, God in heaven is

judge: he alone, 'tis true, is judge of the right. But every man is judge for himself, as in all other cases, so in this, whether another hath put himself into a state of war with him, and whether he should appeal to the supreme judge, as Jephtha did.

242. If a controversy arise betwixt a prince and some of the people, in a matter where the law is silent, or doubtful, and the thing be of great consequence, I should think the proper umpire, in such a case, should be the body of the people. For in cases where the prince hath a trust reposed in him, and is dispensed from the common ordinary rules of the law; there, if any men find themselves aggrieved, and think the prince acts contrary to, or beyond that trust, who so proper to judge as the body of the people, (who, at first, lodged that trust in him) how far they meant it should extend? But if the prince, or whoever they be in the administration, decline that way of determination, the appeal then lies nowhere but to heaven. Force between either persons, who have no known superior on earth, or which permits no appeal to a judge on earth, being properly a state of war, wherein the appeal lies only to heaven, and in that state the injured party must judge for himself, when he will think fit to make use of that appeal, and put himself upon it.

243. To conclude, the power that every individual gave the society, when he entered into it, can never revert to the individuals again, as long as the society lasts, but will always remain in the community; because without this, there can be no community, no commonwealth, which is contrary to the original agreement: so also when the society hath placed the legislative in any assembly of men, to continue in them and their successors, with direction and authority for providing such successors, the legislative can never revert to the people whilst that government lasts: because having provided a legislative with power to continue forever, they have given up their political power to the legislative, and cannot resume it. But if they have set limits to the duration of their legislative, and made this supreme power in any person, or assembly, only temporary: or else when by the miscarriages of those in authority, it is forfeited; upon the forfeiture of their rulers, or at the determination of the time set, it reverts to the society, and the people have a right to act as supreme, and continue the legislative in themselves, or erect a new form, or under the old form place it in new hands, as they think good.

GLOSSARY

This glossary provides a complete list of Locke's citations of authors and books, together with his references to people from biblical and classical sources and from more recent history, and also his citations from Scripture. I have included instances where Locke clearly refers to somebody though not by name. Readers may therefore turn to these notes for a brief explanation of all Locke's quotations and allusions. The roman numerals I and II refer to the First and Second Treatises, respectively, and the numerals following them refer to the numbered paragraphs of the specified Treatise.

AUTHORS AND BOOKS

Acosta, José de (Joseph) (1539–1600): II, 102. Jesuit priest, naturalist and explorer. Locke quotes from Edward Grimestone's translation of Acosta, *The Natural and Moral History of the Indies* (1604; first published, 1590), which he was reading in 1681. He uses Acosta to prove that there are societies in the Americas that remain in the state of nature and have little or no civil government.

Ainsworth, Henry (c. 1569– c. 1623): I, 28. Puritan divine and leader of a separatist congregation in Amsterdam. He was an erudite rabbinical and Oriental scholar. Locke cites his *Annotations upon the Five Books of Moses* (1622), which he purchased in 1681, to demonstrate that King David interpreted *Genesis* 1:28 as granting mankind dominion over the things of the earth and not as granting Adam dominion over other men.

Aristotle (384–322 BC): I, 8, 14, 15, 21, 154; II, 74. The most influential of the ancient Greek philosophers, especially in ethics and politics, and, despite attacks by Renaissance humanists, still widely regarded in the seventeenth century as the greatest non-Christian thinker. Aristotle was encyclopaedic enough to be claimed by every side: Filmer argues that he upheld monarchy as the best form of government (I, 8, 154); whereas Whigs use him to defend a mixed and balanced constitution. Locke attacks Filmer for hypocritically denouncing those who use pagan philosophers, while himself using Aristotle when it suited him.

Barclay, William (*c.* 1546–1608): I, 4, 67; II, 232, 235, 236, 239. A Scottish Catholic absolutist who settled in France, where he became a professor of civil law. His *De Regno et Regali Potestate* (*On Kings and Royal Power*) (1600) attacked both Catholic and Protestant theorists of resistance, especially George Buchanan, whom he called 'monarchomachs' (king-killers). Filmer, as Locke twice points out, opens *Patriarcha* with an attack on Barclay, Blackwood and Hayward for grounding absolute monarchy (as does Hobbes) on the weak foundation of a social compact, rather than on patriarchalism. Locke shows that even the absolutist Barclay allowed a limited right of resistance against tyrants.

Bellarmine, Robert (1542–1621): I, 6, 12. A Jesuit cardinal and saint of the Catholic Church. The most famous defender of papal power in the Counter-Reformation, he held that popes could depose heretical princes. In *De Potestate Summi Pontificis* (*Of the Power of the Papacy*) (1610) he argued that popes derived their power from God, but that kings drew theirs from the people. He was criticized at length in Chapter 42 of Hobbes's *Leviathan*. Locke notes that Filmer attacked Bellarmine (a fact which reminds us that the divine right of kings was a theory as much directed against Rome as against populist or constitutionalist theories within England).

Bilson, Thomas (1547–1616): II, 239. Bishop of Worcester and Winchester, a strong defender of episcopacy, an anti-Puritan and, according to Locke, 'a great stickler for the power and prerogative of princes'. Author of *The True Difference between Christian Subjection and Unchristian Rebellion* (1585). Locke says that even this book allowed that princes may forfeit their power in some circumstances.

Blackwood, Adam (1539–1613): I, 4, 67. A Scottish Catholic absolutist who settled in France, where he became a judge. His *Apologia pro Regibus* (*Apology for Princes*) (1581) attacked Calvinist resistance theorists, especially George Buchanan. See above under Barclay.

Bodin, Jean (*c.* 1530–96): I, 8, 56. The leading French theorist of absolutism, and particularly of the doctrine of sovereignty. He wrote during the Wars of Religion, against the Huguenot (Calvinist) resistance theorists. His *Les Six Livres de la République* (*Six Books of the Commonwealth*), published in 1576, was immensely influential among English Royalists and Tories. Filmer's *The Necessity of the Absolute Power of all Kings* (1648) is made up of passages from Bodin (see I, 8). *Bodin on Sovereignty* is available in the Cambridge Texts in the History of Political Thought series. The 'happy arguers' in I, 56, probably include Bodin.

Bracton, Henry de (c. 1210–68): II, 239. A churchman and royal justice under King Henry III. In the seventeenth century he was believed (probably mistakenly) to be the author of *De Legibus et Consuetudinibus Angliae* (*On the Laws and Customs of England*). It was printed in 1568 and 1640. Both Filmer and the Whigs claimed that the book supported their theories. Locke cites Bracton for the claim that tyrannical princes forfeit their power.

Buchanan, George (1506–82): II, 233. An accomplished humanist author and heir to John Knox as intellectual leader of the Scottish Reformation. He taught in Scotland and France and was tutor to the young King James VI. He developed his political ideas in defence of the deposition of James's mother, Queen Mary Stuart, especially in his *De Jure Regni apud Scotos* (*The Powers of the Crown in Scotland*) (1579).

Filmer, Sir Robert (1588–1653). Referred to in most paragraphs of I; II, 1, 21, 22, 57, 61. A Kentish gentleman, educated at Cambridge and the Inns of Court. His main work *Patriarcha* is characteristic of English absolutist writing. Written c. 1628–31, it was not published until 1680; until recently it was widely believed to have been written c. 1638–45. He published several tracts on behalf of the Royalists during the Civil War. His works became the textbook of Toryism after their republication in 1679–80. Locke's First Treatise is a minute criticism of *Patriarcha*; Filmer is, however, named only three times in the Second Treatise. There is, additionally, an unacknowledged quotation from Filmer in II, 57; and a reference to him in II, 21. In I, 14, Locke refers to Filmer's book by its subtitle, *The Natural Power of Kings*. Locke's text has some two hundred citations from Filmer, mainly from *Patriarcha*, but also from *The Anarchy of a Limited or Mixed Monarchy* (1648); *Observations on Hobbes, Milton and Grotius* (1652) and *Observations upon Aristotle's Politics* (1652). Four-fifths of Locke's citations occur in just fourteen pages in Sommerville's edition of Filmer in the Cambridge Texts in the History of Political Thought series, and these may be read for the kernel of Filmer's doctrine: pp. 6–11, 138, 144, 217, 236–7, 282–4.

Fortescue, Sir John (c. 1395– c. 1477): II, 239. A lawyer and member of parliament, he became lord chief justice in 1442, but was ejected and exiled in 1461. His chief work, *De Laudibus Legum Angliae* (*In Praise of the Laws of England*) (c. 1460s), described England in terms of an Aristotelian balanced constitution; it was a favourite with seventeenth-century anti-absolutists. Locke cites him for the claim that tyrannical princes forfeit their power.

Garcilaso de la Vega: I, 57, 153; II, 14. Author of *La Commentaire Royale, ou L'Histoire des Yncas, Roys du Peru* (Paris, 1633; originally published in Spanish: *Commentarios Reales*), which describes the life of the South American Indians. Locke often quotes from it in his notebooks. In I, 57, Locke gratuitously likens Filmer's patriarchal despotism to the cannibalism of the Incas. In II, 14, he cites a desert island story to show the existence of a state of nature without government. The reference in I, 153, to Ferdinand Soto may be out of Garcilaso's *La Florida del Inca* (1605); French edition: *Histoire de la Floride, ou Relation de ce qui s'est passé du Voyage de Ferdinand de Soto* (1670).

Grotius, Hugo (Huig van Groot) (1583–1645): I, 18, 50, 51, 76. A Dutch scholar and lawyer, he served as adviser to the statesman Oldenbarnevelt, but was in exile after 1619. A great theorist of natural and international law, his chief work being *De Jure Belli ac Pacis* (*Of the Laws of War and Peace*) (1625). He grounded government in the consent of the people (though drew authoritarian conclusions). He argued that property was originally held in common. Locke agreed with this and Filmer did not. But Filmer did invoke Grotius's claim that parents have a right over their children by procreating them; Locke objected that Grotius limited that right. In I, 76, 'Grotius' is a mistake for 'Selden'.

Hayward (Heyward), Sir John (*c.* 1564–1627): I, 4, 67. A gentleman who devoted himself to the study of history and law. He wrote in favour of the Earl of Essex's rebellion in 1599, but later defended James I's monarchy against Catholic resistance theory. See under Barclay.

Heylyn, Peter (1559–1662): I, 1. An Anglican divine, anti-Puritan polemicist, and friend of Filmer. He wrote an admiring biography of Archbishop Laud, who was executed for treason during the Civil War, and he was a vigorous defender of the divine rights of kings and bishops. Locke alludes to the fact that he was the author of the epistle that prefaced Filmer's *Patriarcha*.

Hobbes, Thomas (1588–1679). Author of *Leviathan* (1651), the most original work of political philosophy in English. There are several points at which Locke may be alluding to Hobbes, but it was not the purpose of the *Two Treatises* to address Hobbes, since it was Filmer who was characteristic of English absolutist thought. There is an explicit reference to 'the mighty Leviathan' in II, 98. Hobbes is mentioned by name in the Preface, as one of the objects of Filmer's criticism. The name also appears when Locke cites Filmer's *Observations on Hobbes, Milton and Grotius* (1652) (Preface; I, 14).

Homer (*c.* 8th–7th century BC): I, 153, 154. The earliest known Greek writer, author of the *Iliad* and *Odyssey*, which tell the story of the siege of Troy and its aftermath. Filmer used Homer to defend the ubiquity of ancient kingship; Locke reminds him that elsewhere he criticized reliance on pagan authors. Locke also refers to several incidents and characters from Homer.

Hooker, Richard (*c.* 1554–1600): II, 5, 15, 60, 61, 74, 90, 91, 94, 111, 134, 135, 136, 239. A theologian and university teacher at Oxford, and, between 1585 and 1591, Master of the Temple, where he became embroiled in an argument with the Temple's Puritan lecturer, Walter Travers. The outcome was his *Of the Laws of Ecclesiastical Polity* (1594–7; later parts published 1648, 1662), a massive defence of the Anglican Church and of a broadly Aristotelian and Protestant Scholastic vision of politics. Locke bought a copy and took notes from it in June 1681. He quotes from it several times (mainly from Book I, Chapter 10) and seems to have given currency to the appellation, 'the judicious Hooker'. Locke uses him to show the similarity of his own doctrine with that of such a highly respected Anglican theologian, and jibes that Churchmen borrow Hooker's ecclesiology while rejecting his politics. Locke uses the same quotation twice at II, 94 and 111. Extracts from Hooker are available in the Cambridge Texts in the History of Political Thought series.

Hunton, Philip (*c.* 1604–82): I, 7. A Puritan divine and political theorist, and briefly provost of Oliver Cromwell's abortive college at Durham. His *Treatise of Monarchy* (1643) was one of the key defences of the Parliamentarian cause in the Civil War, and was reprinted in 1680 and 1689. It argued that the English constitution was a mixed monarchy, in which power is shared between king, lords and commons. Locke notes that Filmer's *Anarchy of a Limited or Mixed Monarchy* (1648) was directed against Hunton.

James I and VI (1566–1625): II, 133, 200. King of England and Scotland. A defender of the divine right of kings. His *Political Works* are available, ed. C. H. McIlwain (Cambridge, 1918), and, shortly, in the Cambridge Texts in the History of Political Thought series (ed. J. P. Sommerville). In II, 133, Locke has in mind the famous speeches of 1603 and 1609 (in fact, 1610), for it is these which he quotes in II, 200, to show that even defenders of absolutism distinguish between a king who serves the public good and a tyrant who serves only his own (McIlwain, pp. 277–8, 309–10). In I, 8, Locke quotes Filmer quoting James's *Trew Law of Free Monarchies* (1598): McIlwain, p. 63.

Justin: II, 103. Locke cites an incident recorded by Trogus Pompeius and known only from Justin, who wrote in the second or third century AD. Cited also in Augustine, *The City of God*, Book IV, Chapter 6.

Juvenal (*c.* AD 60–140): II, 235. Roman satirist. Locke quotes him (*Satires*, III, 299–301) to illustrate the pusillanimity of William Barclay's limited allowance of a right to resist.

Knox, Robert (*c.* 1640–1720): II, 92. In the service of the East India Company, 1680–94, and chiefly known for his book, *An Historical Relation of the Island of Ceylon in the East Indies* (1681), the first account of Ceylon in the English language, which Locke purchased in August 1681. Locke does not name the author; he cites the book for evidence of the horrors of Oriental despotism. Knox and James Tyrrell are the most recent authors cited by Locke.

Livy (59 BC–AD 17): quoted on verso of title page. His *History of Rome* defended the stern and simple virtues of the early Roman republic.

Manwaring, Roger (1590–1653): I, 5. An Anglican divine and chaplain to Charles I. He was chiefly famous for sermons on *Religion and Allegiance* (1627), asserting the king's right to levy taxes. Despite punishment by parliament, he was created bishop of St David's in 1635. Locke makes the conventional point that, in Sibthorp and Manwaring, absolutist doctrine came to full prominence in English clerical writing.

Martial (*c.* AD 38–104): II, 98. Roman epigrammatist and satirist. Locke takes an incident from *Epigrams*, I, Preface.

Milton, John (1608–74): Preface. Puritan poet and polemicist. In the 1640s he wrote for religious toleration and freedom of the press; in the 1650s he defended the execution of Charles I. The name occurs when Locke cites Filmer's attack upon him, *Observations on Hobbes, Milton and Grotius.*

Selden, John (1584–1654): I, 21, 23, 32, 76, 112. An erudite lawyer and member of parliament, he supported the opposition to the king in the 1620s, and was a moderate Parliamentarian during the Civil War. He published works on legal history and natural law; his *Mare Clausum* (1635) took issue with Grotius on the law of the seas and discussed the origin of property. Locke quarrelled with Filmer's reading of Selden on the meaning of God's donation of property to Adam in *Genesis* 1:28. In I, 76, 'Grotius' is a mistake for 'Selden'.

Sibthorp, Robert (d.1662): I, 5. Anglican divine and chaplain to Charles I. He was chiefly famous, with Roger Manwaring (q.v.) for a sermon (1627) on passive obedience. A zealous anti-Puritan in the 1630s, he joined the Royalist side in the Civil War.

Tyrrell, James (1642–1718): I, 124. An Oxfordshire gentleman and close friend of Locke. They collaborated on a defence of religious toleration against Edward Stillingfleet (*c.* 1681). Tyrrell's *Patriarcha non Monarcha* (1681), Algernon Sidney's *Discourses Concerning Government* (published 1698), and Locke's *Two Treatises* were the three chief critiques of Filmer's doctrine. There are close similarities between Tyrrell's and Locke's books. Locke does not name Tyrrell but refers to the 'ingenious and learned author of *Patriarcha non Monarcha*'.

Winzet (Winzetus), Ninian (1518–92): II, 235, 237. A Scottish Catholic Benedictine monk, who resisted the Protestant Reformation in 1561. He retired to France and then Germany, where he published attacks on the Protestant Reformers Knox and Buchanan. His name appears only in Locke's quotations from Barclay, where Locke mistranscribes 'Winzerus' for 'Winzetus'; Locke probably knew nothing about him.

OTHER LITERARY REFERENCES

Don Quixote: I, 79. The character in Miguel de Cervantes' eponymous novel (1615), who is a deluded visionary.

Draw-can-sirs: II, 177. Swaggering characters always ready to draw their swords and kill opponents. From the second Duke of Buckingham's play *The Rehearsal*, composed *c.* 1663.

Drum ecclesiastic: Preface. The pulpit; hectoring clergymen. From the opening lines of Samuel Butler's anti-Puritan poem *Hudibras* (1663).

Encomium of Nero: I, 1. Locke refers to Jerome Cardan's satirical *Encomium Neronis* (1546).

Mirror of Justices: II, 239. Possibly written by Andrew Horn (d.1328) and printed in 1640. A suspect source but popular among constitutionalists. Locke cites him for the claim that tyrannical princes forfeit their power.

Septuagint: I, 25. The Greek version of the Old Testament.

HISTORICAL AND MYTHOLOGICAL FIGURES
Biblical

Information about people and places in the Bible can readily be found in a Bible dictionary.

Aaron: I, 107, 157, 167
Abel: I, 76, 112, 118; II, 38
Abimelech: I, 113, 130; II, 109
Abraham: I, 114, 128, 130, 133, 134, 135, 136, 137, 149, 150, 152, 160, 162, 167, 169; II, 38
Absalom: I, 129
Adam: in most paragraphs of I; II, 1, 25, 36, 39, 56, 57, 61, 202

Adonibezek: I, 149
Ahaz: II, 196
Amnon: I, 129
Athaliah: I, 161
Benhadad: I, 149
Benjamin: I, 95, 155, 161
Cain: I, 68, 75, 76, 99, 111, 112, 118, 142; II, 11, 38
Cham (Ham): I, 77, 142, 144
David: I, 28, 30, 95, 161, 162, 163, 167, 169; II, 25, 109
Esau: I, 48, 113, 115, 117, 118, 119, 130, 137, 138, 149; II, 38
Eve: I, 14, 16, 29, 30, 44, 45, 47, 48, 49, 67, 73, 99, 111; II, 56
Gideon: II, 109
Ham: see Cham
Heth: I, 136
Hezekiah: II, 196
Isaac: I, 113, 114, 115, 117, 118, 128, 135, 146, 150, 152, 160
Ishmael: I, 114, 115, 128, 152
Jacob: I, 48, 111, 113, 115, 116, 117, 118, 119, 129, 130, 137, 149, 150, 152, 155, 160, 161
Japhet: I, 77, 142, 144
Jephtha: I, 163; II, 21, 109, 176, 241
Jesse: I, 161
Jeroboam: I, 161, 162
Jonathan: I, 95
Joseph: I, 115
Joshua: I, 149, 154, 157, 163
Jotham: II, 109
Judah: I, 115, 118, 129, 155, 161; II, 196
Lot: I, 135; II, 38
Melchizedek: II, 74
Moses: I, 111, 115, 154, 157, 163
Nimrod: I, 148
Noah: I, 6, 19, 25, 27, 32, 33, 34, 35, 36, 37, 38, 39, 46, 71, 77, 139, 141, 142, 146; II, 25, 36, 137, 139, 140, 141, 142, 146, 147, 200
Paul: I, 40
Rebecca: I, 113, 118, 135
Reuben: I, 115, 155
Samuel: I, 8; II, 109
Sarah: I, 114, 128, 135, 136
Saul: I, 95, 161, 167, 169; II, 109
Seth: I, 68, 75, 76, 99
Shem: I, 77, 139, 142, 144, 146, 147
Solomon: I, 61, 95, 161, 162, 163
Tamar: I, 129

Classical and Other Ancient

Brama (Brahma): I, 141. In Hindu religion, the creator, the personification of the world soul, from whom the caste of Brahmans claim descent.

Caligula (AD 12–41): II, 235, 237. Roman emperor, notorious for his cruelty.

Cato (of Utica, 95–46 BC): II, 98. An upright Stoic politician who opposed Julius Caesar; Cicero makes him into a martyr-hero of the dying republican cause. Locke takes an incident from Martial, *Epigrams*, I, Preface.

Decemviri: I, 201. The ten patricians who drew up a code of laws for Rome and were deposed in 449 BC. In the same paragraph Locke also alludes to Hiero, tyrant of Syracuse in the third century AD.

Deucalion: I, 54. The son of Prometheus; the Noah of Greek myth, who survived a flood, and who, with his wife, re-peopled the earth by throwing stones behind him.

Hannibal (247–182 BC): I, 144. Brilliant military leader of the Carthaginians who took his army across the Alps to defeat the Romans.

Hercules (Heracles): I, 141. In Greek mythology, a hero of formidable strength, courage and endurance. The Dorians claimed descent from him.

Hymen: II, 80. In Greek mythology, the god of marriage.

Jupiter: I, 141; II, 224. In Roman mythology, the chief god, equated with the Greek Zeus; the god of thunder and lightning; the originator of the Romans.

Nero (AD 37–68): I, 1; II, 235, 237. Roman emperor, notorious for his cruelty.

Ogygis: I, 141. First king of Thebes, reigning at the time of the flood, and hence progenitor of a new race of Greeks.

Palantus: II, 103. Leader of the Spartans who founded Tarentum in Italy in the eighth century BC.

Pharamond: I, 141. Legendary Merovingian king, father of the French.

Polyphemus: II, 228. In Greek myth, a one-eyed Cyclops who trapped and ate several of Ulysses's companions.

Procrustes: I, 60. In Greek myth, a brigand who cut down or stretched his victims to fit the length of his bed.

Salmanasser: II, 101. Assyrian conqueror, ninth century BC.

Saturn: I, 141. God of agriculture, and hence progenitor of Roman civilization.

Spartacus: II, 196. Roman slave and gladiator who led an insurrection in 73 BC; after several successes against the Roman armies he was defeated and slain.

Tamberlain (Tamerlane) (1336–1405): I, 141. Mongol ruler and conqueror whose empire stretched across Central Asia.

Thirty Tyrants: II, 201. The oligarchs who ruled Athens 404–403 BC.

Ulysses (Odysseus): II, 228. The hero of the Trojan War, and the voyager in Homer's *Odyssey*.

Xerxes (c. 519–465 BC): II, 101. King of Persia; conquered Greece but was defeated at Salamis and driven out.

Medieval and Modern

Cade, Jack or John (d. 1450): I, 121. Leader of the Kentish rebellion of 1450, which made remarkable military headway against the crown's forces. His name was a symbol for populist revolt. John Crowne produced a Tory warning about him in his play *The Misery of Civil War* (1681).

Cromwell, Oliver (1599–1658): I, 79, 121. Military genius of the Parliamentarian side in the English Civil War and Lord Protector during the republic, 1653–8. Locke cites him as an example of a usurper, implying a conventional Whig self-distancing from the bloody and levelling revolution of mid-century. He accuses Filmer of allowing any *de facto* strongman to count as legitimate monarch; in fact Filmer did write a tract for submission to Cromwell; Locke, similarly, had once published a poetic celebration of Cromwell.

Elizabeth I (1533–1603): I, 47. Queen of England from 1558. Filmer claimed that God made Eve subject to Adam, and hence all wives to their husbands; Locke responds that nobody thinks that Queens Elizabeth or Mary would have lost their sovereignty had they married one of their subjects.

Hingar (Ingware): II, 196. Apparently, with Hubba, a leader of the first Danish invasion of England in the 860s.

Hubba (Ubba): II, 196. See Hingar.

Jeffreys, George (1644–89): I, 129. Notorious judge and Tory politician who conducted many of the trials against the Whigs, including that of Algernon Sidney (1683). He presided over the 'bloody assize' in the aftermath of Monmouth's Rebellion (1685), and served James II as lord chancellor. The reference in I, 129, is the only sentence in the *Two Treatises* that dates itself, to 1689. Aside from King William III, he is the only contemporary politician mentioned by Locke.

Mary I (1516–58): I, 47. Catholic Queen of England from 1553. See Elizabeth I.

Masaniello (Tommaso Aniello): I, 79. A fisherman who led a temporarily successful revolt in Naples against Spanish rule in 1647. Locke cites him as an instance of a usurper, implying a disowning of populist uprisings. In 1683 there appeared a Tory tract: *Massinello, or a Satyr against the Association*.

Soto, Ferdinand (Hernando de) (*c.* 1496–1542): I, 153. Spanish explorer who, after assisting in the conquests of Peru and Nicaragua, explored what are now the Southern states of the USA.

William I (the Conqueror) (1027–87): II, 177. Duke of Normandy who became king of England after the Conquest of 1066. In Tory historical thought, absolute monarchy was grounded in the Conquest, and parliamentary rights were said to arise from the gracious concessions of post-Conquest feudal kings. Locke denies that the English monarchy is grounded in the Conquest, thereby implying agreement with the conventional Whig view that 1066 did not constitute a conquest and that the Anglo-Saxon free constitution persisted into later times.

William III (1650–1702): Preface. King of England, Scotland and Ireland, and Stadholder of the Netherlands; acquired the crown after his successful invasion of England in 1688 – the 'Glorious Revolution'. Locke calls William 'our great restorer'; elsewhere 'our great deliverer'. It is perhaps significant that he fails to mention Mary II, Protestant daughter of James II, who was, uniquely in British history, made joint monarch with her husband William, in order to placate Tory consciences by preserving hereditary right.

PLACES AND NATIONS
Biblical

Africa: I, 142
Ammonites: II, 21, 109
Asia: I, 142, 146
Assyria: I, 196
Babel: I, 143, 146, 147, 148, 152
Benjamin, tribe of: I, 161, 165
Canaan: I, 58, 128, 147, 149, 162, 167
Edom, tribe of: I, 149
Ephraim, tribe of: I, 157
Egypt, Egyptian: I, 6, 150, 152, 154, 155, 163, 168; II, 239
Europe: I, 142

Classical

Medieval and Modern

Greeks: II, 192
Holland: II, 9
Indians (American): I, 130; II, 9, 14, 26, 30, 43, 108
Ireland: I, 137
Italy: II, 196
Mexico: II, 105
Normans: II, 177
Peru: I, 57; II, 14, 102, 105
Russia (the Czar): II, 91
Saxons: II, 177
Scotland, Scotch: I, 124, 144
Spain: II, 36
Swiss: II, 14
Turks, Turkish: I, 33; II, 91 (the Grand Signior), 192
Venice: II, 102
Welsh: I, 144
West Indies: I, 130, 131, 153

BIBLICAL CITATIONS

Locke did not always provide a reference for passages which he discussed; accordingly, as well as Locke's literal references, this list also includes several which have been interpolated by the editor.

Old Testament

Genesis 1:20–3: I, 27
Genesis 1:24: I, 25, 27
Genesis 1:25: I, 25, 27
Genesis 1:26: I, 26, 27, 30, 46
Genesis 1:28: I, 16, 21, 23, 24, 25, 26, 27, 29, 36, 38, 40, 41, 46, 49, 67, 85, 86
Genesis 1:29: I, 39, 86
Genesis 1:30: I, 39
Genesis 2:24: II, 65
Genesis 3:16: I, 16, 44, 47, 49, 67, 73
Genesis 3:19: I, 45
Genesis 3:23: I, 44
Genesis 4:7: I, 112, 118
Genesis 4:14: II, 11
Genesis 4:16–17: I, 76

New Testament

NOTE ON LOCKE'S ADDITIONS

Locke revised his text until the end of his life, sometimes introducing additions as well as corrections. The first (1690) edition exists in two states, in one of which virtually all of II, 20, and more than half of II, 21, is missing. Some modern editions simply have no paragraph 21. Whether Locke rewrote the missing passage for his printer is unclear. In the second (1694) edition two new passages appeared:

1. II, 141: from 'The power of the legislative' to the end (57 words). Locke here emphasizes that the power of the legislature is limited to the terms of its grant by the people; the legislature cannot alienate its power to others.

2. II, 239: from 'This further I desire' to 'gives the offence' (240 words). Locke emphasizes that even the royalist Barclay allows resistance to tyranny, and that it is the alteration of government (in breach of the public good) not of governors that is the real political crime. This seems to be a commentary on the Allegiance Controversy of 1689–93, during which Tories struggled with their consciences over the deposition of James II.

Near the end of his life Locke wrote corrections in his copy of the third (1698) edition of the *Two Treatises*, the Christ's College copy. He added several passages which reflect his thinking at that time. The most substantial are:

1. I, 58: from 'If precedents are sufficient to establish a rule' to the end (151 words). A sharply ironic passage against Filmer's tendency to take any biblical custom as normative: Locke refers to the practice, recorded in Psalm 106, of sacrificing children to idols.

2. I, 154: from 'whether to the great scandal of Christianity' to 'blindly swallow their nonsense' (63 words). The passage reflects Locke's anger at the charge of heresy and atheism brought against his *Essay Concerning Human Understanding* and his theological writings during the 1690s.

3. II, 37: from 'To which let me add' to 'Devonshire where they are well cultivated?' (211 words). A defence of land enclosure and of intensive cultivation: when common land is enclosed, the common stock of mankind is vastly improved through greater productivity.

4. II, 42: from 'This shows, how much numbers of men' to the end (89 words). A remarkable applause for a 'godlike' prince, presumably William III, who actively encourages 'honest industry' and who recognizes that demographic growth is better than territorial expansion.

5. II, 50: from 'be hoarded up without injury' to the end (80 words). Locke expanded his argument in the process of correcting his text. The additional passage emphasizes that the invention of money licenses unequal property. But Locke retained, in revised form, the final sentence where it is said that under government laws regulate property rights.

6. II, 108: from 'The equality of a simple poor way' to 'there wanted not of justice' (40 words). Locke argues that equality, together with fewness of laws and conflicts, was a feature of primitive economic simplicity.

7. II, 172: from 'the common bond whereby humankind' to 'neither society nor security' (110 words). In revising the text Locke expanded it to give greater force to his condemnation of the noxiousness of a tyrant and the rightfulness of destroying such a 'wild beast'.

Three other elements of Locke's final thoughts are worth noting. First, wherever he spotted it, he altered 'propriety' to 'property'; this probably indicates only a shift in contemporary vocabulary, but it may have a wider significance. Second, in II, 243, in the last line of the book, discussing the people's rights in a revolution, he altered 'place it in a new form, or new hands, as they think good' to 'erect a new form, or under the old form place it in new hands, as they think good'. The intrusion of 'the old form' may imply a more conservative slant on the Glorious Revolution, which had indeed changed the monarch but scarcely changed the constitution. Finally, in the Preface, when referring to the Tory clergy's teaching of divine right doctrine, he changed 'preach' to 'preached'. Thus, in his last days, Locke could feel satisfied that his book, and the Revolution, had made their theory a thing of the past.

SUGGESTIONS FOR FURTHER READING

LOCKE'S PRINCIPAL WORKS

After the *Two Treatises*, students of Locke's political theory should turn next to his *Letter Concerning Toleration* (1689).

Two Tracts on Government, ed. P. Abrams (Cambridge, 1967). Written c. 1660.

Essays on the Law of Nature, ed. W. von Leyden (Oxford, 1954). Written 1663.

An Essay Concerning Toleration (1876). Written 1667.

The Fundamental Constitutions of Carolina. Sometimes attributed to Locke. Written 1669.

Locke's Travels in France, ed. J. Lough (Cambridge, 1953). Locke's journals, 1675–79.

Epistola de Tolerantia, Gouda, written in 1685. Translated as *A Letter Concerning Toleration*, by William Popple, and published in 1689. Modern editions: ed. J. Tully (Indianapolis, Indiana, 1983); and eds. R. Klibansky and J. W. Gough (Oxford, 1968).

Two Treatises of Government. Title page has 1690. Written 1680–3. Two further editions in Locke's lifetime: 1694, 1698. The authoritative modern edition is by P. Laslett (Cambridge, 1960, 1967, 1988).

An Essay Concerning Human Understanding. Title page has 1690. Written over many years, from 1671. Three further editions in Locke's lifetime: 1694, 1695, 1700. The chief scholarly modern edition is by P. H. Nidditch (Oxford, 1975). An abridgment by J. W. Yolton (London, 1976) is available in the Everyman series.

A Second Letter Concerning Toleration (1690).

A Third Letter for Toleration (1692).

Some Considerations of the Consequences of the Lowering of Interest and Raising of the Value of Money (1692). This, and other economic writings of 1695, are in a modern edition: ed. P. Kelly, 2 vols (Oxford, 1991).

Some Thoughts Concerning Education (1693). Written during the mid-1680s. Modern editions: ed. J. L. Axtell (Cambridge, 1968); eds. J. W. and J. S. Yolton (Oxford, 1989).

Some Observations on a Printed Paper, Entitled, 'For Encouraging the Coining Silver Money in England' (1695).

Further Considerations Concerning Raising the Value of Money (1695).

The Reasonableness of Christianity (1695).

A Vindication of the Reasonableness of Christianity (1695).

A Second Vindication of the Reasonableness of Christianity (1697).

A Letter to the Right Rev. Edward Lord Bishop of Worcester (1697). In defence of the *Essay Concerning Human Understanding* against Edward Stillingfleet. He published further defences in 1697 and 1699.

Paraphrases of the Epistles of St Paul (1705–7). Modern edition: ed. A. P. Wainright, 2 vols (Oxford, 1987).

The Conduct of the Understanding (1706).

The Correspondence of John Locke, ed. E. S. De Beer, 8 vols (Oxford, 1976–89).

BIBLIOGRAPHIC GUIDES

Attig, J. C., *The Works of John Locke: A Comprehensive Bibliography* (Westport, Conn., 1985).

Christophersen, H. O., *A Bibliographical Introduction to the Study of John Locke* (Oslo, 1930).

Hall, R., and Woolhouse, R., *Eighty Years of Locke Scholarship* (Edinburgh, 1983). Regularly updated in the annual journal, *The Locke Newsletter*.

Harrison, J. and Laslett, P., *The Library of John Locke* (Oxford, 1965, 1971).

Long, P., *A Summary Catalogue of the Lovelace Collection of the Papers of John Locke in the Bodleian Library* (Oxford, 1959).

Yolton, J. S. and J. W., *John Locke: A Reference Guide* (Boston, Mass., 1985).

INTERPRETATION, BIOGRAPHY AND BACKGROUND

Ashcraft, R., *Revolutionary Politics and Locke's 'Two Treatises of Government'* (Princeton, 1986).

Ashcraft, R., *Locke's Two Treatises of Government* (London, 1987).

Ashcraft, R. (ed.), *John Locke: Critical Assessments*, 4 vols (London, 1991).

Burns, J. H., and Goldie, M. (eds.), *The Cambridge History of Political Thought*, 1450–1700 (Cambridge, 1991).

Cranston, M., *John Locke: A Biography* (Oxford, 1957, 1985).

Daly, J., *Sir Robert Filmer and English Political Thought* (Toronto, 1979).

Dunn, J., *The Political Thought of John Locke* (Cambridge, 1969).

Dunn, J., *Political Obligation in its Historical Context* (Cambridge, 1980).

Dunn, J., *Locke*, Past Masters series (Oxford, 1984).

Franklin, J. H., *John Locke and the Theory of Sovereignty* (Cambridge, 1978).

Gobetti, D., *Public and Private: Individuals, Households and Body Politic in Locke and Hutcheson* (London, 1992).

Gough, J. W., *John Locke's Political Philosophy: Eight Studies* (Oxford, 1950, 1973).

Grant, R. W., *John Locke's Liberalism* (Chicago, 1987).

Haley, K. H. D., *The First Earl of Shaftesbury* (Oxford, 1968).

Horton, J., and Mendus, S. (eds.), *John Locke: 'A Letter Concerning Toleration' in Focus* (London, 1991).

Kendall, W., *John Locke and the Doctrine of Majority Rule* (Urbana, Illinois, 1941).

Laslett, P., 'Introduction' to John Locke, *Two Treatises of Government* (Cambridge, 1960, 1967, 1988).

McNally, D., *Political Economy and the Rise of Capitalism* (Berkeley, California, 1988).

Macpherson, C. B., *The Political Theory of Possessive Individualism* (Oxford, 1962).

Marshall, J., *John Locke: Resistance, Religion, and Responsibility* (Cambridge, 1994).

Parry, G., *John Locke* (London, 1978).

Pateman, C., *The Sexual Contract* (Cambridge, 1988).

Phillipson, N., and Skinner, Q. (eds.), *Political Discourse in Early Modern Britain* (Cambridge, 1993).

Pocock, J. G. A., *The Ancient Constitution and the Feudal Law* (Cambridge, 1957, 1987).

Pocock, J. G. A., *Virtue, Commerce, and History* (Cambridge, 1985).

Schochet, G. J., *Patriarchalism in Political Thought* (Oxford, 1975).

Scott, J., *Algernon Sidney and the Restoration Crisis, 1677–1683* (Cambridge, 1991).

Seliger, M., *The Liberal Politics of John Locke* (London, 1968).

Simmons, J., *The Lockean Theory of Rights* (Princeton, 1992).

Skinner, Q., *The Foundations of Modern Political Thought*, 2 vols (Cambridge, 1978).

Tuck, R., *Natural Rights Theories* (Cambridge, 1979).

Tully, J., *A Discourse on Property: John Locke and His Adversaries* (Cambridge, 1980).

Tully, J., *An Approach to Political Philosophy: John Locke in Contexts* (Cambridge, 1993).

Waldron, J., *The Right to Private Property* (Oxford, 1988).

Western, J. R., *Monarchy and Revolution: The English State in the 1680s* (London, 1972).

Wood, N., *The Politics of Locke's Philosophy* (Berkeley, 1983).

Wood, N., *John Locke and Agrarian Capitalism* (Berkeley, 1984).

Yolton, J. W. (ed.), *John Locke: Problems and Perspectives* (Cambridge, 1969).

Yolton, J. W., *A Locke Dictionary* (Oxford, 1993).

KEY WORD INDEX

This index lists all appearances of selected key words and phrases in the Second Treatise, together with all appearances of a smaller selection in the First Treatise. Although it may serve as a subject index, I have not sought to locate concepts as a conventional index would, but rather, by electronic searching, to list every literal appearance of the selected words and phrases. The roman numerals I and II refer to the First and Second Treatises respectively, and the numerals following them refer to the numbered paragraphs of the specified Treatise. Multiple appearances within a single paragraph are recorded by figures in brackets. Words which occur in Locke's quotations from other authors are included. Some items are disaggregated, so that, for example, entries under 'law' do not include examples of 'law of nature', which are separately listed. For reasons of space the most frequently used words in the First Treatise have had to be omitted: these cases are indicated as 'I, *passim*'.